BUT IF
NOT

THE COMPILATION

Other Books by the Authors

BUT IF NOT

THE COMPILATION

JOYCE *and* DENNIS ASHTON

CFI
AN IMPRINT OF CEDAR FORT, INC.
SPRINGVILLE, UTAH

Publisher's Note: *But If Not* was first published in 2008 in three hardback volumes. We are pleased to bring them to you again, this time in a combined softback edition.

ISBN 13: 978-1-4621-1080-3

Published by CFI, an imprint of Cedar Fort, Inc., 2373 W. 700 S., Springville, UT 84663
Distributed by Cedar Fort, Inc., www.cedarfort.com

Library of Congress Cataloging-in-Publication Data

Ashton, Joyce, author.
  But if not : the compilation / Joyce and Dennis Ashton.
    pages cm
  Previously published in 3 volumes: 1. When bad things threaten to destroy good people -- 2. Enduring loss, illness, and death -- 3. Coping with unexpected loss.
  ISBN 978-1-4621-1080-3
  1. Suffering--Religious aspects--Church of Jesus Christ of Latter-day Saints. 2. Suffering--Religious aspects--Mormon Church. 3. Bereavement--Religious aspects--Church of Jesus Christ of Latter-day Saints. 4. Bereavement--Religious aspects--Mormon Church. 5. Church of Jesus Christ of Latter-day Saints--Doctrines. I. Ashton, Dennis, 1950- author. II. Title.

  BX8643.S93A835 2012
  248.8'6--dc23
                              2012024129

Cover design by Angela D. Olsen
Cover design © 2012 by Lyle Mortimer
Edited by Kimiko Christensen Hammari and Natalie A. Hepworth

Printed in the United States of America

10 9 8 7 6 5 4 3 2 1

Printed on acid-free paper

Contents

When Bad Things Threaten to Destroy Good People

IN MEMORY OF

Vivian Johnson Marsden

MY ANGEL MOTHER

1925–2008

Preface to Part One

As I finished the final spell check for this first section, my angel mother slept nearby. She had been in our home on hospice for the past three months, dying of breast cancer complicated with end-stage dementia.

Dennis and I learned about loss and grief early in our marriage when we experienced infertility, followed by the death of our first full-term baby. We started writing about grief years later after the death of our disabled fourteen-year-old son, Cameron. Additional losses and life's challenges have inevitability continued to roll into our family's lives—miscarriage, disability, death, addiction, illness, and other life challenges. As we sadly watch our sweet mother take her last breaths, we simultaneously experience great joy as we plan for our youngest daughter's upcoming temple marriage.

Each of our lives are full of joy, loss, sadness, and hope, all weaved together. Our personal challenge is to remain faithful, find meaning, and choose to carry on in the face of our own inevitable unique trials and adversities. *But If Not* is offered as a guide and support as you cope with your own life challenges and losses. We wish you ultimate happiness and comfort on your life's journey. It is our hope and prayer that the lessons, techniques, and spiritual insights we have learned as fellow travelers will, in some beneficial way, ease your suffering.

—Joyce and Dennis Ashton

CHAPTER ONE

"But If Not ..."

IN SPITE OF THE JOYS AND BLESSINGS, life is full of challenges. For those rare individuals who haven't yet experienced a significant life challenge, we say, "Oh, they are still in the bubble!" The bubble can be compared to the Garden of Eden or an ideal world where there is no sadness, pain, or problems. We float innocently along as life unfolds exactly as planned. All of our choices and decisions provide us and those around us with perfect contentment and joy. No one is upset or disappointed. There is no sin. No one hurts or betrays us. All of our prayers are answered as we think they should be. We don't feel exhaustion or discouragement. Our children are obedient. We are cheerful, kind, and full of love, and we accept those around us. We are content with our uncomplicated life in the Garden of Eden. We know nothing different.

In the Garden of Eden, Adam and Eve "could not be agents unto themselves; for if they never should have bitter they could not know sweet" (D&C 29:39). However, even when we realize that we must know good from evil to "become as one" with God, it is no easy task (Moses 4:28; Genesis 3:22). Adam and Eve certainly experienced a significant adjustment when they first felt sweat on their brows and pain in their hearts.

As we venture out of our Garden of Eden, or when our bubble bursts, we will likely experience denial, shock, and sadness. We may attempt to find meaning as we wonder what has happened to us. At first we may try to go back. We want things how they used to be.

(Likely there were times when Adam and Eve longed to go back to the garden as well.) We desire everything to be the same again, at times even denying our new realities. We fight for what we consider normal, just, and deserved. As time passes, we sadly realize that we can never go back. We have heard that when one door closes another door opens. However, it is in the hallways where we wait and struggle![1] Our struggles and experiences become part of us and forever change how we look at the world and ourselves. We will likely never be the same again; however, we can find joy, meaning, and a "new normal" as we do our grief work.[2]

These concepts may be confusing for those around us who are still in the safe and peaceful Garden of Eden. They often attempt to justify why bad things have happened to others, but not them. They all too often contribute to another's pain by wrongly suggesting their suffering results from a lack of faith, will power, or motivation. Some judge silently, while others cry out that surely they must have somehow deserved their tragedy. Others bombard those in pain with all sorts of suggestions and clichés: "Perhaps you didn't pray or fast enough." "Where is your faith?" Or, "It must be God's will." Some conclude that those suffering must be guilty of an unrepented sin or have some other serious character flaw that is responsible for their pain and dysfunction.

Knowing good from evil and coming to understand the bitter and the sweet can result from a variety of life challenges (Moses 6:55–56; 2 Nephi 2:11, 15). Perhaps your pain and disappointment came early in your life. Maybe you didn't feel loved as a child, or maybe you were abused.

It might have been as simple as realizing you were not born with as much talent, fame, or fortune as those around you. You may be surrounded by individuals who seem to be blessed with kinder and more faithful families. Others may have inherited greater intelligence or better looks than you.

Maybe you have addictions or live with someone who does. Perhaps your daughter became pregnant out of wedlock or you are unable to find a spouse. Maybe your husband has left you for another woman or even another man. Perhaps your parents got divorced even after you prayed, went on a mission, and placed their names on the temple prayer roll. Perhaps after years of infertility and miscarriages your only child died. It could be that your mission ended before your appointed time in spite of sincere efforts to overcome your unrelenting anxiety and chronic depression. You may live with illness, a disability, or chronic pain. Maybe you were there in the last natural disaster or terrorist attack that has left you without home, employment, or family. Any of these significant life challenges and losses can leave you with heartache, disappointment, and grief. To heal and find meaning, you will likely need to do what is coined by some as "grief work." Grief work is often the hardest work you will ever do.

The scriptures confirm the reality that bad things happen to good people.[3] God "maketh his sun to rise on the evil and on the good, and sendeth rain on the just and on the unjust" (Matthew 5:45).

The scriptures also give ample evidence that good people must endure hard times. Moses had to leave his comfortable life to accomplish what the Lord required of him (Exodus 4). Joseph Smith endured significant physical and emotional pain. Job suffered the loss of family, wealth, and health, and did not quickly find relief. He struggled emotionally with anger, anxiety (Job 3:25), and depression (Job 10:1). One of his losses resulted in spiritual injury as the heavens seemed silent. He questioned why God didn't hear and respond to his faithful, sincere pleadings (Job 30:20).

In the midst of Job's long and intense suffering, he asked the profound question, "If a man die, shall he live again?" (Job 14:14). Then, answering his own question, he gave us a key to find peace amid adversity with this testimony: "For I know that my redeemer liveth, and . . . though after my skin worms destroy this body, yet in my flesh shall I see God" (Job 19:25–6). And, "though he slay me, yet will I trust in him" (Job 13:15). Job's losses were restored to him before his death. Elder Bruce R. McConkie taught, "Anything that befalls us here in mortality is but for a small moment, and if we are true and faithful God will eventually exalt us on high. All our losses and sufferings will be made up to us in the resurrection."[4]

Jacob was another great prophet who suffered much loss. He worked seven years for Rachel, only to receive Leah and a requirement of seven more years of work for Rachel (Genesis 29). Rachel suffered years of infertility and then died after the birth of Benjamin, her second son (Genesis 35). After Joseph was sold into Egypt and presumed dead, Jacob was so grief stricken that he said, "For I will go down into the grave unto my son mourning" (Genesis 37:35). More grief and shame was wrought upon Jacob when his daughter Dinah fornicated with an uncircumcised Hivite man. This angered Jacob's sons Simeon and Levi, who then murdered Dinah's lover as well as other males in the Hivite city (Genesis 34). Jacob was again grief stricken.

President Kimball also endured severe trials. Much of what he learned was through his own multiple losses and sufferings. He, like Job, suffered with boils. He also experienced skin cancer, Bell's palsy, smallpox, and heart pain for years that required open-heart surgery. He endured three brain surgeries and suffered skin and throat cancer, which necessitated vocal cord surgery requiring treatments and resulting in his difficulty of speech.[5]

We may logically understand that bad things can and often do happen to good people. However, when we actually experience a serious crisis firsthand, we may find it difficult to accept or believe that a significant tragedy has actually happened to us. We may ask, "Why me?" "Did I do something wrong?" Or we may reason, "I have faith, I have lived a good life, why can't I handle this better?" One such woman facing a serious challenge was told, "People of real faith don't have trials or crises." The statement caused her a great deal of spiritual injury and hurt.

Most of us are not prepared to understand or deal with all the emotions that flood us. We may have been taught falsely that if we are righteous and faithful, we can avoid serious pain and loss. We might also believe that when something difficult does happen to us, our faith, obedience, and prayer will protect or shield us from having to endure emotional or physical pain. It may be especially confusing for those who have strong faith, believe in miracles, and strive to live the commandments, when they are not protected from tragedy. Unfortunately, not even the righteous are granted all they desire in their hearts or pray for. Many faithful individuals do not receive the miracle they sincerely and desperately seek. Others endure pain as a result of the misuse of agency or the destructive and sometimes sinful choices of others.

When assaulted by a personal tragedy, we may feel ashamed to openly admit our feelings and disappointments to others, or sometimes even to ourselves. Consequently, we may choose to mask our true feelings in order to save face. We may pretend for long periods of time to be functioning well, all in a desperate attempt to fool others and ourselves. This facade is often reinforced and buried even deeper when others compliment us with statements such as, "You are so strong and doing so well." Our desire not to disappoint others precludes us from sharing our real feelings and admitting that we are struggling and need help. We then are forced to grieve in the shadows. We become silent sufferers. We fear we will be judged negatively, especially if we somehow feel responsible for the adversity. Our guilt complicates the grieving process and causes us to feel shame and a perceived loss of control over our lives. Our grief can become "disenfranchised" when no one is aware of, allows, acknowledges, or understands our loss.

Enduring hardship over a long period of time can add to the difficulty. When the suffering goes on and on and we can't see an end in sight, we may experience spiritual injury (see chapter 3). This spiritual injury became a reality for many during the Lamanite and Nephite wars. In the Book of Mormon we read that "many had become hardened . . . and many were softened" because of the length and suffering that resulted from the many years of war. Our life's challenge is to maintain soft hearts and not become hardened (Alma 62:41).

We may feel forsaken at times like Job, who said, "I cry unto thee . . . and thou regardest me not" (Job 30:20). Or, we may experience confusion like Moses, who cried, "Lord, wherefore hast thou so evil entreated this people? Why is it that thou hast sent me . . . neither hast thou delivered thy people" (Exodus 5:22–23). We may wonder why God has allowed us to fall into difficult situations. Even Christ felt forsaken and alone in Gethsemane. When He found His apostles asleep, He asked them, "Could ye not watch with me but one hour?" (Matthew 26:37). And later on the cross He asked His Father, "Why hast thou forsaken me?" (Matthew 27:46).

There may be times when our family and friends disappoint us by not supporting us the way we think they should. We may have to accomplish some of our Gethsemane work without them. Neal A. Maxwell said of such suffering, "There is, in the suffering of the highest order, a point reached—a point of aloneness—when the individual (as did the Savior on a much grander scale) must bear it, as it were, alone. Even the faithful may wonder if they can take any more or if they are in some way forsaken. Those who, as it were, stand at the foot of the cross, often can do so little to help absorb the pain and the anguish. It is something we must bear by ourselves in order that our triumph can be complete."[6] Some may repeat the scriptural pleading, "The Lord hath forsaken me, and my Lord hath forgotten me." Or they may need the reassurance from the Lord's promises to us: "But he will show that he hath not . . . yet I will not forget thee. . . . Behold I have engraven thee upon the palms of my hands" (1 Nephi 21:14–16). "I will not fail thee, nor forsake thee" (Joshua 1:5).

The Lord has assured us that He will be with us: "I will not leave you comfortless" (John 14:18). "Fear not, let your hearts be comforted . . . waiting patiently on the Lord" (D&C 98:1–2). The Savior is our example. He is "a man of sorrows, and acquainted with grief" (Isaiah 53:3). He said, "I have drunk out of that bitter cup which the Father hath given me" (3 Nephi 11:11). We too may have to drink from a bitter cup. The secret is to follow Christ's example and not become bitter. We must choose between two *B*s and be "better, not bitter."

We all cope in different ways. There are several coping variables to consider. We will discuss these variables in detail along with interventions and self-help tools designed to increase our capacity to achieve healing. We especially want to emphasize the spiritual healing found in chapter 3. The Lord has promised His spirit and guidance: "And though the Lord give you the bread of adversity, and the water of affliction, yet shall not thy teachers be removed into a corner any more, but thine eyes shall see thy teachers: And thine ears shall hear a word behind thee saying, this is the way; walk ye in it, when ye turn to the right hand, and when ye turn to the left" (Isaiah 30:20–21).

Sometimes we do get our miracle and the Lord removes our adversity. However, more often the Savior will strengthen and enable us in our adversity. God may not remove our adversity, just as He didn't immediately deliver Alma and his people who were persecuted by Amulon. Instead, in Mosiah 24:14, He said, "I will ease the burdens which are put upon your shoulders, that even you cannot feel them on your backs." Alma the Younger, in Alma 31, discouraged with his preaching prayed "that [he] may have strength, that [he] may suffer with patience these afflictions" (Alma 31:31). In Isaiah 53 we are told that the Savior offers comfort and understanding because He is acquainted with grief. He learned to succor us through his own suffering. Now He can carry our sorrow. In Alma 7 the Savior says He can bear any pain, grief, or sickness.

Dennis and I, like most of you, have had a life of both joy and adversity. We cared for our disabled son, Cameron, for fourteen years. We experienced infertility and miscarriage. We raised another son trapped in addictions. We have learned how quickly life can leave us as we buried three of our four parents and two of our six children. Our oldest son, Darren, had a colon mass removed that resulted in severe complications and several major surgeries. Through suffering he came to appreciate more deeply a phrase from a favorite scripture that we quote to each other when one of us gets discouraged: "But if not."

The scripture tells a powerful story about three righteous and brave men. Shadrach, Meshach, and Abed-nego were to be thrown into a "burning fiery furnace" for worshipping God. They displayed their commitment and faith by responding: "Our God whom we serve is able to deliver us . . . *but if not*, be it known . . . that we will not serve thy gods, nor worship the golden image" (Daniel 3:18; emphasis added).

Elder Dennis E. Simmons reminds us,

> We must have the same faith as Shadrach, Meshach, and Abed-nego.
>
> Our God will deliver us from ridicule and persecution, *but if not*. . . . Our God will deliver us from sickness and disease, *but if not*. . . . He will deliver us from loneliness, depression, or fear, *but if not*. . . . Our God will deliver us from threats, accusations, and insecurity, *but if not*. . . . He will deliver us from death or impairment of loved ones, *but if not*, . . . *we will trust in the Lord*.
>
> Our God will see that we receive justice and fairness, *but if not*. . . . He will make sure that we are loved and recognized, *but if not*. . . . We will receive a perfect companion and righteous and obedient children, *but if not*, . . . *we will have faith in the Lord Jesus Christ, knowing that if we do all we can do, we will, in His time and in His way, be delivered and receive all that He has* (see D&C 84:35–38).[7]

President Hinckley reminds us of this kind of faith: "Faith is something greater than ourselves that enables us to do what we said we will do. To press forward when we are tired or hurt or afraid. To keep going when the challenge seems overwhelming and the course is uncertain."[8]

Elder W. Craig Zwick of the Seventy said, "We must trust in the Lord. If we give ourselves freely to Him, our burdens will be lifted and our hearts will be consoled."[9]

Elder Richard G. Scott reminds us to "trust in God . . . no matter how challenging the circumstance. . . . Your peace of mind, your assurance of answers to vexing problems, your ultimate joy depends upon your trust in Heavenly Father and His Son, Jesus Christ."[10]

Most of us can and will adapt to loss and life's challenges as we discover our "new normal."[11] Our spirits can come to the realization that we will find lasting peace and that "joy cometh in the morning" (Psalm 30:5).

NOTES

1. Elizabeth Kubler-Ross and David Kessler, *Life Lessons: Two Experts on Death and Dying Teach Us about the Mysteries of Life and Living* (New York: Scribner, 2000), 19.
2. Rana K. Limbo and Sara Rich Wheeler, *When a Baby Dies: A Handbook for Helping and Healing* (La Crosse Lutheran Hospital/Gunderson Clinic, Ltd., 1986), xv.
3. Harold Kushner, *When Bad Things Happen to Good People* (New York: Avon Books, 1981).
4. Bruce R. McConkie, in Conference Report, Oct. 1976, 158–60; *Ensign*, Nov. 1976, 106–108.
5. James E. Faust, "The Blessings of Adversity," *Ensign*, Feb. 1998, 2–7.
6. Neal A. Maxwell, *All These Things Shall Give Thee Experience* (Salt Lake City: Desert Book, 1979), 43.
7. Dennis E. Simons, "But If Not . . ." *Ensign*, May 2004.
8. Gordon B. Hinckley, *Standing for Something* (New York: Times Book, 2000), 111.
9. W. Craig Zwick, "The Lord Thy God Will Hold Thy Hand," *Ensign*, May 2003.
10. Richard G. Scott, "The Sustaining Power of Faith in Times of Uncertainty and Testing," *Ensign*, May 2003.
11. Limbo and Wheeler, ibid.

CHAPTER TWO

Loss and Grief

GRIEF IS WHAT WE EXPERIENCE WHEN we lose something. Grief is work. It is the work of thoughts and feelings. It is how we heal from loss. In the beginning phase of loss and grief, we may not have much control over our thoughts or feelings. However, as we acknowledge and actually pursue our grief work, using the tools we will discuss in chapters 3 and 4, we can gain increased control and peace. We will probably still have unexpected experiences with grief, especially during holidays and at other significant times. However, by doing our grief work, we are choosing to be a survivor rather than a victim of our circumstances.

No two people's reactions following a crisis will be the same. The type of loss is one factor. Individual circumstances, former life experiences, and previous loss exposure are a few additional factors that contribute to our particular grief process.

Rana K. Limbo and Sara Rich Wheeler, authors of *When a Baby Dies*, teach, "Grief cannot be compared, measured, or quantified. . . . Healing . . . does not mean a quick cure; healing is putting the loss in perspective."[1]

The Chinese symbol for *crisis* consists of two figures: danger and opportunity. Crisis and adversity provide us with an opportunity to transform our pain into healing.

Most of us have had a physical injury. Healing from some physical injuries can take months or years, and often we are never quite the same. When we say someone can heal from a tragic event, or from

13

a major loss that assaults both body and soul, we need to remember that it takes time and they will likely never be exactly the same again. Their loss becomes part of who they are, and although they can find joy and happiness again, they are different people. They see from a different perspective. Many use the term *recovery* when referring to this process. However, it may be more accurate to say that we reconcile, accommodate, or adjust to our loss.

Because most members of the Church depend on their spiritual strength and religious beliefs to get them through difficult challenges, our next chapter on spiritual healing can be especially important and relevant to them. We are blessed to have the gospel and the gift of the Holy Ghost. Christ offers us comfort and healing even when our adversity is not removed. While our faith and spiritual impressions bring great peace, it is also helpful to utilize and apply additional truths and knowledge inherently entwined in the grief process. These additional healing principles and processes can help us cope with loss and find personal meaning.

Individuals experiencing loss will be affected across the following five dimensions: spiritual, physical, social, emotional, and cognitive/intellectual. We will discuss the possible myriad grief symptoms in each of these areas. Additionally we will illustrate how each of the five dimensions interacts and affects the others.

Emotional Symptoms Resulting from Adversity and Loss

One of life's most meaningful emotions, happiness, is often compromised for a time by serious adversity and loss. Symptoms that are associated with acute grief include disbelief, denial, shock, and numbness.

SHOCK, NUMBNESS, AND DISBELIEF

"How can this be? I can't believe it is really happening!" Your assumptive world has been violated. This is not what you wanted or expected. You may want to say, "Life is not fair!" or "Why me?"

You may feel numb or in a state of confusion. The disbelief may initially overpower you. It may be difficult to experience happiness, joy, love, or spirituality for some time. It may be difficult to concentrate on even simple tasks. Your normal coping behaviors become depleted. The depth of your grief is often proportional to the depth of your love and time previously invested in those things or loved ones we have lost. The quality and quantity of your love, time, and service (emotional investment) may coincide with the difficulty and duration of your grief. Grief often takes more time, patience, and energy than most expect or feel capable of enduring.

DENIAL

For some of us, denial may remain for weeks, months, or even years. Sometimes friends and relatives contribute to this denial. They may reason, "Let's not bring it up or talk about it and maybe it will go away." Some may experience a deeper level of denial in their attempt to cope. This is called repression. It is an unconscious forgetting of the traumatic event. We may stuff the loss far from our conscious memory. Unfortunately, emotions not dealt with on a conscious level may appear as physical illness, generalized anxiety, panic attacks, or post-traumatic stress syndrome.

Some individuals use avoidance patterns to deny their grief. These are behaviors and attitudes that cause individuals to delay feeling pain. Avoidance patterns include purposely postponing, displacing, or minimizing the emotions or event. Some become obsessed with shopping, working, eating, intellectualizing, traveling, exercising, crusading, or drugging their pain.

There may be secondary losses resulting from changes and adjustments that might be denied initially. The divorcee who tries to maintain the same financial status finally realizes that she may need to sell her home or make other standard of living adjustments to survive financially. Children already struggling with the loss of a parent may additionally have to adjust to a new school, loss of friends, and a shared bedroom. Some divorced mothers will have to return to work to support their families. Divorced fathers may be forced to take on a second job to cover the expenses of two households. As a result of divorce, many children will lose their fathers' and mothers' consistent presence, guidance, and support in their home. These secondary losses may be more troublesome over time for the children than the primary loss of an absent parent.

One divorced woman said, "I had no idea there would be so

many other changes and adjustments following my divorce. If I'd had to face it all at once, I would have never made it. Step by step, I have accepted my new life."

DEPRESSION

When you're depressed, you might say, "I feel like I'm in a big black hole. Nothing feels or looks good to me. I'm afraid I can't keep going."

Sadness is a normal reaction to a traumatic event and a common component of grief. It is different from depression. Depression can involve our thoughts, moods, and behaviors. When events seem beyond our control, the helplessness we feel can lead to depression. We may feel worried, overwhelmed, and anxious. Intense anxiety can lead to depression. We may feel empty, tearful, helpless, hopeless, worthless, and abandoned. We may move slowly or feel intense anger. Depression can also result from anger turned inward.

Some depressive symptoms can bring changes in our body's ability to function. We may see a change in weight, sleep, or appetite. We might not be able to perform as we used to at home, school, or work. If our situational depression persists, it can become a clinical depression (major depressive disorder), which means we'll likely need professional help or medication to recover.

One woman suffering from depression said, "I've lost my song." Another said, "The worse thing in life is to be alive . . . but dead inside."

Major depression involves not only changes in our ability to function, but it can actually lead us to a total inability to function. In extreme forms, individuals become incapacitated and are unable to care for themselves. Fortunately, even serious depression can be successfully treated by a professional. Major depressive disorders do not usually respond to the basic self-help tools alone (emoting, exercise, sunlight, diet, journaling). We may need psychotherapy and medications. Each year more than 11 million Americans suffer from serious depression. Of these, about 2 percent are children and 5 percent are adolescents.[2]

ANXIETY

Anxiety is a common symptom of loss and grief. Sometimes it is helpful to identify what is being threatened. It may be love, security, esteem, integrity, control, or success. During loss it is probably a combination of many.

Anxiety may appear in a variety of behaviors. One woman wrote: "As part of my grief work, I dove into overactivity. It seemed to be an attempt to validate my worth and redefine my purpose. I used my busyness and doing tasks in an attempt to find relief and a feeling of acceptance through my accomplishments. Through my overactivity, I was determined to make my life significant, meaningful, and productive in spite of my pain. All of this overactivity helped me cope as best I could. However, at first nothing seemed to make me feel better."

If we stay in overactive or avoidance modes for long periods of time, we may become stuck in the grief process, unable to totally resolve our issues. Research has shown that overdoing or overactivity can increase our anxiety and stress. We might take on more responsibility than we can realistically handle. Even small challenges can seem stressful during a crisis.

Many physical symptoms accompany anxiety. One mother writes about her anxiety after the loss of a baby: "My pulse raced, I couldn't breathe, sit still, or concentrate. I tried to do a hundred things at once. I got a lot of things done, but my anxiety never left me."

Another mother feeling vulnerable displays the same anxiety: "The other night the storm picked up so violently. I panicked and ran to find my three-year-old son. He is the only child I have left. I cannot bear another loss. I am angry I have these fears."

Job describes his anxiety as he faced his sufferings: "For the thing which I greatly feared is come upon me, and that which I was afraid of is come unto me. I was not in safety, neither had I rest, neither was I quiet; yet trouble came" (Job 3:25–26).

If anxiety persists or turns to panic attacks, professional help may be needed.

ANGER

Anger is a common emotion with any loss and can signal the beginning of acceptance. On the other hand, if your anger turns to rage, you should seek professional help, especially if there is danger of hurting yourself or someone else.

Women typically display less demonstrative anger than men. Society and likely biology have influenced women not to openly express their anger. Many will find ways to hold onto their anger. Anger repressed, ignored, shelved, or turned inward can lead to depression, confusion, guilt, or even physical illness. Some of us strike out at the very people we love. We may not be sure where to productively direct our anger.

Anger is usually a secondary emotion that can hide other deep emotions. A father who lost a child said to his wife, "When I act mean and angry, it just means I'm feeling sad and hurt inside."

Anger can also be a sign of unmet needs or expectations. Our assumptions of how our life should have been are lost. The loss of a safe, predictable world becomes a secondary loss. We may feel vulnerable and afraid of the future. Our anger can be a sign of healing, so we don't want to stuff it.

We may feel anger toward relatives, medical staff, and others for all the suffering we or our family has experienced. For a time we may feel life is meaningless. We might be angry at God for allowing us and our family to suffer. Even Job, whom God loved and accepted as righteous, expressed his anger toward God: "Let the day perish wherein I was born. . . . Why died I not from the womb? . . . Why is light given to a man whose way is hid, and whom God hath hedged in?" (Job 3:3, 11, 23). "I cry unto thee, and thou dost not hear me: I stand up and thou regardest me not. Thou art become cruel to me (Job 30:20–21).

Anger toward deity or leaders representing God following a crisis is common among all faiths. It can be more intense for the faithful who believed that God should have prevented their tragedy. We may become confused because we know that God is good and loves us, yet we wonder why our suffering continues. Experiencing feelings of anger toward God can produce guilt, which further complicates the grieving process. (See spiritual injury in chapter 3.) It can be overwhelming to face a serious loss while also experiencing a loss of faith or comfort from God.

GUILT

Guilt is another emotion that is common with any traumatic event or serious loss. For some people, this is the most exhausting and difficult emotion to deal with. According to B. Bush, "Guilt feelings are often a combination of many different feelings rather than one simple feeling . . . it's a messy mixture of insecurity, self-doubt, self-condemnation, self-judgment, anxiety, and fear."[3]

Following a traumatic experience, we often blame ourselves for not doing things differently to prevent the loss. A father writes: "If I had just noticed that something was wrong earlier and caught it sooner; I know I could have prevented this whole event."

A mother said: "I did so many things wrong. If I had just done things differently, this wouldn't have happened."

Another mother writes: "Since my child has died, I keep remembering how I got angry at him a few months before. What he did was really not his fault. I made him cry. He went to school late with red eyes. Even though I apologized when he got home, it hasn't erased the painful guilt from my memory."

Children experience guilt too: "If I hadn't wished my sister dead, she wouldn't be dying today." "If I had been a better boy, I wouldn't have gotten sick."

Guilt is a painful component of grief that manifests itself when we feel we should have been able to avert the tragedy that happened through our faith, prayers, or righteous living. We may ask ourselves, "What did I do wrong? Am I responsible for this event?" The guilt ridden words "I should have" may haunt us. It is an overwhelming burden for many to carry and endure.

Guilt was a strong emotion for Dennis and me following the death of our fourteen-year-old disabled son, Cameron. We felt responsible for his safety and care, and we experienced guilt when our decision to subject Cameron to surgery resulted in his early death.

We had been surprised by our doctor's advice. He informed us that Cameron's hips had deteriorated and he would need to have surgery within six months. I could see tears swelling up in Cameron's big brown eyes. I tried to reassure him. I told him that during the surgery he would be asleep and it wouldn't hurt and that when he woke up, he would get medication to keep him comfortable. The surgery could possibly remove his pain so he could ride his adapted tricycle better.

Dennis's guilt was intense. He was the one lying next to Cam when he died. He had kissed him good night shortly before and was relieved Cameron was resting so well with less pain. Had Cameron tried to call out to him? Should Dennis have noticed something was wrong? Had Cameron aspirated or choked, as one nurse and doctor thought, while his father slept next to him? Why didn't he hear something? The nurse was always in the room. Why hadn't she watched or listened closer?

How could Dennis ever let go of this painful blame and guilt? He sincerely felt that by falling asleep he had not protected Cameron. Neither our other children nor I could comfort him. He and Cam had showered, dressed, brushed teeth together, and often shared the same fork for fourteen years. The void and guilt he felt were beyond measure. He was a professional counselor and had helped others through their grief, yet he felt lost at first and unable to help himself.

We had both presented grief workshops and had experienced guilt before. We now realize we may have intellectually understood guilt; however, we hadn't emotionally felt or known this intense pain before. We had no idea that guilt could hurt so much and for so long.

We learned through this loss that there are no clear-cut answers for everyone on how to relieve guilt and pain. For us, talking about it and reframing it was helpful.

Cameron trusted the doctor's and our decision that surgery was best for him. In the 1992 movie *Robin Hood* with Kevin Costner, Robin had made what he thought was the best decision in behalf of his beloved and trusted blind friend, Duncan. He sent him away from the fighting and danger . . . only to find that he had been ruthlessly murdered anyway. Robin Hood felt enormous sorrow and guilt. Duncan was so perfect and obedient; Robin didn't feel he deserved to die. The guilt he felt for his decision was apparent and disabling. Then his mentor, the Great Azeem, seeing Robin's anguish counseled, "There are no perfect men, just perfect intentions." Most of us have "perfect intentions" for those we love. Sometimes beyond our control, something goes wrong. Even with the best plans, accidents happen and our loved ones can become ill or die.

It took a long time to work through our guilt, painful emotions, and questions; however, with time, work, and faith, we ultimately reconciled most of our grief.

Unresolved guilt is not healthy for any of us. If we do make a true mistake, we must remember that "to err is human."[4] None of us are perfect, and we all make mistakes. In fact, we may wish we had done something different. These guilt feelings need to be expressed and then hopefully we can let go and forgive ourselves.

One might also consider eliminating "shoulds" from their vocabulary. (If someone else shames you with too many "shoulds," you could respond back with, "Don't *should* on me!")

FALSE GUILT

In many instances, individuals are experiencing false guilt (blaming themselves for events and circumstances they are not really responsible for). They might say, "If I hadn't fallen asleep, I know I could have prevented his death."

After her child committed suicide, a parent asked, "Didn't I instill hope in my child?" This false guilt is a negative cognitive message that can delay recovery. False guilt can be resolved over time by integrating and expressing healthy and accurate thought processes and then by integrating them cognitively. A professional may need to assist you in this process.

CONTROL ISSUES

Many situations and circumstances in our lives are not controllable. The realization that we have little control over parts of our lives can make us feel vulnerable and afraid. To compensate for this fear, we may attempt to overcontrol others, especially those we may feel concern or responsible for.

A mother writes after her adversity: "I know I am driving my husband and children crazy. They claim I expect perfection from them. I become so frustrated when they don't do what I think they should. The need to control is an overpowering force since the death of my child. Some of it may be the vulnerability I feel. Like an over-protective instinct that something else bad might happen. I realize I am actually pushing the people away that I love the most. I feel the same frustration when someone tries to control me."

When we experience stress and frustration, we should ask ourselves, am I trying to control someone or something outside of my control, or is someone trying to overcontrol me?

Longing, Yearning, Pining, and Searching

For many, this stage of grief lasts the longest. We miss our loved one or our old life and how things use to be. Earth life may seem like a long time to wait before things improve or we see a deceased loved one again. We may have faith in the next life, but the spirit world seems far away right now. We may continue to ask, "Why me?" wishing to resolve questions that seem at first to have no satisfying answers. Even though we may have great faith and tap into the power of the gospel, we may still experience many of the painful symptoms associated with the grief process. Many of us will yearn for the way we thought things could or should be, and now may never be. We search for answers, yearning for hope or peace to return to our lives. We start to wonder if we will ever feel any better. We might conclude that we must be going crazy or doing something wrong to still be in so much pain. These feelings can be very confusing. The fear of something else going wrong hangs over us. Everyone thinks you are better, and you hate to admit you're not. You find it hard to believe that it may take eighteen to twenty-four months[5] to find relief, and then depending on the loss, additional time to achieve a functioning recovery.

Hurt and Confusion

Your friends, relatives, ward members, and coworkers may feel uncomfortable around you. They may seem to ignore you because of their awkwardness. They may not understand the intensity and duration of your grief or may feel helpless to console and comfort you. Consequently, many offer clichés or platitudes in an attempt to heal you. These sayings often bring hurt and confusion even though they are offered by people who sincerely want to help. Because others have not had your experiences, it is difficult for them to understand the depth and length of your grief.

Bargaining

Bargaining during adversity is common. We may make promises to ourselves, others, or God. In return we seek acceptance, answers to our prayers, improved health, or some other miracle.

Disorientation and disorganization

Any traumatic event can cause confusion, disorientation, and disorganization in our lives. The intense reactions can cause a lack of concentration or absent-mindedness.

Withdrawal, Isolation, and Loneliness

When we feel no one can understand or respond to our pain, it is common to withdraw from community, church, friends, and family. However, it becomes unhealthy if isolation becomes a permanent solution to our mourning.

We may isolate ourselves to the point of no return. We may refuse help and stop reaching out to others. We stop sharing our concerns and feelings. Soon we find no one calls or comes around. This self-imposed isolation may feel safer initially. Yet, with time, we may become lonely and bitter, unable to function and find healing. We might lose our ability to feel joy, interact with, or help others.

Ultimate loneliness may occur when we feel separated and misunderstood not only by others, but by God. (See spiritual injury in chapter 3.)

Physical Effects Resulting from Stress and Loss

The list of physical symptoms is extensive. We may feel physical pain or aching as the shock and numbness wear off. We may experience a tightness or hollowness in our stomach or chest, breathing difficulties, or a dry mouth. Our heart may pound so fast and hard that we feel we could surely die, or wish we would! We may be restless, unable to sit still, or so weak and exhausted we cannot possibly move. Many people experience changes in bowel, appetite, and sleep patterns. Some experience headaches, blurred vision, and nervous twitches. The immune system is often suppressed with grief and stress. Individuals experiencing a traumatic situation have a higher incidence of physical illness and death, up to two years following their loss.[6] Physical symptoms may also be intensified by emotional reactions, such as guilt, depression, anger, anxiety, resentment, or bitterness. The majority of individuals seeking medical help or hospitalization have in their recent history experienced a major loss.

Intellectual/Cognitive Processing Following a Loss

Grief affects us cognitively through our thoughts. It includes the process that we experience as we attempt to comprehend or understand what has happened to us. We may repeatedly ask the same questions. We may be trying to intellectually make sense out of what has occurred. Through this mental rumination we sift through each bit of information in an attempt to intellectually assimilate, grasp, or understand the events. This mental repetition is often an attempt to substitute different solutions that would have altered our outcome. We may think, "What if I had done this?" or "What if we had gone there?" We mentally search for a way that we could have a different or better conclusion, diagnosis, or prognosis. It can become very frightening as the mind tries to regain some control by recreating or replaying parts of the experience. These repeated thought processes may eventually help us accept what has happened. We will have to make cognitive adjustments to process this new information.

We may feel irritable with noise or other stimulation, as it is difficult to concentrate on anything except what has happened to us. This preoccupation may cloud our brain and limit our ability to function at previous levels of competency and for extended periods of time.

We may also try to intellectualize the details of our loss without allowing for feelings or emotions. When we are ready to do our grief work, we may need help transferring this knowledge from our heads to our hearts so we can experience greater congruency with our emotions. As A. D. Wolfelt puts it, we may need to "feel it to heal it."[7]

It may take weeks, months, or even years to sort it all out. However, with time, we slowly begin to comprehend what has happened and what it means for our future.

How Men and Women Process Grief

Men and women grieve in the intellectual and emotional dimensions differently. The majority of women are right-brain dominant, meaning they function more from the brain's right hemisphere, which is associated with feelings and emotions. Many men, on the other hand, are left-brain dominant and are more likely to be governed by logic and reasoning. Women are often better at emotionally expressing grief than men. Men usually do better sorting out the intellectual details of their loss. Both men and women do best when they utilize an appropriate balance of cognitive reasoning, while allowing themselves to emote.

Grief is felt inside; mourning is the outward manifestation of grief. Men often grieve inwardly, not displaying the outward signs of mourning. Some may express themselves through tears, while others are very quiet and stoic. Others busily start planning and doing many tasks.

The Social/Behavioral Process During Loss

During a crisis, we often experience grief symptoms that will affect our social interactions. Adversity affects our behaviors and how we function at work, home, church, and in other social settings. In the beginning we may feel uncomfortable around others and at social events, causing additional or secondary losses. Because our church membership represents a way of life within our community, the social interactions among close church associates has a greater potential to help or hurt our healing.

We may isolate ourselves from friends, family, and church members. We try to protect ourselves from the constant reminder of what others still have and we have lost. We might feel shame and embarrassment, especially if we are not living up to our own expectations or the expectations of those around us. We may force ourselves to appear strong, acting as though we are healing rapidly. We might not feel comfortable sharing the details of our painful emotions and circumstances. We fear that others will not understand our pain, or will judge us harshly. We may feel vulnerable and fear that more loss will occur in the future. These social challenges are often damaging to our self-esteem.

Identity/Self-esteem

Our identity includes personal characteristics, body image, talents, and disabilities. Many of our perceptions are learned as we interact with our environment and others. When there are changes in our physical body or environment, we have to make emotional, behavioral, and mental adjustments. This may include viewing ourselves differently.

During trials and adversity, we may also experience a loss of identity and feel as if part of us has died. One sufferer writes: "After my crisis, I think I lost some of my self-esteem. I tried to feel I was still useful and valuable. I felt that others at church expected me to move on as if nothing had happened. I tried to do this in a variety of ways. However, I felt lost for a long time."

We may lose our confidence, feeling that others are judging us as inadequate, which leaves us feeling vulnerable and afraid.

Abuse and other destructive experiences may cause us to feel unaccepted. We then turn to pleasing behaviors that we hope will secure us the love and attention we need. Many professionals call these pleasing behaviors masks or facades because we don't accurately portray our true self.[8] We may appear emotionally healthy, yet on the inside we are confused, lonely, anxious, or depressed. *Identity crisis* is another term used to describe this loss of self-esteem.

We may have to confront past pains that have been hidden away. Honestly acknowledging the hurt and pain is often an important step as we begin our healing. It may be helpful to relive and reclaim past behaviors, qualities, or feelings in a safe environment with a competent gospel-centered psychotherapist. If we repress or suppress grief, we may experience a similar loss of self. We try to hurry and get through our pain and pretend to carry on as usual. Some encourage our denial by complimenting us on how strong we are or how much faith we must have to recover so quickly. We then continue to project this false self in an attempt to save face and look as strong and healthy as we perceive others believe and want us to be.

Caregivers who give so much of themselves to another for an extended time may feel part of their own identity or self-image is lost at the death of the person for whom they are caring. This void can be enormous and adds a unique dimension to their grief. This is true of any worthwhile endeavor or any person who has occupied much of our time, thought, or worries for months or years.

One caretaker writes, "After caring for him for so many years, I wondered, what will I do now? Where do I turn? As I tried to regain or redefine my identity, it seemed more than I could endure at times."

Disenfranchised Grief

People experience disenfranchised grief when they incur a loss that is not or cannot be openly acknowledged, publicly mourned, or socially supported.[9] For example, one of our associate's husbands had divorced her and also abandoned much support of their children. He died soon after their divorce, and she and the children stood at the casket. They were not really mourning his death since their grief had taken place much earlier during the divorce. However, in the shadows, in the back of the room, was a grieving woman. She had hoped to marry him the following month. Her grief was disenfranchised because no one acknowledged or accepted her sorrow.

I felt a twinge of disenfranchised grief last week at my daughter's wedding, which was three and a half weeks after my mother's death. I had worked hard to make it a happy, picture-perfect day, which it turned out to be. No one really mentioned that my mother wasn't there. At one point when the grandparents were taking pictures with the bride and groom, I wanted to shout out, "Ashley's grandma would be here in the pictures and supporting us all, but she died three weeks ago!"

Complicated or Prolonged Grief

Somewhere between 10 and 20 percent of those mourning a serious loss will experience prolonged or complicated grief. Grief may become complicated for a variety of reasons. Common situations resulting in a complicated bereavement include (1) a loss that is preventable or the family member feels responsible for the illness or death of their loved one; (2) a loss resulting from suicide or murder; (3) the loss of children; (4) if someone's illness, death, or suffering is prolonged; (5) when the loss conflicts with spiritual expectations; and (6) multiple losses or deaths. Any one or a combination of the above complications can increase the duration and intensity of our grief.

Adjusting and adapting to significant loss can take many months or years. It may be appropriate and helpful to refer families or individuals for psychotherapy and medication support at any time if you see any of the following symptoms: (1) refusing social support; (2) chronic or persistent depression; (3) failure to provide needed self-care; (4) persistent thoughts of suicide; (5) addictions; (6) history of mental illness; (7) lack of trust; (8) excessive anger or rage; (9) excessive anxiety or panic attacks; and (10) inability to plan one's future and move forward.

Complicated grief symptoms form the following cluster, which is distinct from depression and anxiety symptom clusters:

- Intense yearning and heartache
- Guilt about moving on
- Lack of acceptance
- Lack of trust
- Excessive anger or bitterness
- Numbness and detachment
- Inability to move forward
- Feeling that life is empty and meaningless
- Lack of hope for future happiness
- Irritability and agitation[10]

A diagnosis of complicated mourning using the above symptoms would generally not apply until six months following the loss. Complicated mourning increases the risk for suicidal thoughts and behaviors, cardiac events, high blood pressure, cancer, and other physical symptoms.

Professional support and assistance will be helpful for individuals and families grieving and is especially beneficial for those experiencing complicated or chronic bereavement.

Harold B. Lee said, "Members may need counseling more than clothing and members who, through bishops, are referred to an agency in our [family] social services program should feel no more hesitancy in asking for help of this kind than we should in requesting help through the priesthood welfare program."[11]

Even with intense or complicated grief, we can adjust, adapt, and reconcile our loss. Human beings are highly resilient to loss and trauma. We can help ourselves by acknowledging our loss and grief and finding meaning in our sadness or suffering. Facing loss and finding personal meaning will enable us to identify hope for a positive future.

NOTES

1. Rana K. Limbo and Sara Rich Wheeler, *When a Baby Dies: A Handbook for Helping and Healing* (La Crosse Lutheran Hospital/Gunderson Clinic, Ltd., 1986), xiv.
2. Michael D. Yapko, *Hand-Me-Down Blues* (New York: Golden Books, 1999), 8.
3. B. Bush, *Guilt—A Tool for Christian Growth* (St. Meinrad, Indiana: Abbey Press, 1991).
4. C. Thurman, *These Truths We Must Believe* (Nashville: Thomas Nelsen, 1991), 23.
5. Glen W. Davidson, *Understanding Mourning* (Minneapolis: Augsburg Publishing House, 1984).
6. Ibid.
7. A. D. Wolfelt, "Lessons in Caregiving for the Dying," workshop handout, Dallas Market Center, Aug. 22, 1996.
8. Joan Borysenko, *Minding the Body, Mending the Mind* (Reading, Massachusetts: Addison-Wesley, 1987), 57.
9. J. K. Doka, ed. *Disenfranchised Grief: Recognizing Hidden Sorrow* (Lexington, Massachusetts: Lexington Books, 1989), 3–7.
10. *Bereavement Care Journal*, Winter 2004, vol. 23 no. 3, 3–7.
11. Harold B. Lee, Seminar for Regional Representatives of the Twelve, Oct. 1, 1970.

CHAPTER THREE

Spiritual Hurt and Healing

ONE OF THE MOST HURTFUL ASPECTS OF coping with loss and adversity is that it can impact us spiritually. Spiritual injury results when life experiences contradict our previously held spiritual assumptions. Spiritual pain can occur when someone feels abandoned or forsaken by God. Some plead for a miracle healing, realizing in the end that they must ultimately adjust, suffer, endure, and even die.

How can we prevent the negative events that happen to us from having a negative impact on us? It may be helpful to remember that painful trials and tribulations are part of our earth life experience. Church leaders and latter-day scripture suggest we agreed or were made aware that trials would accompany our mortal existence. New Testament scripture also promises comfort for those suffering in a future estate: "The sufferings of this present time are not worthy to be compared with the glory which shall be revealed in us" (Romans 8:18).

Many bereaved members of the Church indicate that their first step in healing from spiritual injury occurred when they felt safe enough to honestly and openly express their fear, anger, and doubt. A mother whose daughter died of cancer said, "I may not know what I believe about God any longer." The following insight, love, and acceptance expressed by her church leader helped her through the healing process: "God can handle your anger, fear, and doubt. You are not the only person to ever question your beliefs during a tragedy."

What a relief for this woman experiencing spiritual injury to find someone willing to listen and accept her confusion and pain without condemning judgment. She was then able to start the process of spiritual healing and forgiveness. With unconditional love and support, many can begin to nourish their faith again by returning to prayer, scripture reading, and church attendance. Most grieving individuals heal and return to their faith with sufficient time, support, and grief work.

An active LDS wife and mother reluctantly shares her spiritual injury: "After my loss, I had to start all over again with my testimony and beliefs. At first I was so hurt that God had not prevented my tragedy that I couldn't read LDS doctrine or much from the Book of Mormon. I wanted to learn what others believed. Slowly my spiritual pain improved and I returned to my own faith, doctrines, and a love for the Book of Mormon."

A grieving, committed member shares her anger toward God: "If I didn't believe in God, I wouldn't be angry at him now for not protecting me from this tragedy."[1]

Belief in God also allows us to feel His power and comfort. Some who ask, "Where is God?" in their personal crisis may over time benefit from opening their heart again to truly find His love. After expressing confusion and anger, many will be able to let go of their fears and look with reassurance and hope again to Him.

Faith and Grief Coexist

After our son Cameron's death, we were confused at first because we hoped that if we had enough faith we wouldn't hurt. We hoped that we would be shielded from the painful feelings of grief. We came to realize that faith and grief can coexist. Knowing Cameron still existed in the spirit world was very comforting, but that didn't stop us from missing him here and now.

As Dennis and I have worked with other grieving individuals, we have discovered many deeply faithful Church members who wonder why they were feeling such profound pain when they had been obedient and faithful. Some have been hurt or confused when they were referred to 1 Corinthians 10:13: "God is faithful, who will not suffer you to be tempted above that ye are able; but will with the temptation also make a way to escape, that ye may be able to bear it." In Alma 13:28–29 we are cautioned to watch and pray "that ye may not be tempted above that which ye can bear."

These scriptures use the word *tempted*, which may have a different connotation than physical or emotional suffering. The phrase "tempted more than we have strength to resist" may have more to do with sin than adversity, pain, and grief. Dennis and I have met many who feel they are not guilty of sin, yet acknowledge they are barely hanging on as they face adverse circumstances and suffering. If individuals do give in to temptation and sin, it is generally not our place to judge whether they had the emotional or mental strength to resist their personal temptations. Only God knows what their current mental, physical, and spiritual strengths and weaknesses are. It is often more helpful to recognize and understand that exercising faith and obedience does not preclude individuals from experiencing grief.

Mourning for our loss does not mean that we are weak or that we have lost our faith. Grieving, crying, and feeling pain for our situation is not evidence that we don't have sufficient faith or are weak. We can believe in God, life after death, and all the truths of the gospel and still experience profound pain, grief, and sadness in our mortal life.

During the grief process, it is also common to question God and some of our previous beliefs. Some have embraced false interpretations of doctrine that should be altered and reframed. This is especially difficult if these false beliefs or traditions were ingrained through reinforcement by our parents or other significant individuals. The following scriptures discuss how the traditions of our fathers influence us: Mosiah 1:5, Matthew 7:8, Alma 3:8, and Alma 9:16.

A confused member of the Church experiencing a significant trial stated: "My mother taught me I would be protected and blessed if I lived the gospel. I interpreted this to mean, because I was a good person living all the commandments, this tragedy would never happen to me."

It is helpful to understand that being protected and blessed doesn't necessarily mean being exempt from trials. It does mean we can receive direction and be strengthened to endure our trials in ways similar to Christ, Joseph Smith, and other prophets. It might be well to remind ourselves that we will "receive no witness until after the trial of [our] faith" (Ether 12:6).

Attempting to console those who have lost loved ones or endured serious trials by saying, "It will be better in the next life," tends to minimize their immediate pain. "It's like you're on a desert and you are dying of thirst, and someone says, 'Yes, you can have a drink, but not for thirty years!' "[2] Yes, we will see our loved one again or be relieved from our adversity in the next life. However, that ultimate destination for many follows a long and at times very painful earthly journey!

Elder M. Russell Ballard said,

> Life isn't always easy. At some point in our journey we may feel much as the pioneers did as they crossed Iowa—up to our knees in mud, forced to bury some of our dreams along the way. We all face rocky ridges, with the wind in our face and winter coming on too soon. Sometimes it seems as though there is no end to the dust that stings our eyes and clouds our vision. Sharp edges of despair and discouragement jut out of the terrain to slow our passage. . . . Occasionally we reach the top of one summit in life, as the pioneers did, only to see more mountain peaks ahead, higher and more challenging than the one we have just traversed. Tapping unseen reservoirs of faith and endurance, we, as did our forebears, inch ever forward toward that day when our voices can join with those of all pioneers who have endured in faith, singing, "All is well! All is well!"[3]

God Provides Miracles and Allows Agency

It is healing for us to believe that God can and does intervene in our lives and that miracles do happen. The scriptures teach us that "God has not ceased to be a God of miracles" (Mormon 9:15) and miracles have not ceased (Moroni 7:27–29; Mormon 9:19).

It can be equally healing to understand that in most instances, God allows natural laws and consequences to run their course. Many will have to endure earth life experiencing significant illness, disabilities, or other loss and emotional pain. Our miracle or healing may not occur in this life, and our faith will be tried (3 Nephi 26:11).

Often we refer to miracles as guaranteed, predictable events when they are, in reality, hoped for examples of how God can work in our lives. Following the shooting at Columbine High School, the bombing of the Oklahoma Federal Building, the September 11 terrorist attack, and the Salt Lake City Trolley Square shooting, many questioned why some victims survived and others did not. Some of those interviewed said, "I am grateful that God protected and spared my life and the life of my loved one." Consider the unsaid message conveyed to those who lost loved ones. This may sound harsh; however, what many victims heard was, "God did not protect my loved one," or "We were not worthy of His protection."

The same unsaid messages often apply to other kinds of loss and adversity. Bereavement counselors who interviewed individuals following the Oklahoma City bombing concluded that those who were coping best believed God did not cause or intend this horrible event and that God was, in fact, grieving with them. Those who were not coping as well believed that God controls and orchestrates all events and thus was responsible for the bombing and the deaths of their loved ones.

Many have asked, "Why does God allow good, innocent men, women, and children to suffer?" If their suffering is caused by someone else, it is helpful to explain that God permits individual agency. God allows choice (Alma 60:13). Evil individuals can hurt and even murder other innocent victims who are living gospel-centered lives. Moral agency is an important doctrine and principle of the gospel. It was Satan's plan to destroy our agency. With our agency, we are free to make good or poor choices. Alma and Amulek watched as faithful believers were burned. Amulek was tempted to use God's power to save them. However, Alma restrained him and said, "The spirit constraineth me. . . . The Lord . . . doth suffer that . . . people may do this thing . . . that the judgments which he shall exercise upon them in his wrath may be just; and the blood of the innocent shall stand as a witness against them" (Alma 14:11).

Moroni taught that in some circumstances the Lord permits the righteous to suffer or even die as a result of another's sinful use of agency so that "His justice and judgment may come upon the wicked" (Alma 60:13).

At times Dennis and I have felt we had witnessed miracles. At other times we felt that we really needed a miracle and it seemed to be withheld. We witnessed miracles in our oldest son Darren's illness. We also experienced times when the promised blessings didn't seem to come in the way we had hoped for. He endured lengthy physical suffering, emotional despair, and spiritual disappointments. Understanding the reasons seven surgeries weren't successful was difficult, but we went forward with hope that the total healing promised through blessings would eventually come. Sometimes we felt as Job did, that no one could understand our suffering. On two different occasions we were told by well meaning friends and relatives, "Will you just tell Darren to learn what he is supposed to learn so he can get better?" The unsaid message came through loud and clear: "Your son's medical illness is caused by God. It results from Darren not knowing something he must learn through his suffering." Clichés and unkind words from individuals that cause spiritual injury or "enlarge the wounds of those already wounded" do not flow from God, Christ, or the Holy Ghost (Jacob 2:9). Two years and eight surgeries later, Darren was finally completely healed.

God Has Given Us the Comforter

We are less likely to become overwhelmed if we can focus on God as our source and author of all spiritual tools. He gave us the Atonement through His Son and the companionship of the Holy Ghost as His voice. The scriptures testify that Jesus Christ understands our grief: Christ is a "man of sorrows, and acquainted with grief" (Isaiah 53:3). The Holy Ghost is a comforter and the revealer of truth. All insights and reassurances that can bring spiritual healing originate from Godly sources.

God is always there to comfort and support us through our trials: "I will not leave you comfortless. I will come to you" (John 14:18). "Look unto God with firmness of mind, and pray unto him with exceeding faith, and he will console you in your afflictions, and he will plead your cause" (Jacob 3:1).

"He hath sent me to bind up the broken hearted . . . to comfort all that mourn; to appoint unto them that mourn in Zion, to give unto them beauty for ashes, the oil of joy for mourning, the garment of praise for the spirit of heaviness" (Isaiah 61:1–3). God hears us in our affliction (Alma 33:11). "And God will wipe away all tears from their eyes" (Revelation 21:4).

Although we may not understand why some people are healed and others are not, it is comforting to know God does have the ultimate power to heal us physically, mentally, and spiritually. Alma taught that "He will take upon him . . . the sicknesses of his people" (Alma 7:11) and He will succor us in our weaknesses (Alma 7:12).

There Is a Balance with Justice and Mercy

President John Taylor taught, "There may be circumstances arise in this world to pervert for a season the order of God, to change the designs of the Most High, apparently, for the time being. Yet they will ultimately roll back into their proper place—Justice will have its place, and so will Mercy, and every man and woman will yet stand in their true position before God."[4]

Mortal life can seem endless for those facing long-term adversity. Earth life is not necessarily fair. According to Neal A. Maxwell, "If it's fair, it is not a true trial."[5]

It can be helpful for innocent victims to know that God is just and merciful and that there will be justice for those who use their agency inappropriately. The principle of God punishing the wicked is taught throughout the scriptures: "The wages of sin are death" (Romans 6:23). Spiritual death results in a separation from God. The Lord will judge and punish the unjust (Deuteronomy 24:16; 2 Peter 2:4; Mormon 4:5; Alma 42:22).

Why Me? Why Now? Why This Way?

The following letter was written by a mother to her teenage son who was killed in a bike/truck accident. It displays the common confusion and questions when adversity strikes: "I love you so. I'm so sorry that I wasn't there that morning, to not let you ride, for not making you go with me that terrible day. I love you so much. All I want for you is to be happy. Please, please be happy. Please be with us in Eternal Life. Was this the way it was supposed to be?"[6]

The *whys* are a common and painful part of adversity. We think we have finally resolved them, and then we ask again. There seems to be different kinds of *whys*: "Why did this happen, God? Why did this happen logically or medically?" Dennis and I asked those questions. We wanted to know the details of what happened when Cam's heart stopped, why Darren's surgeries failed, and when another son would overcome his struggle with addictions.

The irony of our *whys* is this question: "How often in happy times did you ask, why?"[7] Many have found, "He who has a Why to live for can endure almost any How."[8]

Elder Neal A. Maxwell explains that trials come to us from three general categories:[9]

Type 1: *Trials we bring on ourselves by the sinful choices and mistakes we make.* Some blame God for trials resulting from our personal choices and overly identify with Job, when in actuality our trial is self-imposed. A scriptural example of the consequences of a sinful choice is found in the story of King David. David made a series of choices that ultimately resulted in an act of adultery with Bathsheba and the death of her husband, Uriah (2 Samuel 11:2).

Type 2: *Trials that are part of earth life.* For example, people get sick, have accidents, endure old age, and die. We could also add to this category those who suffer innocently from the sinful choices of others—those abused, murdered, and betrayed. Most of the suffering we experience here is a product of the vulnerabilities and realities of earth life, including the misuse of agency by others. The Lord doesn't fly airplanes into international trade centers or drive the car of the alcoholic who takes the life of an innocent child playing in his path. Nor does God, in most instances, though He could, prevent these events from occurring.

Type 3: *Trials God uses to refine us.* "But he knoweth the way that I take: when he hath tried me, I shall come forth as gold" (Job 23:10). When Christ was asked if a man's blindness was the result of sin, He answered: "Neither hath this man sinned, nor his parents: but that the works of God should be made manifest in him" (John 9:3).

Dennis's and my personal experiences and observations over years of counseling have caused us to conclude that the vast majority of the challenges and suffering we face on this earth are Type 2 suffering, resulting from the realities and trials of earth life.

Elder Maxwell further stated, "The sudden loss of health, wealth, self-esteem, status, or a loved one—developments that may stun us—are foreseen by God, though not necessarily caused by him."[10]

It is not our place to decide which of the three types of adversity our neighbors are experiencing. Our tendency to judge others more critically than ourselves is humorously illustrated in the following definitions:

- **Punishing:** what the Lord is doing to your Gentile neighbor when misfortunes come.
- **Chastening:** what the Lord is doing to your LDS neighbor when adversity hits.
- **Testing:** what the Lord is doing when a bad thing happens to you.

When he was a member of the Quorum of the Twelve, Spencer W. Kimball authored a pamphlet called *Tragedy or Destiny*. He humbly cautions that the pamphlet contains many of his own thoughts and personal beliefs. Nevertheless, Elder Kimball's personal revelation is insightful and poses some challenging questions for each of us to ponder. He asks, "Does the Lord cause tragedies in people's lives?" and "Why does the Lord let these terrible things happen?" A child drowned, several people were killed in a plane crash, and a young elder was killed in the mission field. Elder Kimball asks, "Was it the Lord who directed the plane to crash or the drowning to occur?" He raises the question, "Could the Lord have prevented these tragedies?" He confirms that the answer is definitely yes. The Lord is omnipotent with all power. However, Elder Kimball poses additional questions: What if the Lord always punished the wicked and blessed the righteous? How would the gospel law of moral agency work? Wouldn't we always choose righteousness if we were immediately blessed? Wouldn't the wicked choose righteousness if they were immediately punished? Would they continue to choose to be wicked? Should the righteous be protected from hardship, pain, suffering, sacrifice, or tragedy?

Elder Kimball concluded:

> But if all the sick were healed, if all the righteous were protected and the wicked destroyed, the whole program of the Father would be annulled and the basic principal of the gospel, free agency, would be ended. If pain and sorrow and total punishment immediately followed the doing of evil, no soul would repeat a misdeed. If joy and peace and rewards were instantaneously given to the doer of

good, there would be no evil—all would do good and not because of the rightness of doing good, there would be no test of strength, no development of character, no growth of powers, no free agency, only satanic controls. Should all prayers be immediately answered according to our selfish desires and our limited understanding, then there would be little or no suffering, sorrow, disappointment or even death, and if these were not there would also be an absence of joy, success, resurrection, eternal life and Godhood.[11]

Would God have protected Paul from his "thorn in the flesh" (2 Corinthians 12:7)? The Lord said unto him, "My grace is sufficient for thee: for my strength is made perfect in weakness. Most gladly therefore will I rather glory in my infirmities that the power of Christ may rest upon me" (2 Corinthians 12:9).

Would we have allowed Jesus to stay on the cross? Would we have allowed the Prophet Joseph Smith to suffer in Liberty Jail, and later die in the Carthage Jail if we had all power?

Sometimes when we ask *why*, we are really saying, "Lord, let me be in control, give me the reigns, everything will work out better if I'm in control. I doubt God's goodness because He does not use His power exactly as I wish."[12]

Orson F. Whitney taught: "No pain that we suffer, no trial that we experience is wasted. It ministers to our education, to the development of such qualities as patience, faith, fortitude and humility. All that we suffer and all that we endure, especially when we endure it patiently, builds up our character, purifies our hearts, expands our souls, and makes us more tender and charitable, more worthy to be called the children of God."[13]

Is It God's Will?

One mother asked, "Was it God's will that my daughter was raped and murdered?" Many hurting members of the Church have struggled when they were told their adversity is God's will. It seems helpful when we say something like this to them: "It is certainly God's will that we experience earth life and return to Him. God created this world where we experience pain, sickness, accidents, and death." "However, to say to the suffering individual that God's finger was on the trigger or that he caused someone to be murdered, raped, abused or betrayed is a cruel and unreasonable false doctrine."[14]

Am I Being Punished?

Some fear their tragedy is a punishment for past sins. Belated confessions to extramarital affairs, Church inactivity, breaking commandments, and dishonesty are common when personal tragedy occurs. These shortcomings often come quickly to mind when life's circumstances seem out of our control. When we receive blessings from God, it is through obedience to eternal laws (D&C 130:20–21). Conversely, some of us may inevitably reason that when we don't receive blessings or protection from God, it is always a result of our personal weakness and sin. After a crisis, these and other perceived truisms quickly flood our minds, complicating our grieving. We may search for some wrong we did in the past to explain our present loss. The association of loss and shortcomings may actually increase the complexity of our grief process. However, if our adversity is indeed a result of sin, then it is important that we utilize repentance as a healing tool.

As we confront adversity, we must evaluate each situation and when appropriate eliminate incorrect and erroneous thinking.

A grieving father experiencing multiple losses asks, "Would God punish or teach me by causing my daughter to experience abuse, my wife to get cancer, or my child to die, or does he allow these events and provide the resources and support necessary for our personalized growth and development toward Godhood?"[15]

The Prophet Joseph Smith taught, "It is an unhallowed principle to say that such and such have transgressed because they have been preyed upon by disease or death, for all flesh is subject to death and the Savior has said, 'judge not' lest 'ye be judged.' "[16]

If we accept that living the best we can inevitably falls short of all that is ultimately required, we will question less that we are responsible for all of life's disappointments and tragedies that come our way.

Elder Merrill J. Bateman, an emeritus member of the Quorum of the Seventy, said, "When one understands that trials are not necessarily the result of one's own doing, the test may be easier to endure."[17]

Refining

We should be hesitant in telling someone else that God is refining them as He refined Job. "I will refine them as silver is refined, and will try them as gold is tried" (Zechariah 13:11).

Examples in scripture of how God uses trials and affliction in specific instances may not be a representative sampling of how most of our life's trials originate. "Nevertheless the Lord seeth fit to chasten his people; yea, he trieth their patience and their faith" (Mosiah 23:21).

Elder Neal Maxwell explains that "there may be those who choose to debate . . . whether . . . God gives us a particular trial or simply declines to remove it."[18] If we can be patient and endure, the Lord can consecrate our afflictions (2 Nephi 2:2) and support us in our trials (Alma 36:3).

Am I Being Tested?

Some have also answered their "why me" questions by concluding that God is testing them, trying to see what they are made of. The previous conclusions could apply. Certainly we believe that all life has meaning and purpose and is a test. But should we look to God for inflicting every challenge or thorny problem directly on us as an assignment from Him, or are most of our trials a result of living in a world where adversity exists?

Some members of the Church are offended when they are told during a crisis that God is trying to tell them or teach them something. God certainly does allow us to learn and grow through adversity. However, making God responsible for divorce, accidents, or illness may result in serious spiritual injury.

A spiritual nonmember client in her late twenties was sure that the two miscarriages following her marriage were a direct punishment from God. She reasoned that because she had an abortion as a sixteen-year-old, she needed chastisement. She also carried a lot of guilt because she had never told her parents about the abortion. The repentance process proved healing for her, and she eventually did have a healthy full-term baby. However, the question remained, was her miscarriage inflicted on her because of her sin, or had the abortion she chose caused physical damage to her body that resulted in her compromised ability to maintain a full-term pregnancy?

Repentance and the Atonement

The previously mentioned client's crisis did, fortunately, encourage her to go through the repentance process and experience God's forgiveness. In John we are told if we confess our sins, God will forgive (1 John 1:9). If we don't repent, God is slow to answer our prayers and deliver us from afflictions (Mosiah 11:23–25). Through the Atonement we can be turned into another man and receive a new heart (1 Samuel 10:6, 9). "Faith and repentance bringeth a change of heart" (Helaman 15:7).

Elder Boyd K. Packer gives a beautiful parable of the Atonement, repentance, justice, and mercy. He tells of a man who wanted more material things than he could afford to buy. He promised his creditor that he would work hard and pay his debt off slowly with time. However, when the deadline came, the debtor was lacking and could not pay. The creditor put chains on his hands and feet and was ready to send him off to prison. As the debtor was crying and mourning the justice of his fate, a compassionate friend stepped forward, offering the debtor mercy by paying his debt. The chains were removed and the debtor was told he was free to go. With gratitude he agreed to finish paying his debt to this new creditor who had shown him mercy. This allegory teaches us that in spite of all we do, we are all lacking and come up short until Christ steps in to pay our debt with His Atonement as we repent.

Christ suffered "the pains of every living creature, both men, women, and children" (2 Nephi 9:21). This suffering is not just limited to sin, "but also the cumulative burden of all depression, all loneliness, all sorrow."[19]

The Savior has felt the pain and suffering brought about by living single, losing loved ones, facing illness, and enduring disabilities. He knows the pain and disappointment following a difficult divorce. He is no stranger to life's many losses. He willingly bears all these burdens and as our personal Savior understands our every suffering. Isaiah taught, "In all their affliction, he was afflicted, and the angel of his presence saved them: in his love and in his pity . . . he redeemed them, and carried them" (Isaiah 63:9).

Elder David A. Bednar said, "The enabling power of the Atonement strengthens us to do and be good and serve beyond our own individual desire and natural capacity."[20]

Forgiveness

"Forgiveness can increase emotional and physical healing. Being unwilling to forgive can 'FREEZE' you."[21]

Forgiveness can be part of our spiritual healing. However, it may take time and a lot of spiritual grief work to accomplish such a task. How do you forgive someone who has hurt you? Acts of betrayal may be especially painful.

Many have asked, "Can I forgive a perpetrator if they have not repented? Can I forgive without hearing the words 'I'm sorry'?"

"The reality of the situation is that no amount of talking, no analysis of why the betrayal occurred will completely do away with the hurt. No penalty can be handed down that will satisfactorily pay off the debt. No matter how cruelly you've been treated, the power to forgive does not lie within the person who hurt you . . . the blocks to forgiveness are ultimately within you. Forgiveness can stop the cycle of hurt."[22]

As we hope for God's forgiveness through the Atonement, we must also offer forgiveness to others and ourselves. Many of our struggles originate from someone who has hurt us. It is important to remember that Christ has assumed the unpaid balance of wrongdoings and imperfections incurred by those who have hurt us. We can find peace by allowing Christ to intervene and by letting go of our pain. As difficult as it may seem, we no longer need to focus on others' sins. This letting go is not only for them but, more important, for us.

The following false beliefs and biases can limit our ability to forgive someone who has hurt, abused, or betrayed us:

1. Forgiving allows perpetrators to get away with something.
2. Forgiveness is a sign of personal weakness.
3. Forgiving will cause the abuse to occur again.
4. Not forgiving helps punish the perpetrator.

5. The perpetrator must repent or apologize before I can forgive.

Forgiving someone is difficult, but it is possible. One woman said, "My spouse has been unfaithful. After our divorce he remarried and divorced again. We have now decided to try and to put our temple marriage back together. It's been so hard to trust and forgive. However, I feel I need to try."[23]

How do you forgive the man who robbed, raped, or murdered your loved one? One parent said, "My daughter was raped and murdered. It has been seven years. I will never forget or get over it. However, I am trying to forgive."[24]

Only through the power of Christ and the Atonement can one heal from such trauma. The Lord commanded: "Ye ought to forgive one another; . . . it is required to forgive *all* men" (D&C 64:9–10; Matthew 18:35; emphasis added).

The following tools have proven helpful to those attempting to offer forgiveness:

1. Write a letter to the offender; the letter may or may not be mailed.
2. Keep a journal of your feelings and memories, which may be personal or shared with trusted others.
3. Visualize and confront the offender (in an empty chair or through guided imagery with a professional counselor).
4. Pray, study, and receive priesthood blessings.

"Forgiveness is an ongoing process. It is a gift you give yourself. Christ offered us forgiveness . . . before we ever needed or asked for it."[25]

The Lord has said that "vengeance is mine, I will repay" (Mormon 3:15) and that Satan is the author of not forgiving (2 Corinthians 2:10–11).

Opposition

In the Book of Mormon Lehi teaches, "For it must needs be, that there is opposition in all things . . . righteousness . . . wickedness, holiness . . . misery . . . good . . . bad" (2 Nephi 2:11).

"And they taste the bitter that they may know to prize the good" (Moses 6:55–56).

"Only the soul that knows the mighty pain can know the mighty rapture."[26]

Omnipotence

God not only weeps with us as we experience pain, but He also loves and comforts us through His power. We must remember His omnipotence even when the answer to our prayer is no, or when the comfort comes in delayed or different ways than we expected.

Personal Revelation and Impressions

Personal revelation and impressions can bring healing and comfort. These spiritual impressions are provided to us by a loving Heavenly Father through the gift of the Holy Ghost, one of the most powerful spiritual tools available.

Dennis and I had impressions that caused us to believe that we might lose Cameron. We often feared that through our neglect he would die from an accident. He regularly fell off his tricycle, and even with his helmet on he seemed vulnerable. However, we didn't anticipate that he would slip away in his sleep in a close observation hospital room with bright lights on and with Dennis and a nurse nearby.

Two years after Cameron's death, both of us were surprised how much we still missed and mourned for him. One day as I was feeling particularly sad and discouraged, I cried out in prayer, "How long will it hurt so much? Why does the pain keep coming back?" Then I heard a still small voice in my heart and mind that directed me to read in the Bible. I turned to Jeremiah 31. *A strange place to read*, I thought. I knew I hadn't read much from here before. When I got to verses 15–17, I felt the Lord was trying to comfort me and all those who have or ever will lose a loved one. "Thus saith the Lord; A voice was heard in Ramah, lamentation and bitter weeping; Rachel weeping for her children refused to be comforted for her children, because they were not. Thus saith the Lord; Refrain thy voice from weeping, and thine eyes from tears: for thy work shall be rewarded, saith the

Lord; and they shall come again. . . . And there is hope in thine end, saith the Lord, that thy children shall come again."

This scripture hit me with great force and power. I realized later that this counsel was given to the mothers who were mourning for their children whom King Herod had ordered to be killed. These inspired words gave me hope and strength to endure the long earth life without two of our children.

"Fear not, let your hearts be comforted . . . waiting patiently on the Lord, for your prayers have entered into the ears of the Lord . . . all things wherewith you have been afflicted shall work together for your good" (D&C 98:1–3).

"But they that wait upon the Lord shall renew their strength; they shall mount up with wings as eagles; they shall run, and not be weary; and they shall walk, and not faint" (Isaiah 40:31).

Impressions and revelations have blessed many during adversity. Some are surprised by the answers they have received. One woman shares: "I have tried for many years to keep my temple marriage intact. I have received comfort from the Spirit and many impressions on how to do this. Even after my husband had left us and was excommunicated, I believed we would work things out and stay together. I was shocked after much fasting and prayer when I received an impression to file for divorce."[27]

Another woman, surprised by her answer, said: "My husband had been unfaithful, divorced me, remarried, and divorced again. I was shocked when I received a answer after much fasting and prayer to give him another chance and put our temple marriage back together."[28]

An unwed mother writes: "As much as I want to keep my baby, I received a strong impression that if I really love and care about him, I should place him for adoption so he can be sealed and have both a mother and a father."[29]

Faith and Hope

Having faith and hope does not mean things will always come out how we'd like. It does mean we can trust the Lord to comfort us. A Kosovo high school senior living as a refugee in Albania shared with Dennis the reason for his family's desire to return to their destroyed home in Kosovo. When Dennis attempted to return a picture of the boy's home (given to him as a thank you gift for the Church's humanitarian aid), the teen refused to take the photo back. He said, "You keep the picture so you won't forget our people. I don't need the photo because faith, hope, and Kosovo are in my heart and no man can take it from me."

In Romans 8 we read, "For we are saved by hope: but hope that is seen is not hope: for what a man seeth, why doth he yet hope for?" (v. 24). In Nephi 31 we are counseled to "press forward with a brightness of hope" (v. 20).

Faith can be a healing tool for grief recovery: "The only way to meet affliction is to pass through it solemnly, slowly, with humility and faith, as the Israelites passed through the [Red] sea. Then its very waves of misery will divide, and become to us a wall, on the right side and on the left, until the gulf narrows before our eyes, and we will land safe on the opposite shore."[30]

The scriptures also testify that not all have faith (D&C 88:118) and that faith is a gift (1 Corinthians 12:9). We all have different gifts, and we are not to judge the faithless (Romans 14:1–5).

Pilots enjoy a clear sky when they fly above the clouds, even though down below we might be buried under a blanket of dark clouds. At times our lives seem buried under a blanket of despair and discouragement, and all we can see is the darkness. The reality is, the sun is always shining. The *Son* is also always shining for us, even when we find ourselves in the black pit of despair.[31] We can have faith and tap into spiritual tools to know His power and see clearer.

The definition of faith in the Kings James Bible Dictionary reads: "Faith is to hope for things which are not seen, but are true." The apostle Paul taught, "Now faith is the substance of things hoped for, the evidence of things not seen" (Hebrews 11:1).

In the Book of Mormon we are taught that we "receive no witness until after the trial of [our] faith" (Ether 12:6). The brother of Jared displayed great faith. He progressed beyond faith when he asked the Lord to touch the stones that they might have light. His faith transcended to pure, absolute knowledge when he saw his Savior. Our faith may not be as fruitful as the brother of Jared. However, His example can encourage and even increase our faith.

After Cameron died, we hoped he would appear to us and offer comfort. When he didn't return, we found peace reading the following scripture: "Blessed are they that have not seen, and yet have believed" (John 20:29).

By faith Abraham offered up Isaac. By faith Moses refused the life offered by Pharaoh and followed God to deliver his people. By faith Joseph of Egypt survived and made the best of being kidnapped and sold by his brothers. By faith the walls of Jericho fell. By faith Joseph Smith survived emotionally and spiritually his personal trials and persecutions.

We can find strength in the parable of the mustard seed and nurture our faith: "If ye have faith as a grain of mustard seed . . . nothing shall be impossible to you" (Matthew 17:20). The mustard seed is one of the smallest seeds, yet if nourished it can grow into a large tree. After adversity we may have to start over again by replanting a tiny seed of hope. We can let our desire for faith work in us as we nourish and exercise faith (Alma 32). However, we must remember that having faith does not preclude us from experiencing grief.

Service

Service can be a healing tool that offers relief both to ourselves and others. Helping others helps us to forget our problems as we discover that there are others suffering. Sir James Barrie said, "Those who bring sunshine to others cannot keep it from themselves."[32]

Christ was an example of service during his trials: He "poureth water into a basin, and began to wash the disciples' feet, and to wipe them with a towel wherewith he was girded" (John 13:5). He then said, "If I then, your Lord and Master, have washed your feet; ye also ought to wash one another's feet. For I have given you an example, that ye should do as I have done unto you" (John 13:14–15).

On Cameron's first birthday after his death, we were feeling really down and missing him. Someone in the ward called to see if we would take a meal in to a homebound widow. We made ourselves go, and on our way home, after delivering the food and visiting with the widow, we noticed our grief had lifted some and we felt a little better.

During our oldest son Darren's serious complications from colitis and bowel surgeries, he struggled daily for two years to regain his health. However, he felt he should keep trying to push himself to serve and work. As he offered counseling and support to others who needed him, he found peace and eventually healing for himself.

Church Attendance

We may find it difficult to attend church during and after a crisis. The hymns and lessons that once offered us comfort now may flood us with tears and remind us of our loss. For many years following Cameron's death, it was very difficult to watch the sacrament being passed without him. He had been able to pass the sacrament with the use of a special metal tray attached to the arm of his electric wheelchair. We loved watching him go row to row.

A widower said: "It's so hard to sit on the pew without my wife next to me."

A grieving woman in Relief Society said: "I felt like I was under glass, like everyone was staring at me, wondering how I was doing. The lessons seemed so trite compared to what I was facing."

There are also many who find increased peace and comfort at church following a crisis. "I am just loving going to church, Sunday school, Relief Society, etc.! I am soaking up every word. I am craving the spirit right now."

Eventually most of us can return to church as we find and accept our "new normal." The peace, comfort, and fellowship of worship can with time bring lasting happiness and comfort.

Sacrament Blessings

Do we only find God during times of peace, happiness, and abundance? Do we miss out on growing experiences and God's love when we look for it only in times of smooth sailing? Do we believe God loves us unconditionally? Are we only blessed when things are going well? Some experiencing adversities have asked if they are "still blessed." It is a common phrase we hear often during fast and testimony meetings. When people say, "I am blessed," what does that mean? Does it mean they have no problems in their lives or that they are focusing on the good things? If we are having a lot of adversity, can we still be "blessed"? When we ask God to bless us, are we seeking something specific, or asking for protection? Are we actually seeking His Spirit to be with us? The sacrament prayer confirms this when it says to "always remember him and keep his commandments . . . that they may always have his Spirit to be with them" (D&C 20:77, 79).

We can have His spirit with us even during adversity. We can feel "blessed" even amidst our tragedies.

Commandments

Living the commandments is a spiritual tool that can also bring comfort when we are grieving. It may seem difficult to focus on them. However, "consider on the blessed and happy state of those that keep the commandments of God" (Mosiah 2:41).

Temples

Temple attendance is a service. It also can bring answers to our prayers and provide us with comfort. Many have found the temple to be a safe and peaceful refuge during adversity.

Elder Dallin Oaks teaches, "One of the purposes of building a temple is to present to the Lord a house in which He can reveal Himself and His mysteries to His faithful children."[33]

Although some of us have had profound spiritual experiences in the temple and have felt the presence of deceased ancestors, others may not get the miracle they hoped for. One of my childhood friends recently confided in me, "I have wanted to feel the presence of my deceased son in the temple. It seems odd that others tell me they feel him there and I do not."

We don't understand all of the workings of the Spirit in the temple. There may be many reasons someone does or does not receive a particular spiritual gift. The apostle Paul tells us, "Now there are diversities of gifts . . . For to one is given . . . To another." He lists wisdom, knowledge, faith, healing, tongues, working miracles, prophecy, and discerning of spirits (1 Corinthians 12:4–11). Moroni lists additional gifts in the Book of Mormon: teaching and "the beholding of angels and ministering spirits" (Moroni 10:13). Not all people are to receive the gift of beholding angels and spirits.

Mysteries

Many of our spiritual frustrations don't end with us saying, "Okay, Lord, now I understand, and I see why these terrible things are happening to me." Rather, we must file many of life's challenges away as mysteries or something we just can't understand. Nephi taught us that God loves his children, but Nephi did not know the meaning of all things (1 Nephi 11:17).

Part of faith is knowing there are mysteries. Our natural eyes cannot see and understand all. The Greek term *mystery* means "to close the eyes or to close the mouth."

The word *mystery* appears in the New Testament twenty-four times. Paul speaks of "the mysteries of God" (1 Corinthians 4:1). "The mysteries of God's will" is found in Ephesians 1:9.

Although there are many mysteries, we are blessed as members of Christ's Church to have the restored gospel, which reveals additional spiritual knowledge.

Elder Oaks teaches, "The Melchizedek Priesthood gives us access to the mysteries of God . . . through this priesthood we receive the gift of the Holy Ghost, by which we are taught the things of God."[34]

Scriptures

When we found out that Cameron had cerebral palsy, his grandpa sent this scripture to comfort us. I have since learned the power of letting the scriptures guide, speak, and bring comfort.

> Who shall separate us from the love of Christ? Shall tribulation, or distress, or persecution, or famine, or nakedness, or peril, or sword? . . .
>
> Nay in all these things we are more than conquerors through him that loved us.
>
> For I am persuaded, that neither death, nor life, nor angels, nor principalities, nor powers, nor things present, nor things to come, nor height, nor depth, nor any other creature, shall be able to separate us from the love of God. (Romans 8:35, 37–39)

As members of the Church, we often take for granted these spiritual tools. Many of us have heard them from our childhood. Nevertheless, the most profound comfort often comes through the gifts of the Spirit. These gifts of the Spirit could include scriptures, prayer, priesthood blessings, visions, impressions, and so forth. The comfort of the Holy Ghost has given Dennis and me the strength to endure many of life's challenges. When our oldest son, Darren, was enduring surgery after surgery, impressions came as "the eyes of my understanding was opened, and the spirit of the Lord rested upon me" (D&C 138:11).

It literally felt like "the spirit like a dove descend[ed] upon" me (Mark 1:10).

Fasting and Prayer

Do we pray as fervently during good times as we do during adversity? Even the Savior seemed to turn to God more fervently during His agony and suffering,: "Being in an agony he prayed more earnestly" (Luke 22:44).

We can reach the Lord through praying, fasting, and receiving priesthood blessings. However, many struggling individuals cannot initially turn to these spiritual tools during their crisis. Some individuals following their tragedy have reluctantly shared their heartfelt disappointments: "It is so difficult to pray to a God who allowed this to happen to my family."

It's important for us to keep trying and not give up. Remember that eventually most will be able to return to their faith and reach out to God again. It will then be possible for us to tap into the power of the Holy Ghost, who is literally the Comforter. One member of the Church described it well when she wrote, "I have prayed, fasted, attended the temple, and received a priesthood blessing in hopes of being relieved of my adversity. However, my adversity still remains. Now I pray, fast, attend the temple and receive blessings to help me *endure* my adversity."

How Do We Endure to the End?

One great example of enduring is found in the story of Job. Job's many losses were intensified by the long duration of suffering he experienced:

Time's leavening must sharpen his pain, deepen his disappointment and intensify his discouragement, to see if heightened tension would break his spirit and drive him from the Lord . . . time was assigned to chew away at Job's inner strength until he became miserable—miserable in spirit and body, so miserable in fact, that death appeared in his mind as a coveted, comforting, liberating friend. Who can imagine the state of his mind at this point? Perhaps some of us, maybe none of us.[35]

Job said he was weary of life, bitter in soul, and longing for death (Job 3:20–22; 10:1)

Enduring to the end is an important spiritual tool. Of course, most of us don't really understand the meaning of those words. We never know what challenges we might eventually have to endure or for how long.

Enduring to the end may mean a variety of things to each of us. Sometimes accepting our adversity is the first step to enduring and healing.

Enduring is a principle of the gospel. Many righteous people have had to endure. Ten of Christ's twelve disciples were executed. Stephen was stoned. Joseph Smith, Job, and many other great men had to endure adversity. It is helpful to look to Christ as our example. He too had to experience earthly pain and suffering of His own free will: "Though he were a Son, yet learned he obedience by the things which he suffered; And being made perfect, he became the author of eternal salvation unto all them that obeyed him" (Hebrews 5:8–9).

The Prophet Joseph Smith also called out to the Lord in Liberty Jail for relief from suffering: "Oh God, where art thou? . . . Yea, O Lord, how long shall they suffer these wrongs and unlawful oppressions, before thine heart shall be softened toward them, and . . . [thou] be moved with compassion toward them?" (D&C 121:1, 3). In verse 7 the Lord told him: "My son, peace be unto thy soul; thine adversity and thine afflictions shall be but a small moment."

The Lord provided support as He continued to discuss Joseph's afflictions. However, He didn't immediately remove them. He told Joseph:

> If thou art called to pass through tribulation . . . If thou art accused with all manner of false accusations; . . . and thou be dragged

to prison, . . . and the sentence of death passed upon thee; . . . if fierce winds become thine enemy; if the heavens gather blackness, and all the elements combine to hedge up the way; and above all, if the very jaws of hell shall gape open the mouth wide after thee, know thou, my son, that all these things shall give thee experience, and shall be for thy good. The Son of Man hath descended below them all. Art thou greater than he? . . . Fear not what man can do, for God shall be with you forever and ever. (D&C 122:5–9)

After one of Darren's colon surgeries, he had to return to the hospital with a painful abscess. He was very sick and discouraged. All of his blessings had assured him that he had made the best decision in choosing to do the initial surgery. The blessings also assured him of a quick recovery. If a day is a thousand years in the Lord's time, what is a quick recovery? I recall a hospice patient asking the Lord if she could have more time (she was young). Through a personal spiritual experience, she was told she could have two extra seconds! After her death, one of our social workers did the math and felt she had received precisely the extra earth days she had prayed for.

One night after a family fast, our youngest son prayed that the blessings that had been promised to his older brother could be fulfilled. We felt renewed faith that these blessings would eventually flow down from heaven. We felt healing would eventually come, and we needed to be patient and endure. Healing was still a long time in coming, but it eventually occurred. Although Darren's brush with death was one of the hardest, most emotionally draining experiences we have endured, it was also very spiritual.

I have grown to admire those I work with in hospice. Many suffer day in and day out, week after week, month after month, wondering when death will bring relief. It's not only hard on those suffering, but also on the caregivers watching, loving, and often providing backbreaking care at the bedside. Caring for my own angel mother in our home was hard work mixed with many blessings.

Elder Maxwell taught, "When in situations of stress we wonder if there is any more in us to give, we can be comforted to know that God, who knows our capability perfectly, placed us here to succeed.

No one was foreordained to fail or to be wicked. When we have been weighed and found wanting, let us remember that we were measured before and found equal to our tasks; and, therefore, let us continue, but with a more determined discipleship."[36] "If thou endure it well, God shall exalt thee" (D&C 121:8).

Patience

Paul outlines some benefits for our tribulations to help us cope. "Tribulation worketh patience; And patience, experience; and experience, hope" (Romans 5:3–4; see also D&C 54:10).

"Patience is not to be mistaken for indifference. It is to care very much, but to be willing, nevertheless, to submit both to the Lord and to what the scriptures call the 'process of time.' "[37]

Patience is a difficult attribute for many of us to obtain. "We often expect instantaneous solutions, forgetting that frequently the heavenly virtue of patience is required."[38]

"Be patient in afflictions, for thou shalt have many; but endure them, for, lo, I am with thee, even unto the end of thy days" (D&C 24:8).

Forsaken

It is helpful to remember that at times in their adversity, Job, Moses, David, Joseph Smith, Joseph in Egypt, Jesus, and many other righteous individuals have felt forsaken by God during their suffering. At times it may be difficult for us to understand why He doesn't intervene in the way we think is best or fair. Some may wonder if the Lord has forgotten them. They might say, "The Lord hath forsaken me, and my Lord hath forgotten me." And then comes the answer: "He will show that he hath not." Christ Himself then says, "Behold I have graven thee upon the palms of my hands" (1 Nephi 21:16).

When Christ was in the Garden of Gethsemane, He prayed, "Let this cup pass . . . nevertheless not as I will, but as thou wilt" (Matthew 26:39). This letting go and acceptance is a powerful example.

Covenants

We make covenants at baptism. We renew these covenants each week as we partake of the sacrament. Three of the eight covenants

Alma taught at the waters of Mormon involve helping others experiencing loss and adversity:

1. Being willing to bear one another's burdens.
2. Mourning with those that mourn.
3. Comforting those that stand in need of comfort. (Mosiah 18:8–9)

Christ exemplified these covenants following the death of Lazarus. In John 11:35 we read, "Jesus wept." It appears that the Savior of the world, who learned obedience by the things He suffered, was willing to *mourn* with those who were *mourning* the death of Lazarus (including a distraught and somewhat frustrated Mary). The next verse makes clear the impact of the Lord's willingness to bear another's burden and stand in comfort to those present. Verse 36 reads, "Then said the Jews, behold how he loved him."

The Savior of the world knows our pain; He loves us and is there to comfort us. May God give us the strength, courage, and commitment to keep these covenants. May we be able to proclaim as Paul: "I have fought a good fight, I have finished my course, I have kept the faith" (2 Timothy 4:7).

Notes

1. Joyce and Dennis Ashton, *Jesus Wept* (Springville, Utah: Cedar Fort, Inc., 2001), 129.
2. Deanna Edwards, *GRIEVING: The Pain and the Promise* (American Fork, Utah: Covenant Communications, Inc., 1989), 151.
3. M. Russell Ballard, "You Have Nothing to Fear from the Journey," in Conference Report, Apr. 1997, 82; or *Ensign*, May 1997, 61.
4. John Taylor, *The Gospel Kingdom: Selections from the Writings and Discourses of John Taylor* (Salt Lake City: Bookcraft, 1987), 346.
5. Neal A. Maxwell, *All These Things Shall Give Thee Experience* (Salt Lake City: Deseret Book, 1979), 31.
6. Ashton, *Jesus Wept,* 135.
7. E. A. Grollman, King's College Bereavement Conference, May 1995.
8. Friedrich Nietzsche (quote public domain over 100 years old).
9. Maxwell, *All These Things Shall Give Thee Experience,* 29–31.

10. Ibid., 28.

11. Spencer W. Kimball, *Tragedy or Destiny* (Salt Lake City: Deseret Book, 1982); *Faith Precedes the Miracle* (Salt Lake City: Deseret Book, 1972), 97.

12. J. Hunt, "Hope for the Heart," Newsletter, Sept./Oct. 1996, 3.

13. Spencer W. Kimball, *Faith Precedes the Miracle*, 98.

14. Charles Meyer, *Surviving Death: A Practical Guide to Caring for the Dying and Bereaved* (Mystic, CT: Twenty-Third Publications, 1991); see also Ashton, 139.

15. Ashton, *Jesus Wept*, 141.

16. Lyndon Cook and Andrew F. Ehat, *Words of Joseph Smith* (Salt Lake City: Deseret Book), 141.

17. Merrill J. Bateman, "Living a Christ-centered Life," *Ensign*, Jan. 1999, 15; see also Ashton, 139.

18. Maxwell, *All These Things Shall Give Thee Experience,* 31.

19. Tad R. Callister, *The Infinite Atonement* (Salt Lake City: Deseret Book, 2000), 104.

20. David A. Bednar In the strength of the Lord we can do and endure and overcome all things, 10-23-2001.

21. M. Gamblin with permission to quote Dr. Paul W. Coleman.

22. Ibid.

23. Ashton, *Jesus Wept,* 146.

24. Ibid., 146–47.

25. *Church News*, Salt Lake City, Utah, 15.

26. Earl A. Grollman, *Living When a Loved One Has Died* (Boston: 1997).

27. Ashton, *Jesus Wept,* 151.

28. Ibid.

29. Ibid., 151–52.

30. Dinah M. Mulock, The Compassionate Friends Newsletter, Carrollton-Farmers Branch Chapter, Feb. 1999.

31. Ryan J. Hulbert, *The Sun Is Always Shinning* (Parma, IN: Eptic Enterprises).

32. Earl A. Grollman, *Living When a Loved One Has Died*, 90.

33. *Church News*, Oct. 31, 1992, 11.

34. Ibid.

35. Religion 302 2nd edition, prepared by the Church Educational System, The Church of Jesus Christ of Latter-day Saints SLC, Utah 1981–1982, 24–25.

36. Maxwell, Ibid.

37. Ibid.

38. Thomas S. Monson, "Peace in Our Savior," *Ensign*, June 2005, 4.

CHAPTER FOUR

Healing Our Bodies, Minds, and Emotions

HEALING FROM A LOSS OR LIFE CHALLENGE is no easy task. It may be the hardest work we ever do. Grief requires us to work on our thoughts and feelings to be able to heal. It also requires time and patience. We cannot simply make the pain of loss and emotional injuries go away any more than we can mend a broken leg with will-power alone.

Antoine de Saint-Exupery said, "You cannot plant an acorn in the morning and expect that afternoon to sit in the shade of the oak."[1]

How do we cope and heal from the hurts and challenges of earth life? The answers are as varied as our circumstances, and our grief is as unique as our thumbprints. In this chapter we will identify a variety of principles and interventions designed to help us maximize our individual healing. Some coping strategies encourage us to accept and endure our adversity. Others strive to treat our symptoms and validate our suffering. Remember, suffering can be physical, emotional, cognitive, and spiritual. It is often important to find personal meaning in our suffering to maximize our healing.

According to Viktor E. Frankl, "Man is not destroyed by suffering; he is destroyed by suffering without meaning."[2]

"To live is to suffer, to survive is to find meaning in the suffering. If there is a purpose in life at all, there must be a purpose in suffering and in dying. But no man can tell another what this purpose is, each must find out for himself."[3]

"He who has a why to live for can bear with almost any how."[4]

Trying to find meaning behind what has happened may be a difficult task. It often takes a combination of grief work, prayer, and healthy thought processes to discover one's own meaning and reconciliation.

Coping Variables

There are many variables that affect the way we cope and heal. We will discuss ten common ones:

1. The type of loss or challenge we are experiencing: a. loss of possessions, b. loss of identity, and c. loss of relationships. Sometimes our challenges involve all three kinds of loss. Generally it is not helpful to compare challenges by saying or thinking, "My tragedy is more difficult than yours!" However, you can compare and recognize the cumulative importance of your own losses and challenges. For instance, the loss of Dennis's and my first full-term baby and a fire that destroyed half of our dream home resulted in a more complicated grief than the death of our parents. The birth of our child with a disability was more difficult for us than our infertility and miscarriage. And all of our previous challenges combined did not compare in difficulty or prepare us for Cameron's sudden death.

2. Another coping variable is the anticipation time. This is the amount of warning time we have (if any) to prepare for our loss or tragedy. Before their death, many patients on hospice are able to say to family members that they love them, that they're sorry, and that they'll miss them. However, others must express these important sentiments through writing or talking to the "empty chair" when their loved ones suddenly die.

3. How close was our relationship or attachment to the person or lost object? Generally the more time, love, and energy that we have invested into a relationship, object, or particular accomplishment, the more painful will be the loss. The sadness and pain we feel after a loss is part of the love and joy we feel before the loss. We can't take the sorrow out of loss unless we take the love out of life. In hospice care, we often observe caregivers getting very attached to their loved ones. They often invest enormous amounts of compassion, love, and energy. Once the loved one is gone, they usually experience myriad emotions.

4. Our personalities and past coping styles contribute to how we will react and cope with life's challenges. For example, as a child I experienced separation anxiety whenever my mother went anywhere. I noticed as I grew up and experienced a variety of life's challenges, my primary reaction continued to be anxiety. How we have coped in the past often predicts how we will cope in the future. There are also personality types and disorders that can compromise someone's coping abilities. Any mental illness can also affect one's coping abilities and style.

5. Age, gender, and maturity also influence how one responds to stress and loss. One example of gender difference is that men more often than women openly display anger when expressing loss. An example of age difference becomes obvious for many when we contrast losing a grandparent who has lived a long, happy life to losing a young child whose life has been shortened and whose future happiness on earth has not been realized.

6. Previous losses and experiences can have a cumulative effect on one's grief and coping abilities, especially if the losses occur back to back. Multiple losses engender feelings of vulnerability and thoughts about what might happen next. When our oldest son had to have his colon removed, which resulted in serious complications, we relived Cameron's death. We probably overreacted to the event because of our vulnerability and fear that surgery would result in burying a third child.

7. Evidence has shown that our physical, spiritual, and emotional health affects our coping abilities. If someone is already vulnerable with a mental illness, they probably won't cope as well physically or emotionally and visa versa. For example, if you are rested and exercise regularly, you are not as likely to lose control of your emotions easily, and difficulties are less likely to make you irritable or angry.

8. Having a working knowledge and understanding of the grief process can help individuals cope with trials. My anxiety doesn't trigger panic like it used to because I now understand the physical process and have learned the necessary tools for coping.

9. The grief process can be complicated when our expectations are altered or shattered. If we grew up believing, "If I am good I can

prevent trials," then we probably won't cope as well as the person who expected and anticipated challenges in life.

10. Our beliefs, values, and family background color our grief experience. For example, the atheist's anger is not directed at God when he is not protected from tragedy.

It may be helpful to remember that one step before being obsessed is being passionate. We all need to be reminded to stay balanced as we cope and strive to heal from our losses.

Elder Richard G. Scott taught, "Satan has a powerful tool to use against good people. It is distraction. He would have good people fill life with 'good things' so there is no room for the essential ones."[5]

There are many interventions and self-help tools that can aid individuals as they endeavor to cope with their personal adversities. We discussed spiritual tools in the last chapter. We will now offer additional tools as they relate to the emotional, physical, cognitive, and social dimensions of our lives.

Emotional Interventions

Acknowledging our feelings is the first step in mastering our emotions. If we don't acknowledge and honestly express our painful feelings, we deprive ourselves of the means that allow us to eventually abandon them. Because our emotions affect our physical and mental health, we need to express them in a healthy fashion. Giving voice to our fears and emotions can soften the impact. Often we don't want to feel the intense emotional pain and sadness of grief, so we ignore or shelve the feeling, hoping it will go away. Unfortunately grief usually doesn't magically go away, and if ignored, our painful emotions manifest themselves as physical or mental illness. What we repress may be expressed later in unhealthy ways.

Sharing and Talking

Keeping negative feelings hidden is very draining. We may not want anyone to know that we are hurt, disappointed, or angry at God because of our tragedies. We may not want our bishop or home or visiting teachers to know that we harbor hurt and negative or bitter feelings as a result of our challenges. Over time, if we continue to hide these negative feelings, we will limit our opportunity to work on them.

Denial of intense unresolved emotions can lead to increased stress, depression, anxiety, or physical ailments over time.

Sharing and talking with others can soften our emotional and intellectual symptoms. We can share feelings with a friend, family member, counselor, bishop, or in a support group with others who have experienced a similar loss. Having someone listen is often all we need. One of best gifts anyone can give us is to lend an understanding, nonjudgmental listening ear. Maybe that is why God gave us one mouth and two ears.

At times we may be afraid of the intense emotions we experience. We might fear that we are going crazy or losing control. We may need a safe place to express these emotions.

Once we acknowledge our emotions, we also give ourselves permission to accept them. Acknowledging and accepting an emotion occurs most often when the emotion is expressed and validated in a safe environment. Sharing may help us face the pain and process our grief. The following four A's are interventions that can be used to facilitate our grief work:

1. *Admit* what you are feeling. Don't stuff, repress, or bury it.
2. *Analyze* the feeling. Determine where the negative or painful emotions are coming from—yourself, the event, medical professionals, judicial system, family, church, friends, or God.
3. *Act* on the feeling through talking, crying, journaling, and working to resolve the issues. If you are angry at someone, you could write a letter expressing your concerns and issues. You don't have to mail your letter; you can burn it or save it for later. At a future time you may look at your letter and gain added insight and perspective. Try to focus on acting, not reacting. Thinking is too passive.
4. *Abandon* the intense or negative emotions. With sufficient time, active emotional expression, and grief work, most individuals can eventually abandon or soften destructive or self-incriminating emotions.[6]

If our emotions are intense and abnormal, we may need professional help.

Gratitude Therapy

Gratitude therapy is a practical self-administered tool that can be used after the four A's. When someone has acknowledged their negative emotions and worked on them, then they can focus on gratitude, as they reflect on and review the positive events and choices in their lives. Gratitude can be a powerful healing tool.

Crying

Crying is not the only way that we show our grief. However, it is often beneficial both physically and emotionally. According to Limbo and Wheeler, "Tears shed during grief have more toxins than do regular tears. Tears actually can be healing."[7]

Nearly three centuries ago, Dr. Samuel Johnson wrote, "Sorrow that hath no vent in tears, maketh the organs of the body weep."[8]

Journaling and Writing

Another self-help tool that allows individuals to process their thoughts and feelings is journaling. Studies have shown that those who write about their traumatic experiences have fewer illnesses, spend less time off work, require fewer doctor visits, and have a more positive outlook on life. As members of the Church, we are encouraged to keep personal and historic journals. However, in therapeutic journaling, we may not want to save all of our writing for our progenitors. In fact, many individuals use therapeutic writing to remove negative thoughts from their minds by writing the painful words on paper and then symbolically (or literally) destroying the pages. Through writing we can then get our painful, destructive feelings out on paper rather than harbor them inside. Repressing or stuffing our feelings can be damaging. What we resist sometimes persists. We may want to keep a loss journal for our eyes only. This allows us to regularly record inner thoughts and feelings where they can be frequently read and evaluated. If we do keep track of what we have written, it is often helpful to review and evaluate where we were in the beginning of our experience in relation to where we have progressed after weeks or months of journaling. We should be able to see some subtle, yet significant progress in our healing, reflected as a reduction in our destructive and self-incriminating feelings.

Control versus Letting Go

When we feel vulnerable and afraid, we are more likely to attempt to overcontrol ourselves (such as through an eating disorder), others, or our environment. We may find ourselves frustrated and angry with those around us who won't do things or think the way we desire. It may cause us to feel hurt, rejected, and unloved. The more we try to control others, especially our children and spouses, the more they pull away from us.

Once we realize we don't need to overcontrol, our anxiety decreases or often leaves altogether. In addition, many of those around us will quit resisting our influence and direction. The power struggles between ourselves and others will soften as we let go. We will actually get more of what we want by letting go of the need to control.

Stephen Levine said, "When attempts at control become a prison only letting go of control will result in freedom."[9]

It may be helpful to remember that God never forces us to do anything. We are free to choose. Agency was given to us as part of His plan (Helaman 14:30; Moses 3:17; 2 Nephi 2:27).

It also helps to let go of unrealistic expectations. We then may reduce our frustration level and avoid some of the side effects of attempting to influence issues and people outside our control. Often in working with others we may need to *accept*, not *expect*.

"God grant me the grace to accept with serenity the things that cannot be changed. The courage to change the things which should be changed. And the wisdom to distinguish the one from the other."[10]

Why Me?

We may find it helpful to change our "why me?" to "what?" "when?" and "where?" We may not understand *why* something has occurred; however, we can identify *what* has happened, *what* we can do now, and *where* we can go from here. This technique will allow us to reduce our feelings of vulnerability and will empower us.

Pearl S. Buck asked herself why she had to raise a mentally disabled child. She then chose to change her views and used her positive attitude to find personal meaning: "Why must this happen to me? . . . To this there could be no answer and there was none. . . . My own resolve shaped into the determination to make meaning out of the meaningless and so provide the answer, though it was of my own making . . . her life must count."[11]

Music and Massage Therapy

Many have used a combination of massage and music to comfort those suffering. Many have discovered that touch can heal both physical and emotional pain.

Stress Management

Many individuals think that rushing and doing two or more endeavors at once (multitasking) will help them finish their tasks faster and reduce stress. However, research has shown that this technique does not always help. Trying to think of or do more than one thing at a time causes our mind to race and often creates more stress and anxiety.[12]

Stress management may mean you have to learn how to say no and then stop long enough to think before saying yes and overcommitting yourself, especially while grieving. This is hard for active Church members who want to serve others. We may have to let others serve us for a season as we rebuild our capacity to serve others once again.

Little Pleasures

It is important while enduring loss, stress, and grief to try doing the things that previously brought us happiness and pleasure. This may be as simple as ordering a pizza. After Cam's death, our family tried to do the fun things we enjoyed; however, at first nothing felt very enjoyable. With time, work, and patience we slowly started to feel better and began to once again enjoy previous activities.

Physical Interventions

EXERCISE

Physical interventions include regular exercise, which enhances the reuptake of serotonin in the brain and the release of endorphins, giving individuals a feeling of well-being. Exercise can also improve sleep if not done too close to bedtime. The type and frequency of exercise should be approved by your physician. Most professionals recommend working out four to five times per week, thirty to forty minutes per session. Exercise should begin with a warm-up and end with a cooldown period. Heart rate goals are figured based on our age. Heart rate monitors and charts are available to help you meet your goals safely.

SUNLIGHT

Sunlight also can affect brain chemistry and mood. Many individuals find that sitting near a window or walking outside regularly is helpful. Seasonal Affective Disorder (SAD) is most common in the northern states where the length of sunlight hours is diminished. Artificial sun lights are expensive but often beneficial in the treatment of SAD.

DIET

A proper diet can stabilize blood sugar and brain function, which then affects mood. Do not go for long periods without food. Complex carbohydrates (fruits, vegetables, and whole grains) have especially been shown to facilitate serotonin reuptake.

SLEEP

Proper rest is important for healing our bodies. If sleep has become a problem (a red flag for depression), we recommend that individuals try progressive relaxation, meditation, and visualization. The quality and quantity of sleep is important. During grief or stress, individuals may sleep too much or too little, either of which can produce fatigue. It is important to get back to our normal sleep cycle. Most people need seven to nine hours of sleep each night. If the following self-help sleep tools do not work, professionals may offer over-the-counter or prescription sleep aids. However, after prolonged use, some types of sleep medications may disrupt the deep sleep cycle in some individuals. New research has suggested that people taking prescription sleeping pills are many times more likely to have a sudden death. For long-term insomnia, many doctors recommend a low dose of trazodone or other mild sleep aids that don't seem to disrupt the REM sleep.

A few adjustments to your bedtime routine may also help. It is important to unwind before going to bed. Arrange a quiet time before attempting to fall sleep. Try to go to sleep at the same time each night and arise at the same time each morning. Try a warm bath or milk before going to bed. Dairy products and proteins contain tryptophan, a natural amino acid (L-tryptophan) found in the body that usually causes one to feel relaxed or sleepy.[13] Other natural foods that have been shown to induce better sleep are Scottish oatmeal, cherry juice, pumpkin seed/powder, and fresh dandelion greens that can be steamed like any vegetable.[14]

Avoid exciting television programs or novels before bedtime. Avoid napping during the day. Often we can walk or exercise instead of napping to get rid of a sluggish feeling. Daily exercise is helpful because a fatigued body requires rest at bedtime. Avoid cola or any food containing caffeine, especially before bedtime. Additionally, some medications have side effects that disrupt sleep. Some individuals report benefits from taking melatonin, a natural hormone produced in our body that promotes sleep, or herbs like valerian. These can be found at your local health food stores. However, always confer with your physician to determine the recommended doses and possible individual side effects.

MEDITATION

Relaxation and meditation may help us heal emotionally. When we are stressed at work or away from home, we can try the following quick stress management techniques: count to ten, take a deep breath, leave the situation, or take a short walk.

Relaxation and meditation can also be used as sleep tools. Instead of counting sheep, you can use concentrative meditation to focus on a word, object, or both. This prevents our mind from ruminating on problems or planning our next day's activities. Some individuals meditate best while focusing on their own relaxed breathing, a candle, flowing water, or saying a relaxing word, such as *peace, sleep,* or *calm* repeatedly. We must concentrate on the word, object, or breathing until we fall asleep. We can also use this technique when we wake up in the middle of the night or have a hard time falling back asleep.

The following relaxation technique may soften some troublesome symptoms as well as sleep. This technique involves lying flat on your back and tightening and relaxing each muscle group throughout the body. Take several deep, slow breaths through the nose, exhaling while moving the stomach or diaphragm. Next, tense, tighten, or contract each muscle group one at a time from head to toe, holding them tight and then relaxing the muscle after counting to ten. Relax each muscle group completely as you exhale. This technique can be done several times while picturing the body sinking deeper and deeper into the bed, until totally relaxed. It may be helpful to use relaxation techniques with meditation (concentrating on an image or word). Some people claim that this dimming of the sympathetic nervous system relaxes them better than taking an anti-anxiety drug. It can also slow the heart rate and lower blood pressure. If we still cannot fall asleep, we may need to get up and do something and quit worrying about the fact that we are currently not able to fall sleep.

Cognitive/Intellectual Interventions

Some individuals may try to intellectualize the details of their situation without allowing and recognizing feelings or emotions. When they are finally ready to do their grief work, they need help transferring this knowledge from their heads to their hearts so they can experience appropriate emotions. It is usually true that we need to acknowledge, feel, and express our emotions to heal.

A cognitive tool that may be helpful is called the think/feel/act process. Some people call this process thought control, positive affirmation, or a form of cognitive therapy. When we put a positive or constructive thought in our mind, we usually feel positive emotions that bring about positive behaviors. This process can also work in reverse. Our positive actions and obedient behaviors can transcend to feeling and thinking of ourselves more favorably.

Stress reduction therapies may also help individuals who are confused, disorganized, absentminded, or disoriented.

With time, acceptance, and cognitive processing, most distressed and grieving individuals will eventually be able to let their minds rest and experience some mental closure and peace.

Social Interventions

Helping ourselves in the social dimension can be difficult. It may require getting outside our comfort zone and actually accepting another's help. It may also mean eventually reaching out to help someone else. Joining a support group is a helpful intervention for many. Sharing feelings and experiences with others who have had similar losses is often therapeutic. The power of friendship and helping others can be a powerful healing tool.

Self-esteem and Self-worth

During loss and adversity our self-esteem can appear diminished. Increasing our self esteem and, more important, understanding our self-worth can help us cope.

Self-esteem is often controlled by our actions. It is based on society's standards of what our behavior or performance should be. Self-esteem focuses on doing or having things. Because self-esteem is often shaped and controlled by the opinions of others, our goals often focus on ways to impress others.

Abraham Lincoln said, "If you do good, you feel good." Doing good things has its place. However, what about disabled, ill, or elderly individuals who can't "do"? We may need to remember and remind ourselves, "We are human beings, not human doings."

Self-esteem is often based on our accomplishments and performance. Self-worth, on the other hand, is focused more on "being" rather than our outward "doing." Self-worth is gaining confidence, peace, and happiness based on our personal attitudes and beliefs. It is not controlled by the opinions, evaluations, or approval of others. It comes from the inside out rather than the outside in. It is based on who we are and how we view ourselves. Self-worth requires understanding that our existence is not by chance, that we are created with a purpose, and that our goals and aspirations can be character-based. It requires knowing we are children of God.

If we become so ill, disabled, or incapacitated to the point that we cannot perform in any meaningful way, we can still maintain our character and our self-worth. Stephen Covey said, "Internal security simply does not come externally."[15]

Research indicates that when we feel self-confident, we function better at work, home, and church. We have more friends and view our relationships with others more positively.

Self-love precedes our ability to love and accept others. Oftentimes, if we are critical of ourselves, we project this critical view onto others. We also tend to compare our worst qualities with others' best qualities.

Christ's love is unmerited and is not predicated solely on our performance. Our Savior died for us and loves us unconditionally. When we feel and accept His unconditional love and sacrifice, we in turn feel more self-love and self-worth. We are then free to love and forgive others as He forgives us.

"You can't always try to earn love. In its fullest state, it is given freely to you. It is the love that is there in spite of your faults that you can trust."[16]

Negative Labels

A positive self-concept is important for all of us. How we feel about ourselves influences how we respond to others and how we perceive they respond back. A poor self-image may set a negative pattern for a lifetime. It may be helpful to understand that we are in charge of our thoughts and feelings as well as our actions. In reality, no one can make us feel sad or angry. We choose to feel that way.

"Through our lives we tend to maintain many unnecessary and burdensome recurring thought and behavior patterns."[17] Often we learned these behavior patterns as children. These behaviors may initially have helped us cope with particular situations. They continue with us long after the original situation changes or no longer exists. These situations from the past can also result in our attaching negative labels to ourselves. Our children also do this. If they tell themselves something long enough, it can become a self-fulfilling prophecy that results in enduring personality beliefs and characteristics. In the Bible we read, "For as he thinketh in his heart, so is he" (Proverbs 23:7). Many of us think degrading thoughts that hinder our progress: *I've tried it before. I can't. I'm afraid. Others will laugh.*

A pessimist sees difficulty in every opportunity. An optimist sees an opportunity in every difficulty.

With work, we can dispel, or even avoid, instilling these labels. We can displace them with new positive labels.

Our lives have purpose and meaning, no matter how short or how limited. Cameron helped us recognize that all human life has value and meaning. We are all children of God with self-worth and value in spite of how limited our abilities may be.

You can test your own self-esteem by asking yourself some simple questions.

1. Am I happy when others are successful?
2. Am I comfortable meeting new people?
3. Do I hide my true feelings?
4. Am I confident with my appearance?
5. Do I like new experiences, changes, and challenges?
6. Do I recognize when I do well?
7. Do I blame others for my problems?
8. Do I accept criticism well?
9. Am I overly aggressive or inhibited?
10. Am I afraid of close relationships?

The answers for a good self-esteem would be:

1. Yes
2. Yes
3. No
4. Yes
5. Yes
6. Yes
7. No
8. Yes
9. No
10. No

President Ezra Taft Benson lists the following tools for healing: repentance, prayer, service, work, improving our health, reading good books, blessings, fasting, good friends, good music, endurance, and setting goals and accomplishing them.[18]

Professional Therapy

Knowing when someone needs more than personal insights and self-help tools is not always easy. If someone has an abrasion, cut, or a broken arm, we physically see the wound and send them to the hospital to have it treated. We put them on antibiotics and pain medications. When someone has a broken heart and soul, we can't always see it visually; however, those suffering adversity will often tell you their emotional pain hurts more than broken bones or other physical pains they have experienced. Because emotional wounds are not always visible, individuals often fail to seek or receive the help they need. Often their body and soul have been damaged, bruised, and shattered by their loss. Professional therapy may help. There are techniques designed to address specific types of challenges. Medications have also been improved and can help a great deal. If in doubt, seek professional help and advice. LDS Family Services offers counseling and referrals to LDS professionals in your community.

When one's emotions, thoughts, or behaviors become debilitating, distorted, or exaggerated, professional help should be seriously considered. Warning signs of serious emotional distress include experiencing sadness that turns to clinical depression, anger that turns to prolonged bitterness or rage, fear that turns to anxiety or panic attacks, and guilt that turns to shame. Be aware of siblings trying to take on grown-up roles and children or parents trying to replace the deceased by imitating them. Self-pity, fear of failure or rejection, and prolonged inability to function at home, school, or work are also potential warning signs. The absence of grief can be another warning sign. Everyone is vulnerable to substituting other behaviors in place of the grief process. Substitutes may include avoidance behaviors, under or overdoing, and any type of obsession or addiction.

Different kinds of professionals with varying degrees and therapeutic specialties are available. Psychiatrists trained in medicine may view depression through a biology lens and determine a need to correct a chemical imbalance. Psychologists trained to identify the environmental and developmental influences may view pathology as a long-term consequence of childhood trauma, faulty thinking, or poor relationships. The family or marriage therapists trained in systemic thought may focus on unhealthy behaviors as a product of dysfunctional families, marriages, or gender and social inequities.[19]

Resource lists of available LDS counselors in your community are maintained by your local LDS Family Services office. Bishops are also aware, in many instances, of counselors whose therapy does not conflict with gospel standards.

Victor L. Brown said, "There is a proper place for these professionally trained specialists. The Church has an organization for this purpose. It is called LDS [Family] Services. There are also other faithful Latter-day Saints in public and private practice who can be called upon as a bishop feels the need."[20]

If your child is struggling, seek help from a licensed professional play therapist who has experience treating children. If you are having marital problems, seek an experienced marriage and family therapist. Therapists become licensed after several years of supervision following their graduate training. They then are required to receive hours of approved training each year thereafter. Therapeutic experience with clients, coupled with their post-graduate training, will ultimately have the greatest impact on their skills and effectiveness in therapy.

Helping Others

Many individuals wonder, "How do we help our friends, relatives, or ward members who are struggling and dealing with adversity and grief?" This scripture gives us guidance: "Weep with them that weep" (Romans 12:15).

The scriptures also give a great example of how hurtful it is when our friends and family don't offer the support we need. Job had lost nearly everything important and of value in his life when he experienced a loss that, in its own way, may have been more significant than any of the other losses. He lost the support that loyal friends and loving kinsfolk might have given had they but rallied around him in this trying season of Job's life. But, sadly, this was not to be. In his deepest need, Job, like the Savior, stood awesomely alone. "Betrayal is a cruel loss to endure. . . . The knife was twisted and turned as his friends came to his side to comfort him and instead accused him of deserving his suffering because of sin. . . . The comforters, though saying much, had misjudged his situation, and consequently said nothing relevant."[21] In Job's words, "How then comfort ye me in vain, seeing in your answers there remaineth falsehood?"

(Job 21:34). "Miserable comforters are ye all" (16:1). "If your soul were in my soul's stead, I could heap up words against you, and shake mine head at you. But I would strengthen you with my mouth, and the moving of my lips should asswage your grief" (Job 16:4–5).

M. Dickson, a religious leader, explains why we desperately need support and comfort from our church leaders and ward family: "For reassurance . . . our need for reaffirmation that God still does care for us, that God is still with us and that God is still forgiving and loving and merciful. Our world has crumbled and the one constant we need to be reminded of is the constancy of God's love, as shown in Jesus Christ."[22]

A member of the Church in the midst of loss expresses a commitment to remain active and forgive those who lacked empathy or failed to express it helpfully: "I realized there were few people who could understand the intensity or duration of my grief. I felt hurt, angry, sad, and guilty on different occasions. I did not want to allow any of these emotions to drive me from my friends, family, God, faith, or church. With time, work, and patience, I, like many, found I could return with love and forgiveness to my friends, relatives, and faith family, who were unable to understand my grief. I was then able to offer help and support to others."

Some feel injured because of what they perceived God allowed or even caused to happen. To help them we must first accept and validate their feelings. When individuals tell us that they are no longer sure they believe the principles of the gospel because of the hurt and pain they are experiencing, we must listen and assure them that this can be a stage of the grieving process. If we try to rescue or correct their vulnerability and doubts prematurely, it may only cause further spiritual injury. We need to overcome our fears that these people are apostatizing and allow them time to rediscover or redefine their faith. We should refrain from prematurely pitting our testimony with theirs, or from giving them advice when they are not ready to receive it. When someone feels love and acceptance, they then feel free to explore the Spirit and rediscover their God, church, faith, and testimony.

After someone experiences a crisis, we may feel nervous the first time we see them. However, we should never ignore them or act as if nothing has happened. We should acknowledge their loss as soon as possible. A call, card, flowers, or another gesture will mean much to those suffering. A physician who lost one of his own children said that before his loss, when he would hear of a child's death, he would send a card; now he sends himself. Another way we can help the bereaved is to assist with their basic life chores. Cleaning, laundry, yard work, child care, and providing food are almost always appreciated. If a death has occurred, attending the funeral shows love, care, and concern.

Often we don't know what to say. A simple statement, "I'm so sorry you have to go through this," is usually enough. Most bereaved individuals just want you to *listen* and acknowledge and accept their pain. If they have lost a loved one, be available to talk about their loved one and reminisce. Whatever the adversity, you might ask if they would like to talk about it; however, don't pry or ask for specific details. A helpful question might be, "What aspect is most upsetting or hurts the greatest regarding your loss?" Don't worry about making them cry. Oftentimes, that is what they need to do. In *Henry VI*, William Shakespeare wrote, "To weep is to make less the depth of grief." Having someone they feel comfortable crying with can provide a beneficial release of pent-up emotions.

We must avoid telling the bereaved how they should feel, and avoid sharing our own experiences unless invited by those mourning. We should avoid saying, "We know how you feel," even when we have personally experienced similar challenges. Remember, we are all unique and may experience the same trials differently. We shouldn't contrast losses by telling about someone else in a worse situation, nor should we expect them to "get over" their loss. We can let them know we'll help them through their difficulties as long as they need us. We shouldn't expect the bereaved to call us if they need anything. They will seldom call; they are too overwhelmed and have no energy to reach out for our help. Instead, we must reach out to them for a longer duration of time than we have traditionally thought. Accept and acknowledge their feelings. Don't try to negate or minimize their loss or experiences by offering clichés. The following is a list of common hurtful clichés.

Secular Clichés

1. You're young; you'll have another opportunity to marry, have children, etc.
2. Put it behind you; get on with your life.
3. Time will heal everything. (Time alone does not heal. What one does with that time can facilitate healing. It's called grief work.)
4. Be strong; keep your chin up.
5. Get over it; move on.
6. There are worse things.
7. Don't cry.

Clichés are not usually helpful for those struggling. We often say them because we've heard them ourselves and don't know what else to say. Even though those grieving may believe some of these clichés are true, the personal application must come from those experiencing loss themselves—not by others repeating them. Let the bereaved find their own *why's*. If a death has occurred, don't be afraid to share memories of their loved one's life.

Remember that most people do not hurt by choice; they are trying their best to cope. It will be a long, hard walk for most. It may be overwhelming and frightening for many initially to think of living with such pain.

"Do's" and "Don'ts"

- Do let your concern and caring show. Don't expect too much and impose "shoulds" on those in mourning.
- Do be available to listen or run errands.
- Don't let your own sense of helplessness keep you away from those hurting.
- Do say that you are sorry about what happened.
- Don't avoid them because you are uncomfortable.
- Do allow those grieving to express their feelings.
- Don't say you know how they feel.

- Do allow them to talk about and express what happened.
- Don't tell them how they should feel and that they should be better now.
- Do give special attention to children.
- Don't change the subject when they want to talk about their tragedy.
- Do allow them to do as much as possible for themselves.
- Do respect their need for privacy.

Additional "don'ts" to be aware of:

- Don't avoid mentioning a deceased person's name.
- Don't try to find something positive about their tragedy; they can do that for themselves. Don't point out their blessings; they can do that for themselves.
- Don't suggest that they should be grateful for other loved ones.
- Don't moralize or offer theology unless invited to do so.
- Don't say things that will intensify feelings of doubt and guilt already present.
- Don't use clichés.
- Don't give advice about what they should feel. There are no right or wrong feelings; they are just feelings.
- Don't share things that were intended to be kept in confidence.
- Don't tell them other stories of tragedy and catastrophe when they are already feeling vulnerable.
- Don't make light of things sacred or meaningful to them.
- Don't continually question their decisions.
- Don't label their feelings or behavior as abnormal, childish, neurotic, and so forth.
- Don't encourage self-destructive behavior.
- Don't be embarrassed by tears.

Most important, remember that we can send ourselves instead of a card.

Offer Love, Time, and Support

Never hesitate to share your love and memories with the living concerning their departed loved ones. Remember, many individuals who have experienced significant loss are not grieving less over time; they're just grieving less often with the passage of time.

Some individuals seem to cope better than others. What might be a huge trial for me or someone else may not challenge you to the same magnitude. It is healing and mutually beneficial to listen to another's struggles without judgment. I didn't do this very well years ago when we moved into a new ward. We were told by several ward members about the unfriendly harshness and bitterness carried by a young mother in the ward. She had a young child diagnosed with cancer who, after suffering for more than a year, died a long and painful death. We soon had some encounters with her and agreed she was unfriendly, cold, and bitter. This added our critical judgment to that of the other ward members. This experience happened before we understood loss, suffering, and death. We know now that this woman faced many sleepless nights in which she watched her frail child cry in pain as she felt helpless to save her. A couple of years later when we buried Cameron, this woman was one of the first to send flowers, food, and eventually her listening ears and compassionate heart to wipe away the tears that few could understand.

"Comfort Those That Stand in Need of Comfort"
(Mosiah 18:9)

We have buried two of our six children. Weeks after Cameron's death, Dennis ran into a good friend and neighbor while walking our dog. They talked on the corner about the fun and spiritual aspects of Cameron's life. Dave had taken the time to know Cameron and see past his limitations. When their reminiscing ended that day, Dave ended the conversation with a statement that brought great comfort. He simply said, "I want you to know, I will never grow tired of hearing you talk about Cameron." Others had shared more profound messages about death and dying that were appreciated. However, none of the counsel and expounding had the impact of these sincere words of comfort.

With time, patience, and grief work, most individuals come to understand that grief is a process; adaptation is possible, and resolution as a difficult yet worthwhile destination.

Notes

1. Earl A. Grollman, quoting Antoine de Saint-Exupery, *Living When a Loved One Has Died* (Boston: Beacon Press, 1977), 58.
2. V. E. Frankl, *Man's Search for Meaning* (New York: Simon and Schuster, 1946).
3. Ibid., 9.
4. Ibid., 85.
5. Richard. G Scott, "First Things First," *Ensign,* May 2001.
6. M. Dickson, quote from recovery seminars, Dallas, Texas 1991, 21.
7. R. K. Limbo and S. R. Wheeler, *When a Baby Dies: A Handbook for Healing and Helping* (LaCrosse Lutheran Hospital/Gunderson Clinic, Ltd., 1986), 8.
8. B. D. Rosof, *The Worst Loss: How Families Heal from the Death of a Child* (New York: H. Holt & Co., 1994), 246.
9. Stephen Levine, *A Year to Live* (New York: Bell Tower, 1997), 252.
10. Reinhold Niebuhr (quote over 100 years old).
11. Pearl S. Buck, *The Child That Never Grew* (Bethesda, MD: Woodbine House, 1950), 26.
12. Joan Borysenko, *Minding the Body, Mending the Mind* (Reading, MA: Addison-Wesley Publishing Co., Inc., 1987).
13. Robert Ornstein and David Sobel, *The Healing Brain* (New York: Guilfore, 1990), 109.
14. See http://suppspot.wordpress.com/2012/03/12/foods-for-deep-sleep/.
15. Stephen R. Covey, *Principle-Centered Leadership* (New York: Summit Books, 1990–91), 84.
16. M. Gamblin, American Association of Mormon Counselors and Psychotherapists (AMCAP) Conference, Salt Lake City, Utah, April 1999.
17. J. M. Chamberlain, *Eliminate Your SDB's (Self-Defeating Behaviors)* (Provo, Utah: BYU Press, 1978), 1.
18. Ezra Taft Benson, in Conference Report, Oct. 1974.
19. Michael D. Yapko, *Hand-Me-Down Blues* (New York: Golden Books, 1999), 92–93.
20. Victor L. Brown, "Questions and Answers," *New Era*, Sept. 1978, 16–18.
21. Religion 302, 2nd edition, prepared by the Church Educational System (Salt Lake City: The Church of Jesus Christ of Latter-day Saints 1981–82), 25.
22. Dickson, 21.

PART TWO

Enduring Disabilities, Physical and Mental Illnesses, and Death

FOR

Darren D. Ashton

WHO INSPIRED THE BUT IF NOT
TITLE THROUGH HIS SUFFERING,
FAITH, AND ENDURING

Preface to Part Two

IN THE FOLLOWING PAGES WE WILL ADDRESS coping with disabilities; chronic, terminal, and mental illnesses; and the death of a loved one. Part One discussed the grief symptoms that you may experience as you encounter any type of loss or life challenge. Part I also offered healing interventions to help you cope with your loss.

It was our oldest son Darren's enduring and faith during his two-year illness that inspired the title *But If Not*.

—Joyce and Dennis Ashton

CHAPTER FIVE

Disabilities and Physical and Mental Illness

WHETHER IT IS FOR A PHYSICAL AILMENT OR A MENTAL ILLNESS, the diagnosis of a disability for you or a loved one can result in a major loss and the need to make significant adjustments in your life. Although you may feel you clearly understand that our journey on earth includes confronting illness and suffering, it may still come as a shock when you personally have to assimilate and deal with a serious diagnosis and a life-altering tragedy.

Dennis and I still remember the vivid details associated with receiving the varied diagnoses that accompanied our own children's disabilities and illnesses. We will never forget the shock when our doctor told us that our first seven-pound, full-term baby girl had died. It was our first conceived child after a season of infertility. We could hardly believe what had happened as we looked at her beautiful but lifeless body. A cause for her death was never determined.

A few years later the doctor confirmed that our third child, Cameron, had cerebral palsy. We weren't sure what it would mean to parent such a child. After fourteen years of learning how to feed and care for him, we were heartbroken at his sudden and unexpected death.

We were shaken again when I experienced a TIA, or mini-stroke, at age forty-seven. I woke up in the middle of the night and couldn't move the left side of my body. Although I recovered, I've faced several fearful years as experts attempted to determine a cause, including the discovery of what appear to be MS lesions on my brain.

It was surreal five years later when our oldest, now adult son, Darren, became ill and required several major surgeries. We have other close family members whose struggles with mental illnesses have resulted in drug and alcohol addictions. The negative consequences and their associated behaviors have taken a toll financially, emotionally, and spiritually for our family members. Dennis's mother took her own life at age fifty after overdosing on prescription drugs and alcohol.

Dennis and I have found comfort in the stories and insight given to us by others who have coped with difficult diagnoses. Job comes to mind as well as Paul with his "thorn in the side." We have also been impressed with President Spencer W. Kimball's thoughts on adversity. Much of what he learned was a by-product of his own profound suffering and personal life experiences. As explained in Part I, he, like Job, suffered from boils. He also experienced skin cancer, Bell's palsy, smallpox, and heart pain for years, which eventually required open-heart surgery. He endured three brain surgeries. He suffered skin and throat cancer, which necessitated vocal cord surgery and ultimately led to his difficulty speaking.[2]

Physical and mental illnesses and disabilities affect the family as a whole and each member individually. If you have ever watched someone you love suffer, you now realize that you not only grieve for the dying, but you also grieve for the living.

Physical or Chronic Illness

There are many illnesses and diseases that we might acquire in our lifetime. Living with chronic pain and symptoms is a challenge.

Some individuals who are suffering significant physical or emotional pain report that they would rather die than continue in their suffering. Those watching at the bedside as caregivers may feel similarly. Caregivers, especially parents, often wish they could take the place of their suffering loved one. One mother said, "I would have gladly suffered in place of my son. There is nothing worse than watching someone you love suffer and not be able to change their painful experience."

Our sister-in-law said, "When my mother told me about her cancer I was twelve years old. I was so upset. I ran to my friend's house crying all the way! I just knew she [my mother] would immediately die. This experience, hearing of mother's diagnosis, was more difficult for me than her death seven years later."[3]

This quote reveals that sometimes anticipatory mourning and preparation can soften the impact when death eventually does arrive.

Adolescents are often embarrassed by a parent's or sibling's illness, disability, or appearance. A mother with cancer illustrates this embarrassment: "One day I had to make a quick run to my child's school. I just threw on a baseball hat to cover my bald head. When my child got home from school, he asked if I would please wear my wig when I came to the school."

One of our patients suffering from cancer told of her child's embarrassment: "I lost all my hair during chemotherapy. Sometimes I would take my wig off and swing it around being silly. One of my children would laugh, but the other would ask me to please not do it."

These reactions and comments may later cause the embarrassed individual to feel guilty, especially if the loved one dies from the illness. Discussing ambivalent feelings and helping families realize their mixed and at times conflicting emotions may help them eventually abandon their guilt.

Occasionally our children were embarrassed when our large family would all go out to eat. Cameron was in his wheelchair, and we would have to feed him because it would be too messy if he tried to feed himself in public. His brothers were self-conscious when they perceived others were critically judging them as well as Cameron.

For many, the emotional suffering can be as intense as physical suffering. Each new day can introduce a new set of emotions. These emotions are influenced by medical treatments, test results, and current health status. Individuals' reactions are also influenced and weighed against the quality and anticipated duration of life. A dear friend and relative told us years ago: "My cancer experience left me emotionally drained and severely depressed. There were times it was more than I could bear, and I wanted to die. If my cancer returns I will not go through all the treatments again. I will just take pain medication until I die. I am not afraid of physical pain; it's the emotional pain that I cannot do again."

I don't think Dennis or I totally understood her painful,

emotional recovery until we watched Darren's recovery from what turned out to be several serious abdominal surgeries and months of complications and hospitalizations. There were many times we feared we would be burying our third child. It brought back our grief memories and vulnerability as we remembered our previous son Cameron's surgery and death. It was a long recovery. We found that long after the physical healing was done there was emotional and psychological grief to heal from as well. The long-term effects of emotional recovery were described well by Lance Armstrong. This is what he said a year following his cancer remission: "I was physically recovered, but my soul was still healing. There is no support system in place to deal with the emotional ramifications of trying to return to the world after living in a bottle for your existence."[4]

A part of him didn't want to return to his old life. He wanted a permanent vacation. Darren felt similarly as he fought to come back. He had good days and bad days and wondered if he would ever be the same again. We knew in reality that most individuals wouldn't be the same after such suffering. Loss and life's challenges change us. We see through different eyes.

The constant ups and downs of remissions and relapses can be exhausting. Dennis and I would think Darren was out of the woods, and then he would get another infection with a fever and painful, intense cramps. We would all sink into fear and despair thinking he might have to go back to the hospital. What if he didn't make it this time? I told him I understood the phrase, "A mother is only as happy as her saddest child."

Illness can also cause spiritual injury. We may ask, "Why me? Why hasn't God intervened and healed me? Where is my miracle? Why does He allow me to continue to suffer?" In the midst of Darren's suffering and surgeries, Dennis and I would return to the scriptural passage that helped us cope. We determined that we would continue to hope and pray for a healing, "But if not . . ." we will still remain faithful (Daniel 3:17–18).

Other times during our struggles we may see that someone's spirituality increases. A friend of ours told us, "Since my adversity, I am just loving going to church and lapping up every spiritual moment and lesson I can."

When we first began working with individuals who were suffering from serious illnesses, we assumed we would always see chronic sorrow and depression. However, as with life in general, some patients are able to cope better and discover personal meaning at varying stages in their tragedies and losses. Reactions are in fact very individualized, especially when observed as single moments in time. Conclusions and feedback concerning how well someone is coping in the early stage of mourning often discourage people from honestly sharing their struggles later when their grief returns.

A while back I was visiting a family of seven whose young father was dying after a long, chronic illness. His beautiful wife sat crying at his bedside. The care center and hospice staff worried about her grief. She had a son serving a mission and four younger children still at home. However, her tears were tears of gratitude for the powerful comfort and the Spirit she was feeling. She told me, "I am not a strong person; I am being carried." She had received spiritual peace and was ready to let her husband transcend to his next life. At that moment she was embraced with the overwhelming love of the Savior. She did go through a more typical grief process later. For that time, however, she acknowledged that she was in the arms of her Lord. It's important to validate the spiritual comfort and support an individual may receive, while leaving an invitation to share painful moments that may resurface in the future.

I hadn't totally understood the enormous comfort a grieving individual can receive until I experienced it personally. In the midst of Darren's serious complications from surgeries, I was still able to find peace, comfort, and answers to prayers. It was an amazing experience for me. I understood more fully how the Lord, without removing our trials, can comfort and carry us through them. By discovering these "tender mercies" (1 Nephi 1:20), we will more likely find meaning and peace in our suffering.

Disabilities

Dennis and I came to understand and glimpse into the world of the disabled through Cameron. When he was ten months old, he could not sit up without assistance. The doctor sent a nurse to our home to test the extent of his developmental delays. After she left (although she never gave us a diagnosis) the term *cerebral palsy* came to my mind. I looked it up in my college nursing book and recognized that his delays and birth injuries fit the diagnosis. Receiving the diagnosis of a disability can begin an intense grieving process, and for me, it did. I remember closing the drapes, taking the phone off the hook, and crying uncontrollably. How could we raise a disabled child? What did this mean for our lives?

Later the doctor confirmed the diagnosis. We made many adjustments and over the years learned to care for him. Our lives suddenly included wheelchairs, daily dressing, feeding, toileting, bathing, and countless doctor visits.

The mother of a blind child said, "My child could see normally for many years and had many friends in and out of the Church. After she lost her vision she also lost her friends. It was very difficult for both of us."

The mother of a disabled baby writes:

> When you get pregnant, it's like planning a fabulous trip to a place you've dreamed of all your life, maybe . . . to Italy. You buy a bunch of guide books and make wonderful plans. It's all very exciting. After months of eager anticipation, the day finally arrives. You pack your bags and off you go. Several hours later, the plane lands. The stewardess says, "Welcome to Holland." "What!? I signed up for Italy. . . . I've wanted to go there all my life!" "Well there's been a change in the flight plan, and here you must stay!" It's not a horrible place, just different than you expected. You must learn a different language. And everyone you know is talking about their trip to Italy, and how wonderful it is there. "Yes," you say, I was supposed to go there too. The pain of this change will never go away, the loss of your dream. I will try and see the beautiful things in Holland. They do have tulips and windmills![5]

There are often secondary losses along the way. A young father writes, "I've spent most of my life working hard to get good grades and a good career. I married and started my family before I finished law school. I finally got a job offer with the company of my dreams; however, I couldn't accept it due to the serious illness and disabilities of my child."

Accidents can cause disabilities, adding guilt to our intense grief. One person said, "In a flash I went from a healthy, active young adult to a paraplegic. The panic of not being able to feel and move eventually turned to sorrow. I had to alter all of my goals and plans. It took every ounce of physical, emotional, and spiritual strength to go on."

When Cameron was diagnosed, Dennis and I wondered how we, or anyone, would accept this less than "normal" child. Would he accept himself? Like most parents, we wanted to ensure that he had the opportunity to be the best he could be. We wanted to give Cameron every opportunity available. The professionals could not tell for sure if he would ever walk, so we worked long and hard assuming he would. It took many years for us to realize he would not. We learned that his cognitive and physical growth would be a slow process, and that small accomplishments in those areas would measure his and our successes. The doctors didn't feel that he would be able to talk, so we taught him how to use a communication board. He learned to use it very fast, and then surprised us by developing language skills and eventually speaking.

Here is what I wrote regarding his growth:

> Cameron's first partial sentence was a small miracle to us. He was three years old and this was the first day that he would go to a special preschool without mom, all alone on a bus. As I was dressing him I could see the anxiety in his eyes. His big brown eyes always melted my heart. He looked up at me and asked, "Mamma go?" Tears came to my eyes and I cheered, "You spoke, you spoke!" With great emotion I explained he would be going to school alone, but I would be home when he returned. We were going to have some great communication together and make the most of his limitations! He had communicated and I had understood! This was such a great thrill![6]

It wasn't long before patient friends and relatives could understand Cameron's slurred speech, which replaced his need to use the communication board. We were all thrilled and grateful when others at home, church, and school could understand him over time.

Other parents will have disabled children who will never speak with words. These parents will have to look for other qualities within their children's personalities and spirits that can bring them joy. If they are able to focus on their child's inner qualities, or self-worth, and the importance of their child's existence as a child of God, they will find meaning and purpose.

Caregiving can be very difficult and demanding for families. There is usually more to do than feels humanly possible. Often we can't find or accept all the help we need or desire. A mother writes that after finding little support during her son's illness that she became immersed in the work of caring for him. Over time she was unable to attend to anything else. "I am the main caregiver. My husband doesn't really do much of the necessary care. He has thrown himself into his work and earning the money to enable me to stay at home. This has caused some arguments, because if he would give some of the medications or treatments, I could have a break, or eat hot food!"[7]

Although most of the time my family remained positive, there were some challenges we faced in caring for our disabled son. The following is an entry from my journal when he started school:

> I have been helping Cameron in his classroom. I worry when I see him with other normal children. He doesn't fit in very well. It's sad and emotional for me to watch. It's hard at home too; lifting, feeding and bathing him. Sometimes I get down and discouraged. One day Cameron asked me, "Why am I handicapped anyway? I said, "It's our challenge." He said, "I wanta be normal. I wanta walk, I wanta walk!" I did the best I could to comfort him. I sometimes feel sad for him and for me.

Over the years Dennis and I had learned to accept Cameron's disability and love him immensely. Although it was hard work, we found joy and purpose in caring for him. We spent nearly every day for fourteen years feeding, bathing, and dressing him. And we spent every day addressing his medical and emotional needs. He attended special schools. He was happy and loved living. We spent countless hours trying to find the right wheelchairs, computer, electric bed, prone standing table, eating utensils, and school programs for him.

At age fourteen, six months before his death, Cameron expressed the following ideas and feelings to a class of college students majoring in special education. It took an hour to videotape this fourteen-minute testimony because of his labored speech and limited grammar:

> Hi! My name is Cameron Ashton, and I live at Dallas, Texas, and this is my house and this is my pool. I can swim with a little

help from this [holds up arm floats]. It really neat. It a hot day here. I have a trampoline. It over there [points], and I can jump on it, and I mean I can lay on it and have somebody jump with me [his honesty]. And I have a bike I can use, and it's in the garage. [We get it out for him.] This is my bike that I ride. I ride it to the duck pond. It a little ways from here and my dad helps me get on and my mom too, and it really fun to ride. It like walking for me. Plus my family is really nice too. My dad helps me get dressed in the morning and helps me go bathroom and all that. And I have aide who work good [at] school, helps me at school [his appreciation], and my school is across the street, and my mom helps me a lot. She helps me with my homework.

It not easy being handicapped. It look easy, but not really. It like hard, I guess [realistic]. [But] I get to drive early [finds the positive]! I'll drive it [moves the wheelchair around]. I hope I can go on a mission and be married in the temple. Sometimes hard for me to be handicapped, like for example, I can't play basketball and football like you guys can do. I can't *do* a lot, but I play with my computer [he finds the positive again], and I hope to learn more about the computer and so I can teach my mom and my dad to use it and stuff. [We learned how to use it!] I hope you can understand me okay and learn what it like to be handicapped. . . . I really like Texas, I moved here just a year or two ago, and I like it so far. It big and nice and I really like it. It [Texas] good. Here, oh boy. Here my suggestions about college helpers of handicapped people. Be nice to handicapped. They know a lot just like you, and don't tease handicapped people because it hurt their feelings. I LDS boy and that mean I go to church every Sunday, like today, I just came back from church. . . . I guess I don't have to say anymore, and this is Cameron signing off. (See his concluding testimony on page 79.)[8]

Words cannot describe the profound grief and loss we experienced following his death.

Mental Illnesses

Just as physical illness affects and limits our physical bodies, mental illness can affect and limit our brain's capacity to think clearly and control our emotions. Mental illness can compromise our thoughts, feelings, behaviors, and how we interact with others.

The truth is that many faithful Latter-day Saints, who live the commandments and honor their covenants, experience personal struggles with mental illness, or are required to deal, perhaps over long periods of time, with the intense pain and suffering of morally righteous mentally ill family members. I assure you that Church leaders are in no way exempt from the burden of mental illness, whether as victim, caregiver, or friend.[9]

Experts do not totally understand why some people's brains malfunction. However, faulty brain function is as real as cancer, physical disabilities, or diseases of any vital body organ. Mental illness is usually not caused by sin, cannot be willed away, and often requires professional treatment. Some of the more commonly recognized mental illnesses include depression, anxiety disorders, obsessive-compulsive disorder, bipolar disorder, schizophrenia, attention deficit disorder, and eating disorders. We will define these mental conditions later in the chapter.

Mental illness is usually not as visible as physical illnesses; however, the suffering and impact is just as profound for the patient and the patient's family.

"Most patients would rather have a physical than a mental disorder. . . . Among the more important reasons . . . is the fact that psychological diagnosis often carries a stigma, as many still believe that a psychological problem implies that a person is weak and has not tried hard enough to overcome the problem."[10]

Unfortunately, because of a lack of knowledge and understanding, few families receive cards, flowers, or casseroles when a mental crisis hits or sends a family member to the hospital. It is important for friends, family, and ward members to increase their knowledge and acceptance relative to the complete causes and impact of mental illnesses. The mentally ill and their families desperately need our nonjudgmental love, support, and acceptance.

Many mental illnesses go untreated because individuals are ashamed, in denial, or feel their symptoms can be willed away with their positive attitude.

One woman tells of her struggle being married to a man with a severe mental illness: "I married a returned missionary who I thought had left his past and struggles with adolescence. Unfortunately his mental illness continues to resurface in our marriage. The loss of what I thought marriage and family life would be has left me with a grief I can't describe. I'm not sure I have what it takes to stay married to a spouse with so many problems."

Another person says, "I had no time to study for my bar exam due to the serious mental illness of my spouse. I had to pursue a different career."

The following eleven mental health conditions are frequently diagnosed, treated, or referred to professionals in the community by LDS Family Services. Personal quotes illustrate some of the difficulties faced by individuals suffering and those who love them. Understanding the diagnosis and symptoms is the first step to healing.

Obsessive-Compulsive Disorder: Unwanted intrusive and recurrent impulses, images, or thoughts that one cannot control (obsessions). Repetitive behaviors or mental acts that the person feels driven to perform in response to an obsession (compulsions).[11]

"Before I can leave the house I have several rituals that I must do in a certain order. I try logically to stop but cannot."

"I am so obsessive about certain unimportant details of my life that it keeps me from doing the truly important things and finding contentment or joy."

Major Depressive Disorder: Depressed mood lasting most the day nearly every day. Many people suffering from depression experience changes in sleep, libido, appetite, or weight, as well as a loss of pleasure, interest, or motivation in activities they once enjoyed. They can also experience a loss of energy, hope, and worth. An inability to concentrate, focus, or function as usual is also common. People suffering from depression may be more tearful, irritable, or indecisive. Feelings of anxiety or guilt, or thoughts of suicide, are common.[12]

"My depression limits my ability to give to my family. I hide in my room, reading or sleeping, isolating myself from everyone and everything."

Generalized Anxiety Disorder: Exaggerated worry and restlessness generally lasting for six months or longer. One may experience headaches, dizziness, blackouts, and a difficulty breathing or swallowing. Some may feel nervous, tense, sweaty, or even experience heart palpitations. Some may suffer from panic attacks, which are sudden feelings of terror that often occur unexpectedly.[13]

"I feel anxious about everything: work, school, and friends. I worry I will have a full-blown panic attack one of these days."

Personality Disorders: Enduring patterns of inner experiences and behavior that deviate markedly from cultural expectations. These patterns appear in the following areas: cognitions, affectivity, interpersonal functioning and impulse control. There is a general criteria for personality disorders and those not specific; others are called borderline, paranoid, schizoid, antisocial, histrionic, narcissistic, avoidant, and dependent personality disorders.[14]

Adjustment Disorders: The development of emotional or behavioral symptoms in response to an identifiable stressor(s).[15]

"When I went back to work at the children's ward at the hospital after the death of my child, I started feeling uncomfortable. Sometimes I felt anxiety and panic, fearing I would be responsible for a child's death. I worried my fear could turn into PTSD [posttraumatic stress disorder] so I changed units."

Attention Deficit/Hyperactivity Disorder (ADHD): Common symptoms may include restlessness, fidgetiness, the inability to sit still, the ability to become distracted easily, impulsivity, forgetfulness, and impatience. Those with ADHD often struggle with saying and doing things before thinking. They also have trouble staying focused on tasks or thoughts. Many experience extreme mood shifts from normal to depressed to excited feelings in a short period of time. Some associated features include marital instability, a lack of academic and vocational success, stress intolerance, and alcohol and drug abuse.

"My daughter's ADHD has led her to very negative behaviors. Her teachers call and complain about her conduct. She has trouble keeping friends, making appropriate decisions, and keeping her grades up."

Bipolar Disorder: Alternating periods of depression and manic euphoria. In most cases euphoria is an elevated or irritable mood.[16]

"My daughter will go days with little sleep. Excited about life and goals she wants to accomplish. She seems overly excited and somewhat unrealistic about what she is involved with. Then she crashes and sleeps for days or is unmotivated and depressed."

Delusional Disorder: At least a one-month duration of real life, nonbizarre situations that are delusional. Examples might include the fear of being poisoned, infected, or deceived by a spouse or loved one.[17]

"It took months of therapy to convince my husband that his bizarre thoughts were unfounded. He believed our temple marriage of forty years was being threatened by me being unfaithful to him."

Conduct Disorders: There are different types of conduct disorders. However, it is usually a persistent pattern of behavior where the rights of others or rules are violated.[18]

"My son's conduct disorder began as a young child. He was cruel to animals and experimented with fire. He has spent multiple times in jail."

Eating Disorders: Eating disorders are a complex way to manage emotions. There are three types described here. (1) Anorexia Nervosa: Forced extreme weight loss (25 percent or more of body fat) causing life-threatening symptoms due to severe malnutrition and excessive exercise. Even with extreme thinness, patients believe they are fat. (2) Bulimia Nervosa: Extreme overeating, bingeing, and then purging, which is forced vomiting. Victims may also overuse laxatives and other weight loss products. (3) Binge Eating Disorder: Uncontrolled, impulsive continual eating beyond the point of feeling full. Food addictions (without purging) causing gains up to 50 percent over normal weight.[19] Binge eating disorder produces physical changes in the brain similar to those of drug abuse.

"I used to be thin; I started putting on extra weight last year. I love to eat, but I started to cut back what calories I could. Soon I would overeat and binge, then purge to control my weight. I ruined my throat, hair, and emotional peace."

Schizophrenia: Hallucinations (hearing or seeing things that don't actually exist), delusions, paranoia, and disordered speech and thoughts.

"I have been called by God to travel the world, preaching his word."

Professional resources include your local LDS Family Service agency, faithful Latter-day Saints in public and private practice, the NAMI (National Alliance on Mental Illness) organization, your county mental health agency, and The National Institute of Mental Health (NIMH) 866-615-6464.

Treating these illnesses can be effective, yet complicated. There are studies that compare the effectiveness of psychotherapy such as cognitive, behavior, and interpersonal therapies with and without medication for each illness. It would be impossible to review all the research in this chapter. However, it would be important to seek education and counseling for your specific illness. Most research confirms that medications and psychotherapy are equally effective in treating mental illnesses. However, if both are initiated and used in concert, therapy outcome improves substantially.

"Some persons who are ill, who have received a priesthood blessing and have prayed fervently that their burdens might be lightened, may feel that they suffer from a lamentable lack of faith if they seek professional help for their affliction. They may even stop taking prescribed medication, thinking erroneously that their faith will replace the need for it. Such thinking is quite simply wrong. Receiving and acting upon professional advice and the concomitant exercise of faith are not in conflict. In fact, exercising faith may require following the advice of experienced health professionals."[20]

For spiritual and emotional self-help tools and interventions, see Part I.

Notes

1. Dennis E. Simmons, "But If Not . . .," *Ensign*, May 2004, 73.
2. James E. Faust, "The Blessings of Adversity," *Ensign*, February 1998, 2–7.
3. Joyce and Dennis Ashton, *Jesus Wept* (Springville, Utah: Cedar Fort, Inc., 2001), 31.
4. Lance Armstrong with Salley Jenkins, *It's Not About the Bike: My Journey Back to Life,* audio book (New York: Penguin Putman Inc., 2000).
5. E. Kingsley, "Welcome to Holland" broadcast by Television Works Western Publication Co., 508-750-8400.
6. Joyce and Dennis Ashton, *Loss and Grief Recovery* (Amityville, New York: Baywood Publishing, 1996), 51.
7. Ibid., 26.
8. Ibid., 64.
9. Alexander B. Morrison, "Myths about Mental Illness," *Ensign*, October 2005, 31–35.
10. Elliot S. Valenstein, *Blaming the Brain* (New York: The Free Press, 1998), 219.

11. DSM-IV-TR American Psychiatric Association, Washington DC, 2000, 217–18.
12. Ibid., 168–69.
13. Ibid., 222–23.
14. Ibid., 287.
15. Ibid., 285.
16. Ibid., 179–91.
17. Ibid., 159–60.
18. Ibid., 68–69.
19. Ibid., 263–66.
20. Elder Alexander B. Morrison, "The Spiritual Component of Healing," *Ensign*, June 2008, 47.

CHAPTER SIX

Terminal Illness

WE WORKED ON THIS CHAPTER TWO WEEKS after the death of our dear mother. She came to live with us three months ago on hospice care. She received a terminal diagnosis of inflammatory breast cancer six months before her death. Caring for her was an honor and a privilege. We had a few hard days, but not many. She was the perfect patient, always grateful for everything that was done for her. We hope to endure to the end as well as she has.

A terminal illness is a diagnosis of a disease that will take the life of an individual. Usually it refers to a time period of weeks or months rather than years. One of the most common diseases we see in hospice is cancer. Most of us will know someone who will suffer with cancer. Cancer is not always terminal. Over eight million people are living today with a history of cancer. An additional 1.2 million will be diagnosed this year.[1]

Terminal illness is uniquely different from chronic illness because those affected must now shift from hope for a cure to hope for comfort, peace, and a good death. Focus changes from earth life to eternal life and includes letting go of earthly things. Embracing the idea of death can be a challenge for the dying as well as for their families. Dying is a unique and individual process. Transcending from earth life to a hereafter will involve physical, mental, social, spiritual, and emotional work. We may have to sacrifice what we are for what we will become. This process can be complicated as patients and families struggle to do important end-of-life tasks that may include offering forgiveness, asking for forgiveness, expressing love, saying thank you, and ultimately saying good-bye.

It may take a while for the diagnosis of death to sink in. Some patients actually die with the belief that they aren't dying and thus miss the opportunity to complete important end-of-life tasks. Others wonder, "Do I really have to die?" or "Has my life made a difference?" Many question, "Why, God? Why me? Why suffering?" Half of those facing immediate death worry about not being forgiven by God and not reconciling with others.[2] Others express fears about approaching the unknown, leaving loved ones, and losing control.

Whenever someone's life expectations are altered, it requires adjustments in his assumptive world.[3] One patient said this about the fear of dying: "Life is pleasant. Death is peaceful. It's the transition that [is] troublesome."[4]

It is recommended that a hospice team support anyone receiving a terminal diagnosis of six months or less to live.

The first hospice was started in the United States in 1974. Medicare offers a hospice benefit for anyone sixty-five and older. Its objective is to provide quality end-of-life care. Many insurance companies also offer a hospice benefit for younger individuals who receive a terminal diagnosis. To qualify for the hospice benefit a physician must verify that the individual has approximately six months or less to live because of his terminal illness.

The primary mission of hospice is to provide a "good death" by keeping patients physically and emotionally comfortable. The roots of the hospice movement are spiritual. Dame Cicely Saunders established hospice after watching the spiritual yearnings that preceded the death of one of her patients, who also became a close friend. Ultimately she decided that she could have more influence with end-of-life care by becoming a physician rather than staying at the bedside as a nurse. Her mission statement for hospice care states: "You matter to the last moment of your life, and we will do all we can, not only to help you die peacefully, but also to live until you die."[5]

Families may feel they need to choose aggressive medical treatments for their loved one; however, sometimes less is better. We may have to focus on comfort measures until death comes. Once the patient and the family realize that all has been done to preserve life medically, then comfort may mean stopping aggressive treatments and going home to pass away peacefully.

A mother of a young child who died of cancer wrote,

> My son relapsed after the bone marrow transplant. We were told that all that could be done had been done. I felt such guilt for what I had put him through all these months. There were blood tests, bone marrow aspirations, spinal taps, radiation and chemotherapy that made him so sick. I was with him through them all. They were difficult to watch. Now after all he's been through, it didn't work anyway, I am angry, nervous, uneasy and totally devastated.[6]

Hospice teams can also offer individualized support in hospitals and care centers as well as in patients' homes. Physicians trained in end-of-life care who are experts on pain and symptoms management oversee the care. Registered nurses administer the best symptom management medications available to control everything from pain and nausea to anxiety. Hospice social workers offer counseling, provide help with life review, and discuss relationship issues with patients and their families. These skilled social workers are especially helpful in offering support to the often conflicted and diverse family members. Hospice aides are available to bathe and dress your loved one while also attending to other personal cares. Hospice chaplains will explore the patient's deepest thoughts and fears and offer spiritual support and prayers while guiding patients and their loved ones through important end-of-life tasks. Hospice also offers bereavement support (after death follow-up care) for the grieving family members.

At least 55 percent of those dying desire someone with whom they can share their fears and concerns.[7] Patients often share personal concerns with hospice team members when they are reluctant to burden or worry their family members. It is sometimes easier for patients to share troubling issues and concerns with a caring professional they feel will not judge them.

Some patients may fear choking, pain, or dying from air hunger. Hospice team members assure the dying that the hospice staff are experts in comfort care and can successfully treat these uncomfortable symptoms. In fact, most deaths come as a gradual slipping away. Some say this is like losing their loved one bit by bit. It is interesting that 54 percent of the patients prefer not being alone, 47 percent want someone to hold their hand, and 50 percent want to either have the opportunity to pray alone or have someone pray for them.[8]

A patient's decline becomes especially evident as their appetite begins to diminish. Patients struggle as it becomes progressively more difficult to eat, and food begins to lose its flavor. As the body slows down, food makes the dying feel bloated and nauseated. As they drink less and become dehydrated, the body produces a natural tranquilizer allowing them to feel comfortable. They may sleep more, withdraw from the world, and turn inward.

Some families try to change these natural dying processes by force-feeding their loved one or by holding back medications to keep them more alert. Unfortunately force-feedings and limiting medications can increase the patient's nausea, vomiting, and diarrhea, which results in unnecessary physical and emotional pain. Families and patients generally do better if they can find meaning in death and accept the natural processes of decline. We should assume that even when the patient can no longer talk to us that he can still feel our gentle touch and hear our soft, loving words.

It is helpful to understand the physical changes that occur as the sick go into what is called the active phase of dying. This can last from hours to days. As the body slows and eventually shuts down, we see more sleeping; less eating; less drinking; and, gradually, more labored breathing. You can swab their mouth, but forcing fluids orally when someone can't swallow can cause choking, aspiration, and other uncomfortable symptoms. It is natural for the muscles and tissues in the throat to relax and for mucus to form. This will cause a noisy, rattled sound as patients breathe. Research reports that it is not uncomfortable to the patient, just to the family hearing the disturbing sounds. Suctioning is uncomfortable; however, sometimes medications or repositioning the patient can soften the sound. The lips, hands, and feet often become cold and bluish in color, and a fever might surface.

As patients near death it is not uncommon for them to reach out to or call the names of deceased loved ones. They talk symbolically about needing to catch a plane, find a key, or get dressed to go somewhere. Assuring them that we will help them get ready and find their way is often comforting.

Some families do better than others. Their strengths and qualities as well as their inadequacies will usually present themselves as they care for their loved one. Family members may not agree with each other on how to care for the dying loved one. They may even be upset with the patient's decision to stop further aggressive medical interventions and treatments. Hospice staff try to honor the patient's wishes relative to their personal treatment. When hospice staff walk into a patient's home or room, the staff put themselves away and focus on the needs and wants of the patient, and then the family. Hospice staff may find patients and families experiencing peace, frustration, grief, anger, gratitude, or a combination of many emotions.[9]

A common scenario happens with married couples when one of them is experiencing a chronic illness and poor health that has extended over many years. The healthy spouse has been in the supporting role as a caregiver when, suddenly, the healthy spouse is diagnosed with a terminal illness. This is a shocking turn of events for the couple, since both assumed that the chronically ill spouse would die first. The tables are turned and the chronically ill spouse is caring for the dying spouse. The dying spouse may feel guilty for now needing care and further burdening his already fatigued and ill spouse. He may also feel guilty for abandoning the chronically ill spouse in anticipation of his own upcoming death.

It is difficult for families to hold on and let go simultaneously. This happens when family members get ready for the death of their loved one, only to have him go into remission and his life span extended. It is natural to think the caregiver would be thrilled with more time together. However, often the enormous emotional energy necessary to detach can be so painful that the task of reattaching seems unbearable. The patient becomes confused as well and at times feels everyone has already given up and buried him.

I have often heard people say that we die how we've lived. If someone is social, he may want people around and involved as he passes on. The private individual may approach death in a more isolated fashion. Some are accepting of their fate while others go out kicking and screaming. A hospice staff's goal is to help patients die the way they choose.

Woody Allen put it well when he said, "I'm not afraid to die. I just don't want to be there when it happens!"[10]

The truth is that some of us are very afraid to die. We may fear choking and difficulty with breathing. Some fear leaving loved ones and facing the unknowns or God's judgment.

There are processes families and patients can implement to help enhance a peaceful or "good death." Some helpful end-of-life tasks and processes include the following:

1. Acknowledging our regrets and saying "I'm sorry." No one is or has been a perfect child, spouse, or parent. We have all done or said something that we wished we hadn't. It can be healing to openly talk about these issues and put them behind us.

2. Acknowledging that others make mistakes, and then being willing to forgive them. We can follow the Savior's example by offering forgiveness to family or others who may have hurt us. "Father, forgive them; for they know not what they do" (Luke 23:34).

3. Saying "I love you." "A new commandment I give unto you, That ye love one another; as I have loved you, that ye also love one another" (John 13:34).

4. Remembering. It is valuable to talk about our life memories. This is called life review. It is an important end-of-life task. It keeps the dying's self-esteem intact by remembering who they are and what they have accomplished. This can be done by looking at scrapbooks together, or creating them.

5. Saying good-bye. Saying the final good-bye can be a difficult end-of-life task to perform. We often remind families they can do it every time they say good night. It could go something like this: "I hope I see you tomorrow. If not, know that I love you, Dad. I will really miss you, but I will take care of Mom and carry on in your name."

6. Unfinished business. We're referring to financial and other personal affairs as well as resolving unfinished personal issues. Doing so will put both the patient and his family at ease so they won't have to worry that his death will cause unnecessary burdens for those left behind.

Hospice staff try to help families understand that their loved one has a good chance of dying alone. It may happen when the caregiver goes to the mailbox, grabs a bite to eat, or falls asleep. "When the loyal guard leaves, so does the soul from the body of the guarded."[11]

They also help families understand that "preparing for Death is one of the most profoundly healing acts of a lifetime."[12]

Many individuals with a terminal illness will ask, "Is it my time to go?" The Lord has told us that the sick will be healed if there is sufficient faith and if the person "is not appointed unto death" (Doctrine and Covenants 42:48). Acts 17:26 says there is a determined time and appointed habitation. Hebrews 9:27, Job 14:14, and Alma 42:6 talk about being appointed to death. It was a comfort to many at Richard L. Evans's funeral when President Joseph Fielding Smith said, "No righteous man is ever taken before his time."[13]

Others dying have reported that during their near-death accounts they were told it was not their time to die and they had to return to earth. Some were even given a choice to stay or return. Recently, a hospice patient shared a near-death experience he had a few years previously. After a surgical procedure, he found himself out of his body, viewing it from above. Soon he was joined by a personage in white who reminded him of what he thought Moses might look like. He was told that he must go back into his body because it was not his time to die.

Many dying patients seem to hang on, waiting for a specific time to die. It may be a child's graduation, a loved one's wedding, the coming season, or a special holiday. It sometimes involves the completion of some important endeavor they have worked for. A few years ago, on Easter weekend, three of our hospice patients died on Good Friday, three more on Saturday, and three more on Easter Sunday. I've seen others who seem to wait until someone who is traveling to see them arrives. It's important for them to say their good-byes and have closure. Some seem to hold on to life, hoping to make peace with someone they had experienced relationship problems with in the past.

The Lord may also intervene and extend life. See Helaman 15:4, 10–11 where the Lord "prolonged their days." Alma 9:16 indicates that "the Lord will . . . prolong their existence in the land," and Doctrine and Covenants 5:33 promises "that thy days may be prolonged."

President Kimball said: "I am grateful that even through the priesthood I cannot heal all the sick. I might heal people who should die. I might relieve people of suffering who should suffer. I fear I would frustrate the purpose of God."[14]

He also asked, "What if we did have power to heal? Would we have allowed Abinadi to die in the flames of fire?" Abinadi said, "Touch me not, for God shall smite you . . . for I have not delivered the message which the Lord sent me to deliver . . . therefore, God will not suffer that I shall be destroyed at this time. . . . Ye see that ye have not power to slay me" (Mosiah 13:3, 7).

After Abinadi delivered his message and before he was martyred, he prayed, "O God, receive my soul" (Mosiah 17:19).

At-Death Experiences (ADEs)

At-death experiences (ADEs) have brought spiritual healing to those observing the event as well as to those dying. Some dying non-believers say that they have seen angels or deceased relatives just prior to their deaths. These experiences often convert them to the reality that there is life beyond death.

One interesting story involved a dying woman's ADE. She was anticipating joining her husband who had died some years before. One day she experienced an ADE that had left her puzzled. She asked one of the hospice nurses, "Why is my sister with my deceased husband?" The hospice worker talked with one of the other family members. She asked if the sister was dead. She was told that her sister was in China and had died just a couple of days before. The family had decided not to tell their mother for fear it would upset her. They then decided to tell her about her sister's death because they realized it would give her spiritual comfort and make sense in light of her vision as she herself faced death.[15]

One dying woman awoke with a beautiful smile on her face as she reached for something unseen. She seemed to put her arms together in a cradling position as she looked lovingly into her arms. As her family discussed this event, they realized that her first baby had died just moments after birth. She later had other children and the fact that she had lost a child was hardly ever discussed. This realization was a sweet moment for her family as they concluded that as she died, their mother was allowed to see and hold her deceased spirit baby.[16]

When someone is dying, it is important that we pay attention to everything they say and do because their communications may be subtle and symbolic. We could miss some of these last communications because of our own preoccupations. Sometimes the important messages shared will be vague and confusing. Those present may think that the dying person is delirious or confused rather than trying to communicate something important. Common events occurring prior to death include dying individuals staring through you as if to see something else. In other instances they may seem distracted or offer inappropriate smiles or gestures, pointing or reaching for something unseen, and sometimes calling out names. They may report hearing voices. It is not usually helpful to argue or challenge what the dying are seeing or otherwise sensing.

I was working in the hospital the same day that my paternal grandmother was brought in with heart palpitations. I went to her room on my break to feed her dinner. She visited with me and ate a little. At the end of our visit she looked off into the corner of the room and called out my deceased grandfather's name. We then discussed how she had missed him for the last ten years and how she was looking forward to being with him again. She died a few hours later.

Some dying individuals talk about getting ready to go on a trip. For example, a pilot talked about getting ready to go on a flight. It might be helpful to go along with the symbolism and ask questions such as, "Do you know when it leaves?" and "Can I help you get ready?" If we try to relate to the dying person's world, it can help him experience a more meaningful and peaceful death. If we have trouble understanding, it is okay to say, "I think you are trying to tell me something important and I am trying very hard to understand, but I am just not getting it. Please keep trying to tell me."

One man described missing his trolley. A wise hospice nurse told him that she was sure that the trolley would stop for him soon and that he would be able to get on. The trolley was his symbolic way of saying, "It is time for me to go." It wasn't long after that he died.[17]

Recently I was visiting a hospice patient that we had served for several months. The past month she rarely communicated with her family or our staff. This particular visit I asked how she was. She said, "Not well; I've had a terrible crash." I asked her if she thought she was dying. She nodded her head yes. I asked her if she was ready to go. Again she nodded yes. I asked her if she was afraid and she shook her head no. We shared some other special symbolic communication, and she died a couple of days later.

Many will describe seeing a beautiful place. If they do, it is okay to say, "I'm happy that you see such a beautiful place and that it makes you happy." Others may reluctantly share their fears. It is important to address any concerns: past regrets, strained relationships, unfinished business, a need for repentance, and so forth. Encourage the dying by telling them you want to understand what they are saying. You might ask them, "Can you tell me more?" Pace yourself and don't push them. Let the dying control the conversation.

It has also been helpful to believe those who die are no longer suffering because they are in a beautiful afterworld. It is those of us left behind that struggle through the loss and grief issues. President Kimball reminds us that the Lord does not usually view death as a curse or a tragedy.[18]

The following scripture can also give us comfort: "Blessed are the dead that die in the Lord"(Doctrine and Covenants 63:49).

Because of the veil over our eyes and our limited understanding, it is sometimes hard to realize the Lord's promise that "those that die in me shall not taste of death, for it shall be sweet unto them" (Doctrine and Covenants 42:46).

However, the Lord realizes the pain we experience losing our loved ones. He makes us the following promise about the Millennium and our next life: "There shall be no sorrow because there is no death" (Doctrine and Covenants 101:29).

"And God shall wipe away all tears from their eyes; and there shall be no more death, neither sorrow, nor crying, neither shall there be any more pain: for the former things are passed away" (Revelation 21:4).

He also counsels us to "weep for the loss of them that die, and more especially for those that have not hope of a glorious resurrection" (Doctrine and Covenants 42:45).

He has left us the Comforter and promises, "blessed are all they that mourn, for they shall be comforted" (3 Nephi 12:4; see also Matthew 5:4).

Notes

1. *Cancer Facts & Figures* (Atlanta: American Cancer Society, 1998).
2. Gallup telephone Poll, 1997. National sample of 1200.
3. T. A. Rando (speech, Association for Death Education and Counseling Conference, Chicago, March 1998).
4. Isaac Asimov, http://en.wikiquote.org/wiki/Isaac_Asimov (accessed September 10, 2008).
5. Dame Cicely Saunder, http://mercatornet.com/articles (accessed July 30, 2005).
6. T. A. Rando, ed. *Clinical Dimensions of Anticipatory Mourning: Theory and Practice in Working with the Dying, Their Loved Ones, and Their Caregivers* (Champaign, Illinois: Research Press, 2000), 7.
7. Gallup telephone Poll, 1997. National sample of 1200.
8. Ibid.
9. Kit Jackson (speech, Utah Hospice Palliative Care Organization, Davis Conference Center, Layton, Utah, November 9, 2005).
10. Woody Allen, http://www.brainquote.com (accessed September 10, 2008).
11. Neale Donald Walsh, *Conversations with God: An Uncommon Dialogue,* Book 1, (New York: G. P. Putnam's Sons, 1995) , 80.
12. Stephen Levine, *A Year to Live* (New York: Bell Tower, 1997), 7.
13. Smith, "Funeral Services for Richard L. Evans," *Ensign,* December 1971, 10.
14. Spencer W. Kimball, *Faith Precedes the Miracle* (Salt Lake City: Deseret Book, 1979), 99.
15. M. Callanan & P. Kelley, *Final Gifts* (New York: Bantom Books, 1992), 92–93.
16. Ibid., 179
17. Ibid., chapter 6
18. Kimball, *Faith Precedes the Miracle,* 101

CHAPTER SEVEN

Death of a Loved One

AS MY MOTHER'S MEMORY SLOWLY DECLINED OVER THE YEARS, I wanted her to experience one more trip to the early Church historic sites that she loved. We traveled to Winter Quarters in Omaha, Nebraska, to visit the pioneer sites and monuments there. I was especially interested in the Winter Quarters memorial statue that stands in the cemetery behind the Winter Quarters Temple. I had only seen pictures and smaller replicas of this life-sized pioneer statue that was dedicated in 1936. The statue depicts a pioneer man and woman huddled together with a shovel in hand. They are looking down sadly on a grave they have just dug for a deceased loved one. As I gazed on this beautiful statue, I asked my mother to take a picture of me standing close to the grieving couple. As I got up to the statue for the photo, I looked down and discovered that the artist, Avard Fairbanks, had chosen to sculpt a small child lying on its back in an open grave. I was overcome with emotion as I felt witness to the intense grief and suffering these pioneer parents had to endure.

It was Dennis that had first noticed the backside of this same statue a few years earlier while attending a training seminar for LDS Family Services. He came home and described the large roots coming out of the ground that are attached to the legs and backs of the pioneer couple. It looked to us as if these roots could pull them down and bury them in the ground as well. This symbolism of grief and mourning had a profound effect on both of us since we have buried two of our own children.

Although both of us work with grieving individuals, we were shocked at our own pain and suffering following our personal losses. We had learned much through our study of loss and grief, but we hadn't felt the deep suffering of the heart until we experienced it first hand. We were surprised that research has shown that it can take many months or years to adjust and find one's "new normal."[1]

We wouldn't have believed the time frame if we had not experienced grief firsthand. We realized, as many others have, that we never can be the same following a significant loss. Our loss and all that we have since experienced are now becoming part of our new normal. As our priorities change, we see through new eyes. Finding our new normal usually takes longer than we expect or would like. After losing Joseph with his coat of many colors, Jacob refused to be comforted and said, "For I will go down into the grave unto my son mourning" (Genesis 37:35). I recently heard a mother whose daughter had been murdered express similar feelings, followed by her own reassurance that we can find comfort in knowing where our loved ones are. It is helpful to realize that faith and grief are both uniquely important but separate principles. Each requires actions on our part to fully benefit and sustain us in times of loss. We will always miss and grieve the earthly presence of our loved ones, even when knowing where they are.

The death of a loved one is an experience that most of us will face someday. When that moment comes, we may discover the poignant reality expressed so well in the movie, *Man's Search for Happiness*. "Life's greatest test comes with the death of a loved one, and without faith in the immortality of the soul, the separation of death looms forever comfortless."[2]

In this chapter we hope to give you helpful information as you exercise faith and receive the necessary comfort to survive your loss.

We all experience different types of grief, mourning as we confront different types of death. The death of a parent is considered a loss of our past while the death of a spouse constitutes the loss of our present. The death of a child (often the most challenging) represents the loss of the hopes and dreams for our future.

Loss of a Spouse

Although some professionals feel there is more social understanding and support with the loss of a spouse, losing one's best friend, lover, and life companion leaves many profoundly lonely. Even when we realize that one of us must go first, it is no easy task. We often experience a loss of identity. We were once a married couple and now we are a widow or widower. We may not like the label or the feeling of being alone in the world.

Widowers usually display less emotional grief and have more trouble adapting to the practical problems, like housework and child care. Widows usually experience a sense of abandonment and may require more help with emotional issues. The most common complaint expressed by both is the loneliness felt following the loss of a spouse.

One woman said after the death of her husband, "It is so hard. I need help. I am falling apart. I am not coping. I don't know what to do."

Another widow was asked by friends, "What can we do to help you?" Her reply was, "Undo it!"

A man who lost his wife said, "My wife was so healthy when she suddenly got ill and died. I am still in shock to be left alone so suddenly. I go over and over the details of her death. I am so emotional."

We often struggle to understand the impact of someone else's loss. In our attempt to provide encouragement, we often say the wrong things. A sister in one of our wards lost her husband and son in the same accident. The Relief Society president said to her, "Well, some people lose their whole family. At least you have your daughter." This mother was angered by the statement and went inactive for years. She turned her anger toward the Church because a well-meaning member and Church representative made a hurtful statement. (See Part One for more information on spiritual injury.)

Another widow who had cared for her ill husband for many years was told, "You should be glad, now you can have a life."

Many don't understand that caring for someone so intensely often deepens our bond with them, thus complicating or intensifying our loss. It's also normal to feel relief from the hard work of caring for a loved one and watching them suffer; however, most will still mourn and miss them.

Death of a Parent

Over twelve million Americans will bury a parent this year. Unfortunately, the grief of adult children is often disenfranchised (overlooked). Because society expects, accepts, and discounts the loss of older parents, their children's grief consequently goes unrecognized. In reality, the death of a parent can be difficult at any age.

Young children often struggle as they attempt to make sense of a loss they can't developmentally understand. In addition, some children experience a sense of abandonment after the death of a parent, which may cause anxiety and depression.

A young girl who lost her mother stated, "I know that I should be happy. She's well in heaven. But I miss her so!"

What relief she felt when she learned it was okay and normal to miss her mother and feel sad. She, like many, needed permission to grieve.

A twenty-one-year-old woman said, "My mother died after years of suffering. I felt relieved that her suffering had ended."

My own mother's parents died when she was fourteen. She told us that she would often go in her parents' coat closet and put on her mother's fur coat and weep. She felt comfort by cuddling herself in the coat. The smell and warmth allowed her to feel close to her mother, both physically and spiritually.

I couldn't sleep well for two weeks after my father died. We had traveled many miles to be with him on Christmas Day. He died early that Christmas morning. I couldn't understand how my mother could sleep in the bed where he died that very night. I could hardly walk past the bedroom. It was frightening for me because his bed was where Dennis, my brother, and I performed CPR to keep him alive until the paramedics arrived.

Now, twenty years later, Mother (Vivian Johnson Marsden) died just a few months before the printing of this book. She had the perfect death or a "good death" as we call it in hospice. She was eighty-two years old, living alone, and caring for herself until her cancer diagnosis six months earlier. She had five children, their spouses, and grandchildren who helped keep her at home as long as possible. She experienced a little dementia, which was a blessing because she never realized how sick she really was. As she declined, the family gave Dennis and me permission to care for her at our home with the support of Rocky Mountain Hospice. She lived comfortably for three months, surrounded and supported by her five children, their spouses, and grandchildren. She was a spiritual saint, choosing to be an "instrument in God's hands," as my brother put it. She was a Relief Society stake and ward president for over fifteen years. She served three full-time missions and continued to serve as a ward missionary until four months prior to her passing.

We had just finished watching the first session of general conference when Dennis and I thought her eyes looked different. She hadn't been eating or drinking much for a few days. I went and looked at the calendar to confirm the date—April 6, of course! I thought if she could pick her day to die this would be it. She loved the Restoration of the gospel and she never missed a session of general conference, including this one.

I called my brother and asked if he could come after conference and give her a blessing. I was hoping it would be a blessing of release, if my brother was inspired to do so. After the closing prayer of general conference, we gathered around her bed as a family. At the end of her beautiful blessing, my brother asked, "When did she start breathing like that?" I replied, "As soon as you said amen." She took a few quiet, peaceful breaths and was gone. We all sat in silence and basked in the spirit. Dennis said, "I haven't witnessed many miracles in my life, but I believe we have witnessed a miracle today."

Our youngest daughter got married three weeks later and our youngest son moved out of state for medical school. Our house feels empty now. We miss the three of them living in our home. We are again experiencing loss and grief.

We are also experiencing a new phenomenon, one that has been described to us by our clients, but now we sense it ourselves and understand it more clearly. Having buried our grandparents and all four parents, we are suddenly the "old" generation. We are truly the grandparents, the ones who will die next. For the first time, we see, feel, and fear our own death and mortality. It is lonelier than we expected and more frightening than we imagined. This, like all of life's losses and changes, will require grief work and faith to adjust and find meaning.

Loss of a Sibling

Loss of a sibling can be very confusing for young children as well as adult survivors. It is common for the bereaved to canonize the deceased. It is also common for other siblings to feel unloved, or think that their parents love the deceased sibling more. One child said, "My mother kept saying the joy of her life was gone after my brother died."

Well-meaning comments can also cause pain and damage relationships. A female acquaintance of ours said, "Soon after my brother died, my visiting teacher kept asking if and when my sister-in-law would remarry. This upset me and really hurt my feelings."

Some lack the ability to fully express their feelings. A sibling writes, "When my parents start getting down about the death of my brother, I usually leave the room. I just can't talk to them about him. I don't know how to talk to them. I feel like no matter what I say it comes out wrong and hurts them. I'm not good at saying what I mean. I'm afraid to cry about the death of my brother because it might upset them more. I cry alone most of the time. I can talk to my sister."

After Cameron died, one of our sons shared, "I feel guilty that I hadn't been a better brother. I should have been kinder to him."

Children and Loss:

A child's abnormal, bad behaviors or rebelliousness may be a way of acting out his or her pain and grief. Grief and loss can be confusing for children. They may become angry at God or the Church because they feel God should have prevented their tragedy or protected their loved one. Spiritual injury may result when a child's prayer isn't answered how they hoped it would be. Many young children have earnestly prayed for a loved one to recover, only to watch them eventually die.

Parents should encourage (not pressure) children to express their feelings and fears by allowing them to be active participants in coping with the crisis, illness, or death. Children can usually sense increased stress and anxiety in the home. They may feel and recognize that something is not right. If children are not told honestly or allowed to share in what is happening, they may become confused, frightened, and insecure. They feel secure when parents share their feelings openly and regularly. They may also feel comfort and reassurance when parents share personal testimony, read scriptures, and pray with them.

Family home evenings can be a forum for family sharing and listening. Children should also be involved in the open acknowledgment of family issues and problem solving. Including them in challenges doesn't mean parents should overwhelm them with their own grief, guilt, and unrealistic expectations. Children cannot fully comprehend a parent's pain. They have developmental limitations based on their age and limited life experience. They often remember and regrieve certain aspects of their loss as they grow and mature. They may experience a loss of trust toward their parents if important issues affecting the family are kept from them.

Children look to adults, especially their parents as examples of how to respond to life events. Seeing and sharing our grief and disappointments in healthy ways often validates a child's own sadness, confusion, or other emotions. It's a challenging and sobering responsibility to acknowledge that, "Parents can complicate or facilitate the grief process for children."[3]

A five-year-old was confused with her mother's fluctuating behavior and mood. She would see tears in her mother's eyes and ask, "Why are you sad mommy?" Her mother would reply that she was just tired because she was pregnant. What she didn't share was that she was carrying twins and knew one of the twins would not live due to a serious birth defect.

This went on for a couple of months. A few days before the delivery, their doctor hoped that some reading material and encouraging a more open communication style might help the family.

After reading some grief literature, the mom told her daughter that two baby girls would be born, but that they could only bring home one sister because the other was sick and wouldn't live very long. This curious child asked many questions. When she got the answers she needed, she returned to her play.

When the babies were born, the child was allowed to see, hold, and kiss both babies. The baby with the birth defect died a few hours later. As this five-year-old saw her parents and grandparents cry, she asked additional questions. When she had sufficient contact with both of her baby sisters, she turned her focus back to her crayons and dolls.

The entire family spent time with the deceased baby sister. They had said a brief hello and now had to say good-bye. With time, everyone seemed to adjust to the loss, including the five-year-old.

It has been said that, "Children can't tolerate intense emotions for very long. Children generally have a short feeling phase."[4]

After his brother's death, our seven-year-old son Brandon wondered, "Am I crying enough?" However, he was unable or unwilling to verbalize this guilt until he was fifteen years old. At age sixteen, he wrote a poem about an ornamental pear tree we planted eight years earlier in Cameron's memory. We were surprised at the deep feelings and understanding that he could now express.

The Pear Tree

Death, the disabled brother gone
Crippled, but much stronger than us all
Sadness and grief of the loss
Of a great brother, son, and example
Now planted in the earth his body lies
A small sapling also then planted
Small and weak, could barely stand
Weak as he once was
Year after year it grows
Stronger and taller it points to the sky
A remembrance of joys
That still live on
Beautiful, soft, white, flowers
Blooming on his day of birth
Falling to the earth
The month of his passing
The memorial Pear Tree
A true symbol of Cameron

Standing tall and firm above us
As he is now, while he watches below

In young children, we may see bedwetting, returning to the bottle, clinging, and phobias. Encouraging open communication may aid in the healing process. Remember, young children communicate in many ways. Some may communicate subtly through behaviors and play. Others may communicate through art and music. Young boys often grieve through anger, while many girls become caregivers. We can help children become healthy survivors, rather than victims, by offering support. We can guide children toward letting go of unrealistic blame and rechanneling their energies into meaningful and productive tasks.

The following are age characteristics of grieving children.

Two and Under

These children react behaviorally to stresses around them. They can sense tension in the home and conflicts between their parents. They may react by crying, or through changes in behaviors such as eating, sleeping, bathroom habits, withdrawing, or temper tantrums. They respond best to consistent nurturing from significant others in their lives.

Three- to Five-Year-Olds

These children often react with similar behavior changes as those two and under. In addition, they may be very curious, asking many questions. Answer as simply and honestly as possible. We may see their grief as they color, draw, sing, or play. Many children act out parts of the crisis with dolls and toys as they play house. They may also respond like six- to nine-year-olds, feeling guilty that somehow they caused the crisis. We should allow them to talk and give them extra attention and hugs.

Six- to Nine-Year-Olds

Generally they can understand adversity, illness, and death. They recognize that death is final. They may feel that bad thoughts, wishes, or anger they experienced in the past caused the illness or death. They need hope for a positive future. They may experience negative dreams. We may see them acting out their loss issues through behavior problems or poor academic performance. Their physical symptoms can be similar to teens and adults. They need reassurance and reminders that others love them.

Ten- to Twelve-Year-Olds

They may want more answers about what happened and why. They may kid or joke about illness or death to hide their true fears and anxieties. Provide honest answers to their specific questions, allowing them to set the pace of the discussion.

Adolescents

Adolescents can react as an adult would, with confusion, withdrawal, depression, or intense emotions. However, because of their preoccupation with self, they may not feel the same depth of grief experienced by adults. Their recovery is often more rapid than adults.

After Cam's death, our teenage son reported, "After my brother died, I was afraid to talk to my parents. I decided to go back into the family room where my parents were. I remember sitting on the couch, listening to my parents cry. I didn't cry, I just sat there staring at the balloons that said, 'Get well Soon!' A couple of days later at the funeral, it all got worse. I became more angry and depressed."

Although teens understand death is final for others, they often personally feel immortal. Consequently they may still participate in risk-taking activities as they search for their own personal identity.

Adolescents are often self-focused, which takes most of their time and energy. They are also preoccupied with friends and need our love and support to become free of peer pressure. They are concerned with day-to-day events, and may want to hurry through the grieving process and get their lives back to normal.

We should avoid telling teens how they should feel or react. Lecturing, comparing, or overcontrolling doesn't usually work. They need good role models, encouragement, and a listening ear at crucial moments. It is often after midnight!

Loss of a Child

"The death of a child is like no other. Parents experience the symptoms of grief more intensely and far longer than with any other loss."[5] For many years, Dennis and I worked with parents who had lost children. However, we hadn't fully realized that their suffering and pain was so intense until we lost two of our own. We were shocked at the magnitude of our own grief. We discovered that it can be difficult to understand what someone else is going through until we experience it ourselves. The following excerpts are from parents in a support group who have lost a child.

One person said, "I can still feel today the absolute cold feeling of my son's skin as I kissed him good-bye on the forehead. That will be with me forever as a reminder that he was taken from us so suddenly, and represents the feeling of absence and loss that weigh upon us."

A father lamented, "I miss watching her jump on the trampoline. She always wanted me to spot her. I also miss my old life and how my wife was before this tragedy. We can never be the same."

John Craig, a family therapist, lost two daughters, fourteen and sixteen, in a car-train accident. A few years later, another daughter died of meningitis. He said:

> For me, the night our two daughters died changed everything. I would never be the same, feel the same, or be completely at ease again. And more significantly, neither would the rest of my family. My grief began with outrage. How could God or life be so contemptuous of me? What possible wrong could I have committed that would bring such ruthless destruction to my family? It hit me with a blunt force hard enough that even after eighteen years, I still experience an ache that threatens to undo me, to expel me from among the faithful. Yet I have not yet given in to the demon of discouragement or succumbed to spiritual death—not even when six years later that awful monster, death (2 Nephi 9:10), came again to my home. This time it was my middle daughter taken in one day from the blush of health to the darkness of the grave.
>
> Through yet another siege of overwhelming sadness, way beyond my ability to endure, I remained confused, disoriented, and perpetually dissatisfied with my life, but I didn't and haven't quit. Instead I reach for the Comforter; I pray for peace nightly, and I take heart in the promises extended by the Savior of the World.[6]

A friend of mine said, "It has been almost twenty years since the car accident of our three-year-old son. I know I will be with him in the celestial kingdom; however, I still miss him and wish I could have raised him on earth. Our grief was very intense at first. It almost cost us our marriage. Our grief has turned into mourning, which seems to be staying with us a lifetime."

Hyrum G. Smith said the following:

> There are many of our Latter-day Saint mothers who have mourned the loss of their little children, and many mothers have felt that they themselves had committed some great sin, else their little ones would not be taken from them. Now, to such mothers let me say, do not accuse the Lord of taking your little ones from you, nor feel that you have committed any great sin, that those little ones are taken from you, because the Lord loves little children and he will not treat them unkindly, nor without mercy, for through the blood of his atonement they shall come forth in the morning of the Resurrection with his Saints, and they shall be glorified according to the works they would have accomplished in the earth had they lived."[7]

Professionals are now suggesting that, "Accommodation in contrast to recovery captures more accurately the process that most individuals experience following a major loss. Major losses can be integrated into the rest of life; however, final closure after the death of a loved one usually cannot be obtained and is not even desirable."[8]

An example of this reality is evident in the account of a mother whose child died forty years ago. She recently ran into her deceased daughter's best friend who was shopping with her granddaughter. This mother experienced a grief attack. She mourned again as she realized that she had missed forty years without her daughter and was now also missing her role as grandmother and great-grandmother to lost generations of grandchildren! This account illustrates the developmental aspects of her grief.

A Time to Die?

Typical questions asked by those who lose a loved one are: Does everyone have a specific time assigned to leave earth life? What does appointed time mean? Is it a specific day, month, or year? What about those who die of sudden accidents? What about those who die as the result of murder?

Ecclesiastes 3:1–2 tells us, "To everything there is a season, and a time to every purpose under the heaven: a time to be born and a time to die; a time to plant, and a time pluck up that which is planted."

President Spencer W. Kimball taught that we can die prematurely when he said, "I am confident that there is a time to die. I am not a fatalist. I believe that many people die before their time because they are careless, abuse their bodies, take unnecessary chances, or expose themselves to hazard, accident, and sickness."[9]

Lehi and Nephi, the Sons of Helaman, were protected by God. They were put into prison without food. Their persecutors tried to slay them, but could not. They were encircled about as if by fire, and they said, "Ye cannot lay your hands on us to slay us" (Helaman 5:26, 29).

Christ sensed when it was his time to die. He said, "Mine hour is not come" (John 2:4, 7:30). As his martyrdom drew closer, he announced to His disciples, "The hour is come" (John 12:23) and "It is finished" (John 19:30).

Elder Neal A. Maxwell wrote, "God is never surprised by unexpected arrivals in the spirit world . . . we must always distinguish between God's being able to foresee and His causing or desiring something to happen."[10]

Grieving Variables

Some may use the word recovery as they describe the grief process. However, better words may be that we will reconcile, adapt, or adjust to our loss of a loved one. How we ultimately grieve and cope is as individual as each of our thumbprints.

There are many variables that account for how someone will experience the death of a loved one. Who died, and how close was I to this person? Often, the depth of our love, time, and emotional investments coincide with the depth of our grief. Was the death an expected loss, possibly of an elderly loved one who was at peace and ready to go? I have seen this kind of death with my hospice work and it can be a beautiful experience. We may feel relief that their suffering is over. However, one of my saddest and loneliest patients was a ninety-six-year-old husband who wanted his ninety-eight-year-old wife to just live a few more years.

Heber J. Grant expressed shock and grief when his mother, who was in her eighties and was his best friend, died before reaching one hundred as he had expected.

Another factor in how we may experience grief relates to the amount of time one has to prepare for the death and to say good-bye. We knew our ninety-year-old grandmother was dying and we were able to help her do some end-of-life tasks, express our love, and say good-bye. When my fairly young father died suddenly of heart disease and Dennis's mother took her own life at age fifty, we weren't able to express these heartfelt messages. We had to do these end-of-life tasks vicariously with our deceased son and parents who died suddenly. (It can be done through writing down our thoughts in a letter to our deceased loved ones or talking out loud to them in an "empty chair.")

There are also differences between a sudden death and an anticipated death. Anticipated death is like standing on a street corner as you see someone running toward you. Soon they are upon you, knocking you down as they continue running away; you saw them coming and you knew what hit you. In sudden death, your back was turned and you didn't see the runner coming; you didn't have time to brace yourself. Suddenly, you find yourself flat on the ground with no idea of what hit you. It will take longer for the brain to adjust, and for the shock to soften after experiencing unexpected death.[11]

Paradigm Shift

We need not fear the future; we can still find joy, peace, and happiness again. To achieve future peace, we might consider what Steven Covey calls a paradigm shift. In a paradigm shift, we come to view and define the meaning associated with the same event dramatically differently. An example of looking at an event from another angle became clear to us when we were driving to the mortuary to see our deceased son in his casket for the first time. Dennis found himself sitting through a red light and still didn't move when it turned green. He was moving in slow motion still in shock from Cameron's sudden death the night before. The man behind him started honking, raising his fists, and yelling at Dennis. Most likely, if the angry driver had known where we were going and why Dennis wasn't moving, he would have shifted the way he looked at the event and remained patient. There would be a predictable change in his response if he also had a young child, and a guaranteed shift in his paradigm if he had buried one.

Another example of a paradigm shift occurred when my father died on Christmas. While we were waiting for the ambulance I would go in another room and ask the Lord to let my father live, especially since it was Christmas. My prayer was not answered how I thought it should be. However, my mother helped me reconstruct my view and the thoughts that were upsetting to me. She shared that she felt Christmas was a special day to go to the spirit world and meet the Savior.

Loss of Identity

For a time after the death of a loved one it may be hard to interact with others. We may feel wounded, devastated, and vulnerable. Some withdraw and isolate themselves from the very support they so desperately need. We may also feel deserted and experience a loss of identity. We may feel uncomfortable being introduced as a widow or a widower rather than a married couple. President Hinckley described this process when he spoke following the death of his wife, Marjorie. "Only those who have passed through this dark valley know of its utter desolation. To lose one's much-loved partner . . . is absolutely devastating."[12]

A loss of identity is also common especially if we were a caregiver and had invested significant time and energy caring for our deceased loved one. I felt very lost for a long time wondering what to do with all the time and energy I had previously spent caring for our disabled child. Some feel they are under glass, continually scrutinized and judged for how or how long they are grieving. Consequently, many wear masks, pretending to be coping well. As they mourn alone in the shadows, they are experiencing disenfranchised grief because they feel like few understand their pain. One woman asked, "What would the ward members think of me if they knew I really wasn't coping well with my husband's death?" To cope with these social symptoms, we encourage our patients to decrease their isolation and try to accept others' support. A daily phone call from family or friends asking how we are doing can help a great deal. Many hospitals and mortuaries now offer bereavement support groups where mourners can talk with others who are grieving similar losses.

Service

Service can be a healing tool. You will increase the likelihood of finding meaning and purpose in your loss as you reach out to others who are also hurting. At the last supper, knowing of His fate, Christ asked His disciples to love one another. When He hung on the cross He looked at His weeping mother and said "Woman, behold thy son," and then looking at John, "Behold thy mother" (John 19:26, 27). He encouraged them to care for and look after one another. He asks the same of us today.

On Cameron's first birthday following his death, we were missing him and feeling sad and depressed. We decided to take a meal to a woman who was confined to her home. After visiting with her, we acknowledged that we both felt better and that our sadness had lifted as we helped another.

We remember our first sacrament meeting after the death of Cameron. We used to watch him proudly pass the sacrament with a silver tray attached to his electric wheelchair. The Sunday following his death there was no wheelchair, no silver tray, and of course, no Cameron. This Sunday void stayed with us for many sacrament meetings. Hospice widows and widowers often share with us that sitting alone after many years of marriage and hearing the familiar hymns which used to bring comfort, now bring a flood of tears and grief.

Loving in Absence

We miss our son very much. We have had to learn to love him in absence because we can no longer love him in presence.[13] Because someone has died does not mean the love or relationship ends.

We mourn for others who have lost loved ones. We look forward with great anticipation to claim the hope of the Resurrection and see our son again. We draw comfort from the scriptures that say,

"Because I live, ye shall live also" (John 14:19) and "Whosoever liveth and believeth in me shall never die" (John 11:26).

For coping tools and grief interventions, see Part One.

Notes

1. Rana K. Limbo and Sara Rich Wheeler, *When a Baby Dies: A Handbook for Helping and Healing* (La Crosse Lutheran Hospital/Gunderson Clinic, Ltd., 1986), xv.

2. *Man's Search for Happiness*, original film, directed by Judge Whitaker (Provo, Utah: Brigham Young University, 1964).

3. K. Doka, "Living with Grief" (speech, Hospice Foundation of America National Teleconference, April 14, 1999).

4. A. Wolfelt (speech, Association for Death Education and Counseling Conference, Chicago, March 1998).

5. Barbara E. Rosof, *The Worst Loss: How Families Heal from the Death of a Child* (New York: H. Holt & Co., 1994), 3.

6. Craig, "Surviving the Death of a Child: It Takes Courage to Believe," Essay G5, *Helping and Healing Our Families* (Salt Lake City: Deseret Book/Brigham Young University, 2005), 280–81.

7. Smith, in Conference Report, April 1917, 70–71.

8. T. A. Rando, "Grieving and Mourning: Accommodating to loss," *Dying: Facing the Facts*, edited by H. Wass and R. A. Niemeyer, (Washington DC: Taylor & Francis, 1995), 221.

9. Kimball, *Faith Precedes the Miracle*, 103.

10. Neil A. Maxwell, *All These Things Shall Give Thee Experience*, (Salt Lake City: Deseret Book, 1979), 18.

11. T. A. Rando (speech, Association for Death Education and Counseling Conference, Chicago, March 1998).

12. Ann Bennion Brown, *The Widow's Might*, (Springville, Utah: Horizon Publishers, 2007), x.

13. T. A. Rando, *Clinical Dimension Of Anticipatory Mourning: Theory and Practice in Working with the Dying, Their Loved Ones, and Their Caregivers* (Champaign, Illinois: Research Press, 2000), 192.

CHAPTER EIGHT

Death and Spirituality

SOME SURVIVORS ARE SPIRITUALLY INJURED WHEN they experience the death of a loved one. Spiritual injury results when life's realities contradict previously held spiritual assumptions. The night before our fourteen-year-old's hip surgery, I told him if anything went wrong I hoped he would come back from the spirit world to let me know he was okay. As the mother of a deceased infant and a child with cerebral palsy, I worried and wanted reassurance. However, the look in Cameron's eyes caused me to change my request. I said, "If you can't come back, or shouldn't, don't worry. I will just have faith that you are okay." He died suddenly and unexpectedly in a close observation room at twelve midnight, thirty-six hours after his surgery, with a nurse and Dennis at his side.

Initially I really thought that Cameron would come to visit me. I waited longingly with faith for many nights. I was sharing this story with a man whose wife had died on hospice. He too had hoped for a visit from beyond the veil. I told him that I had experienced many special spiritual experiences that brought me comfort and I was trying to have faith that my son was alive and well without the visitation I had hoped for. He replied. "Well isn't that what you told him you would do?" "Well yes," I responded as the reality of my own words sunk in. I stopped expecting a visitation.

As a young bishop, Dennis had several opportunities to observe the impact of death on those dying and those left behind. A wonderful sister in our stake lost her husband without warning. He was a prominent and loved priesthood leader and physician. All the outpouring of love, support, and testimony provided much-needed strength to this grieving widow. She was comforted and blessed by others, and her willingness to share her testimony as she entered the mission field kept her grief at bay for a season.

Many months following her husband's death and her honorable release from the mission field, a young adult renting an apartment in her basement called expressing concern. His landlord and admired friend seemed depressed and distraught. When Dennis called this grieving sister and asked if he might be of some assistance, her humble response taught him an important lesson. "Oh, bishop, I would love to visit, but I could never allow others to see me in the waiting room of LDS Family Services." This spiritual sister wanted to be a good example to others who had complimented her on how strong she was. She felt she would disappoint them if she admitted that she was still grieving her husband's death. She feared that some would judge her delayed grief reaction and need to mourn as a lack of testimony in the Savior's Atonement.

A mother whose daughter was suddenly and violently killed in a high-speed auto-pedestrian accident was confused at first and angry with a God that would take her daughter from her just two weeks before her twenty-second birthday, and only a month before her appointed time to begin serving her full-time mission. With support, prayer, and grief work, this grieving mother eventually achieved spiritual understanding and comfort. She came to believe that God's hands are most often present to sustain and comfort us in our suffering rather than to remove the trials and suffering from our lives.

Well-Meaning Clichés Can Cause Spiritual Injury

After the death of a loved one, family and church members often reach out in a sincere attempt to comfort those left behind. Unfortunately, sometimes their intended words of encouragement cause spiritual injury. Jacob 2:89 warns us not to "enlarge the wounds of those already wounded" with our words.

The following statements and clichés resulted in spiritual injury according to the grieving members who received them. We might agree with or believe these clichés and some may even be doctrinally true. However, bereaved members frequently list these intended words of comfort as being very hurtful. Some of their specific responses are included in parentheses. These experiences and responses can help us better understand and respect the vulnerability of the newly bereaved.

One family was told shortly after the death of their child that if they did not quit mourning and feeling sad, their child would not be able to progress and do her work in the spirit world.

A mother who lost a child wrote, "The man who drove the car and survived the crash in which my only daughter was killed has several living children. His wife said, 'Look for the silver lining behind your child's death and you'll find it because I have!' She went on to point out, 'You still have your boys.' (Those who have not experienced their own major loss often minimize the impact of such a loss in the lives of the bereaved.)

Another bereaved parent was told by a temple worker, "Your son would be moving out and going on his mission in a few years anyway. This just makes it a little sooner." This mother said, "I felt like I had been slapped in the face."

Those of us who have had a child marry or go on a mission and also lost a child through death know this is a damaging comparison.

Another mother said:

> I was called to be the stake Primary president. The next day my daughter away from home at BYU died suddenly. My father died eighteen days later. Three days after returning from all the traveling and funerals I had my first stake leadership training. However, no one in the stake presidency said a word to me about how difficult this all must be: having a new calling and presenting, so soon after the death of my daughter and father. Fortunately I was able to make a good presentation. However, the pain from their lack of concern has remained with me. Four or five months later, while being interviewed by a member of the stake presidency, the subject of my daughter's death came up and I got emotional. The counselor said, "Oh, you're not over that yet?" I bravely tried to explain that it wasn't something I would 'just get over,' rather I would learn to cope with it.[1]

A bishop's wife posed this question to a father who had just lost a child: "Isn't it odd how Heavenly Father takes the most precious?" This father disagreed as he reflected on the murders, rapists, thieves, drug and alcohol addicts that die daily.

There are, of course, circumstances when the very young appear to be called home. The Prophet Joseph Smith taught of such instances: "The Lord takes many away, even in infancy, that they may escape the envy of men and the sorrows and evils of this present world . . ." [2]

It may comfort some to know that their deceased loved ones are freed from the trials of earth life. However, others may become angry or confused. Some have questioned, "Would God physically take my child or does he allow accidents and disease to occur even among the innocent?"

A well-meaning bishop said, "It's surely a blessing to know your daughter will be spared the trials of this life." Her mother thought to herself, "Send your child. It may seem like a blessing to you, but not to me. I want to raise my daughter here on earth like the rest of you!"

The following additional statements were made by well-meaning members to the bereaved:

"You look like you're doing so well." (She shared later, "You can't see this kind of pain.")

"Well it's not like you don't know where she is!" (Her mother thought, "I would rather be worrying late at night for her to come home by curfew!")

"Well at least he isn't suffering, in a coma, or a vegetable. God loved him enough to take him." His father thought, "Does that mean God doesn't love my aunt who has been in a coma for over a year?" (The "at least" examples usually don't help. They in fact have the tendency of negating another's loss and grief.)

"It was God's will," "God needed him," "His work was done," and, "It was his time."

These statements are all possible explanations for untimely death. Regrettably, even though you may believe one or all of these statements, they usually offer little comfort for those who are grieving.

In a summary, here are some general clichés that might be hurtful to the bereaved:

- We say, "Don't feel bad." (They hear "Don't grieve," which negates their loss.)
- We might say, "It's God's will, he needed them." One mother said, "God has lots of babies, I just had one. I needed her too."
- We might say, "Just give it time" or "Time will heal." (However, time without grief work doesn't usually heal.)
- We might ask, "Did you pray and fast?" (They may hear, "God would have healed me or my loved one if I had prayed more or had enough faith?")
- We might say, "Be strong, put it behind you." (They may hear, "If you show emotion you are weak.")
- We might say, "You just need to get over this." (They may hear, "Your loved one is not worth your sadness and tears.")
- You might say, "She led a full life." (They may wonder, "Does that make me miss her less?")
- You might say, "Just keep busy, the living must go on." (They may feel that you think their loved one is not worth remembering.)

More Helpful things to say would be:
- I'm sorry you are going through this.
- I want you to know I care.
- When you hurt, I hurt.
- This must be very difficult for you.
- I can't imagine how you must feel.
- I'll be there at_____, and bring_____.

The Holy Ghost can, of course, offer comfort through you when you are prompted: "Then can ye speak with the tongue of angels" (2 Nephi 31:13), "Wherefore, they speak the words of Christ" (2 Nephi 32:3). After observing the dilemma of sincere attempts to comfort, a Christian leader warned that inadvertently we often wound those in mourning: "We often bury more people outside the church doors than in the ground when a death occurs!"

In other words, the bereaved are fragile, and at times things are said that hurt them, and in some instances drive them away from our church doors. As previously stated, in most instances, it is safest to simply say you're sorry, and not "enlarge the wounds of those who are already wounded" (Jacob 2:8, 9) with words of intended comfort that minimize the profound grief experienced by those coping with significant loss.

Spiritual Comfort

After the death of a loved one, some individuals receive spiritual healing from personal impressions, visions, dreams, and visitations. Others are spiritually comforted by their own or another's near-death experiences. These same experiences can also serve as helpful death preparations.

Our disabled son, Cameron, wrote the following poem for a school project six months before his death:

If I Had a Wish

If I had a wish I would wish that I could walk!
I would run and play and all the girls would like me.
See, it's hard to be different in some ways.
Like you can't do your homework without someone helping you.
Sports would be fun to do, and I would play basketball.
And I wouldn't miss standing in my prone stander if I could walk.
In some ways not walking is good luck because you get to drive early! (My Wheelchair) and you don't even have to have a license.
You also can have a computer all to yourself.
My wish will come true—in the next life!"[3]

The day Cameron died, his special education teacher in Texas remembered the poem he had written earlier about his wishes. We didn't know her well, and she was initially hesitant to share a poem she had written in response to Cameron's poem. It wasn't until after Cameron's funeral that she decided to share her poetic spiritual impressions. After Cameron's funeral, she quickly went home and returned with her poem. When she shared the poem, she mentioned that during her fifteen years of teaching, she had never been spiritually touched so profoundly by a student. In turn, reading her poem brought us personal comfort.

She told us that she had trouble sleeping after hearing of

Cameron's death. Early that morning she got up and wrote her personal impressions.

The Wish

Written in response to the death of Cameron Ashton and his private wish for his next life.

I felt the breath of death today. It brushed against my cheek, and left me most unconscious, taking thought and words to speak. It left me feeling empty, and lost within myself. It crept about my being like a mouse on pantry shelf. I wandered aimless through the day and half the lonely night, but came a "Great Awakening" at break of morning light. I saw a child in field of green with yellow flowers 'round. He was moving swiftly through the grass on limbs so strong and sound. His laughter rang within my ear as clear as Sunday's bell. His smile did light the broad blue sky and caused the clouds to swell. I watched as one who's privileged eyes had glimpsed through heaven's door, and just as quickly saw it close, revealing nothing more. Then as a wave upon a shore, washes it so clean, my torched mind was cleared to see that this was not a dream. The sorrow felt inside my heart belonged to only me. For how could I be sad for one who's now so free? I swept away a tear that trickled down my cheek, and rose to meet the bright new day that God had given me. I felt witness to a sacred time, not really meant for me. For how often does God grant a wish and allow someone to see?[4]

Cameron talked of death and his next life often. The following is his testimony recorded on videotape six weeks before his death. While Dennis was taping, he had the distinct impression that what Cameron was saying was deeply significant, more than the typical family video session. He worried about Cameron being near death and pled with God in silent prayer that his impressions would not be realized. It took Cameron more than fourteen minutes to meticulously share his life reflections, which after being typed doubled spaced covers less than one page. This is the end of his recorded message. It's the only recorded testimony we have from him.

"I really feel that I can walk in the next life, and that I can talk better. And that I will live forever in the next life after this and that I will see God again. And I get to see my grandma and grandpa again who died a couple of years ago. And you can too someday. I guess I don't have to say anymore. And this is Cameron signing off."[5]

HEALING DREAMS

Most of us dream about one and one-half hours each night.[6] Dreams often contain elements from our past, present, and sometimes our future. Although we might not remember all that we dream, dreams can bring us significant insight. The scriptures contain accounts of individuals being guided by their, or others,' dreams. One of the most familiar accounts is when Joseph is warned in a dream to flee from King Herod with Mary and baby Jesus (see Matthew 2:13).

One week before Cam's surgery, I dreamed his surgery was over and the doctors said they needed to talk to me. They told me he was having trouble breathing and would have to be on life support and would not be able to live without it. The doctors recommended the removal of life support; however, it was my decision. I went into his room and watched the cardiac monitor move with each thump of his heart. I knew that if I told them to turn off the ventilator, the line on the heart monitor would soon go straight. I thought about my choice for a while. Finally I ran out of the room crying. I could not tell them to unplug my child's life! I wanted him alive! The dream was so real, I woke up sobbing. I felt sad and afraid. I shared my dream with my mother and Dennis. He later related having similar feelings, and several impressions (Death Preparations) that caused him to worry about Cameron too.

At family home evening the night before his surgery, we shared a few of our fears and concerns with Cameron. We didn't want to frighten him so we tried to be reassuring. He had just turned fourteen. Most important, we wanted him to know how much we loved him. I asked him that if something did go wrong and he actually died, would he please try to somehow let us know he was okay and happy in the spirit world? He nodded yes. As I looked at his big tearful brown eyes, I realized this could be a hard promise to keep. I then told him if he couldn't return and tell me (visitation), I would try to just have enough faith to know that he was well. He obediently agreed like he usually did when we made requests of him.

Although we had this open discussion during family night, none of us believed it would actually happen.

We'd forgotten about the family discussion and the dream until several days after Cameron's death when my mother reminded us. Remembering the dream brought comfort mixed with guilt. Why didn't we cancel his surgery? Was the dream a warning? However, with time, we chose to believe the dream was a glimpse into our family's eternal future. Over time, the dream became a meaningful death preparation that brought us comfort.

After-death dreams can offer comfort as well. In one dream, I was crying and mourning Cameron's death. I was impressed to get up and read the words to hymn 117, "Come Unto Jesus." The following were the words that brought the most peace and comfort: "Oh know ye not that angels are near you from brightest mansions above?"

Visions

It may be difficult at times to tell the difference between a dream and a vision. Visions can occur when we are awake and able to see what is happening; whereas dreams generally occur in our minds while we are sleeping. Visions may occur in the day or at night. The Bible mentions "night visions" (Daniel 2:19).

The vision and revelation received by Joseph F. Smith concerning the redemption of the dead came following the death of his adult son. President Smith agonized for nine months following his son's death. He wondered why he remained alive in his eighties, while his gifted, worthy son in his forties was gone. He felt grief, and through his loss, sought greater understanding. President Smith's grief, prayer, and searching allowed him to receive many comforting doctrinal truths. He died soon after recording his dream that was later accepted as revelation and canonized as section 138 of the Doctrine and Covenants.

The prophet Joseph Smith had a vision where he saw the gates and the beautiful streets of the celestial kingdom. He wrote, "whether in the body or out I cannot tell" (Doctrine and Covenants 137:1). Joseph was surprised to see his brother Alvin in the celestial kingdom. He received the following revelation that clarified how it was possible for his deceased brother to receive celestial glory, even though he had not heard and received the gospel or been baptized. "All who have died without a knowledge of this gospel, who would have received it if they had been permitted to tarry, shall be heirs of the celestial kingdom of God" (Doctrine and Covenants 137:7).

Many enduring adversity wish they could have a comforting vision, but do not. Sister See desired a vision or visit from her deceased thirteen-year-old. When it didn't happen, she turned to the scriptures for comfort. Doctrine and Covenants 24:4 provided comfort and an answer to her plea: "Murmur not because of the things which thou hast not seen, for they are withheld from thee and from the world, which is wisdom in me in a time to come."[7]

VISITATIONS

A visitation is the act of being visited by a deceased person. Although many visitations seem to occur as dreams, some occur while the person is awake and during daylight hours.

One such visitation occurred to a woman seated at her sewing machine. Her mother, who had been dead for some time, came with an important message for her. She said, "Daughter, you don't know what it has cost me to come to you."[8]

Many have wondered, "What is the cost, and why do some deceased spirits visit while others do not?" Another similar account seemed to be prompted by a deceased individual's strong desire to have her temple ordinances done. She firmly said, "You are the only one I have to depend on. . . . Don't fail in this."[9]

In a therapy session with Dennis, a widower described in detail a visit from his deceased wife. It concerned him much because she had encouraged him to marry a certain woman that they both knew. She explained that he would need someone to help him take care of their children. In the beginning, he wasn't sure he was ready to marry, or that he even wanted to marry this particular woman he hardly knew!

Many who have lost a loved one experience apparitions. Some professionals feel these apparitions are acute grief hallucinations; however, one account seems to rule out intense grief as the cause of a man's deceased wife visiting him eighteen years after her death.[10] His acute grief would no longer be present this long after her death, thus decreasing the possibility of hallucinations resulting from an acute grief reaction.

A comforting experience occurred when a deceased mother who had died from cancer appeared to her grieving daughter and said, "I was allowed to come and tell you not to be worried about me. I don't suffer anymore and I am very happy."[11] This deceased mother made it clear to her daughter that she had received permission to communicate with her.

In one report, 75 percent of parents surveyed who lost children claimed they had an apparition involving their child.[12] On the other side of the veil, some survivors of near-death experiences report asking, while in the spirit world, for permission to communicate with the living and were denied the privilege.

No Visitation

"Blessed are they that have not seen, and yet have believed" (1 John 20:29).

An Amalekite in the Book of Mormon asked why Aaron was allowed to see an angel. "Why do not angels appear unto us? Behold are not this people as good as thy people?" (Alma 21:5). Many members have wondered the same, questioning their worthiness.

Louis E. LaGrand lists possible explanations why some mourners do not have contact experiences with their deceased loved one.[13] He concludes the following: (1) They do not need one. (2) They cannot believe it would occur. (3) Their fear causes repression or suppression of an event. (4) They may have negative states that preclude any positive experience, such as anger, pessimism, or any negative emotion. His 5th suggestion is especially meaningful to us. It is the explanation shared by Paul in the book of Corinthians concerning spiritual gifts. Paul points out that we all have different gifts: teaching, preaching, prophecy, and recognizing angels or spirits. Moroni also lists a number of spiritual gifts, including knowledge, faith, healing, tongues, working miracles, and the beholding of angels and spirits (Moroni 10:9–17). Some of us apparently are not destined to receive the gift of "beholding angels and spirits."

President Wilford Woodruff stated:

One of the Apostles said to me years ago, "Brother Woodruff, I have prayed for a long time for the Lord to send the administration of an angel to me. I have had a great desire for this, but I have never had my prayers answered." I said to him that if he were to pray a thousand years to the God of Israel for that gift it would not be granted, unless the Lord had a motive in sending an angel to him. I told him that the Lord never did nor never will send an angel to anybody merely to gratify the desire of the individuals to see an angel. If the Lord sends an angel to anyone, He sends him to perform a work that cannot be performed only by the administration of an angel.[14]

Near-Death Experiences (NDEs)

Many find spiritual comfort from reading the accounts of individuals' near-death experiences. The Apostle Paul describes an out-of-body vision in 2 Corinthians 12:2–4. More than eight million people have reported having NDEs. Some reports of NDEs occur following an illness or accident where individuals lose consciousness, or where their heart has stopped beating, requiring resuscitation efforts. Some individuals experiencing NDEs report finding themselves traveling outside their body. Others report traveling down a tunnel with vibrating sounds. They may view their physical body from above and report the details of their own resuscitation. Many see a light or spirit being. Some are greeted by deceased relatives. Still others describe a brightness and beauty beyond anything earthly. Most profoundly, nearly all report feeling an unconditional, overpowering love and acceptance. The importance of one's love for his fellow man is also reinforced. Many are allowed to visually review portions of their life. Often the life events viewed, which seem to be of greatest importance, are those where they showed kindness and love to other individuals. Personal accomplishments did not seem as significant. It wasn't the honors or praise of men. Rather, it was the love and charity they showed to other human beings. Most NDEs additionally emphasized the importance of obtaining wisdom and knowledge while on the earth.

A few months after our son Cameron died, our forty-year-old friend and neighbor had to have open-heart surgery. I decided to be brave make a strange request. I wished him the best (with such a serious surgery) and acknowledged his fears of a negative outcome. I asked him if he did have complications or had an NDE and found himself in the spirit world, would he try to locate Cameron and give him my love? He agreed without hesitation. After his surgery, he told us that nothing happened and that all had gone well. He was home recovering for a few days when he got very ill and fainted in the shower. His wife took him back to the hospital and the doctors told her that his gall bladder had failed (probably a complication from his previous surgery). He would now need to have an emergency surgery to remove it. While he was on the operating table, they had some problems maintaining his heart rhythm so soon after his open-heart surgery. Gordon soon found himself outside his own body watching the doctors working on his heart below. He was then led to a very large room full of deceased spirits. It didn't take long to recognize Cameron on the other side of the room. He tried to move toward him; however, he was not allowed. He was told he had to go back. He woke up in the intensive care unit. He was weak and ill, but he sent his wife to tell us what he saw. He said that Cameron looked like a missionary and even had what appeared to be a companion with him. He looked content and busy. It brought us great comfort.

Some of the most profound NDEs are reported by children. Young children are innocent, open, unbiased, and they seldom lie about such experiences. Many report seeing and hearing angels or deceased relatives who call them by name, telling them it is not their time to die.[15] Hearing these NDEs has provided many individuals with hope and has increased their faith in what they might experience when they die.

Final Healing: God's Atonement and Resurrection

Hope of a reunion with Cameron has helped Dennis and I endure. However, we still had to walk through a difficult grieving process. At first I questioned as did Job, "If a man die, shall he live again?" (Job 14:14).

I started intense reading, meditating, and praying. I wanted to rediscover how I had gained a testimony of the Resurrection. I studied the book of Job. He also struggled to understand, yet ultimately bore a strong testimony of the Resurrection: "For I know that my

Redeemer liveth, and that He shall stand at the latter day upon the earth: And though after my skin worms destroy this body, yet in my flesh shalt I see God: Whom I shall see for myself, and mine eyes shall behold, and not another; though my reins be consumed within me" (Job 19:25–27).

Christ said, "In the world you have tribulation" (John 16:33), but He also said in the same verse, "But be of good cheer; I have overcome the world." He told His disciples, "I go to prepare a place for you" (John 14:2). Our hope and belief in an afterlife does not rid us of our challenges and struggles; however, it can offer us great peace and solace as we endure them. "I am with you always to the end of the age" (Matthew 28:20).

We love the example Christ gave us in the book of John. In fact, we liked the story so much we titled our last grief book after it. Lazarus was very ill. His sisters Martha and Mary had called for Christ to come and heal their suffering brother. By the time the Savior arrived, Lazarus was dead. The shortest verse in the Bible and the title of our book is "Jesus Wept" (John 11:35). Although Christ knew the plan of salvation and also knew he would raise Lazarus, he still had great compassion and "mourned with those that mourned" (Mosiah 18:9). Those in attendance, witnessing the Savior's tears, said, "Behold how he loved him!" (John 11:36).

In Acts 26:8 we see more proof that God can raise people from the dead. "Why should it be thought a thing incredible with you, that God should raise the dead?"

Joseph Smith said, "If I have no expectation of seeing my family and friends again my heart would burst in a moment and I should go down to my grave. The expectation of seeing my friends in the morning of the first resurrection, cheers my soul and makes me bear up against the evils of life."[16]

"For a trump shall sound both long and loud, . . . and they shall come forth—yea, even the dead which died in me, to receive a crown of righteousness, and to be clothed upon, even as I am, to be with me, that we may be one" (Doctrine and Covenants 29:13).

The first Easter after Cameron's death, I had to give a lesson to the Young Women organization on the Resurrection. I knew it would be difficult because my grief was still so fresh. I reviewed the lesson the night before and went to bed. I had a special dream that continues to bring comfort to me now, many Easters later:

There was a large-colored rock similar to something you'd see in St. George, Utah. From behind it came Cameron walking briskly toward me . . . no wheelchair which he had spent his fourteen years in . . . he had a smile on his face (usual for him). I was walking toward him quickly, knowing that it was the Resurrection and that I was greeting him after many years of separation. I was eager to get my arms around him; however, before I reached him I awoke to the name of a hymn. The hymn was "Come unto Jesus." I jumped from my bed to find the hymnal and read the words of the hymn:

"Come unto Jesus, Ye heavy laden, care worn and fainting . . . he'll safely guide you unto that haven where all who trust him may rest . . . Come unto Jesus, he'll surely hear you if you in meekness plead for his love." And as previously stated, "Oh, know ye not that angels are near you from the brightest mansions above?"

Yes, I knew! I knew Cameron still existed even though I hurt and missed him. I knew he was near and that I had claim on the Resurrection, and that if I followed Christ's example and lived worthy I would see him again.

I received even more comfort from reading Revelation 21:4, which says, "And God shall wipe away all the tears from their eyes; and there shall be no more death, neither sorrow, nor crying, neither shall there be any more pain; for the former things are passed away."

Attending the temple in behalf of Cameron brought one additional spiritual comfort from a loving Father in Heaven. Dennis had hoped, like many others coping with the loss of a loved one, for a miracle sign, visitation, or at least a reassuring dream. The Prophet Elijah had a similar desire as he sought a dramatic miracle from God to change hearts and prevent the physical and spiritual deaths of those in his stewardship. Instead, he learned firsthand from the Lord that the most convincing witness to the righteous is often much more subtle. "And the Lord passed by, and a great strong wind rent the mountains, and brake in pieces the rocks before the Lord; but the Lord was not in the wind: and after that wind an earthquake; But the Lord was not in the earthquake: And after the earthquake a fire; but the Lord was not in the fire: and after the fire a still small voice" (1 Kings 19:11–12).

This still small voice came at a sacred moment in the temple. As I mentioned before, we had hoped, like many others coping with the loss of a loved one, for a miracle sign, visitation, or vision of some kind. Rather, it was a miracle moment of complete reassurance concerning the immortality of the human soul. That witness came at a sacred location at the completion of Cameron's temple endowment.

Once again we consider the words from the movie *Man's Search for Happiness:* "Life's greatest test comes with the death of a loved one, and without faith in the immortality of the soul, the separation of death looms forever comfortless."[17]

Fortunately, God has not left us comfortless. He has promised: "I am the resurrection and the life and he that believe in me though he were dead yet shall he live" (John 11:25).

NOTES

1. Ashton, *Jesus Wept*, 183–4.
2. Joseph Smith, *Teachings of the Prophet Joseph Smith* (Salt Lake City: Deseret Book, 1976), 196.
3. Ashton, *Loss and Grief Recovery*, 141–2.
4. Ibid., 145–6.
5. Ashton, *Jesus Wept*, 167.
6. E. Linn, *Premonitions, Visitations and Dreams . . . of the Bereaved* (Incline Village, Nevada: Publishers Mark, 1991), 72.
7. Joselli K. See, "I Prayed to See My Son," *Ensign,* January 1977, 62.
8. J. Heinerman, *Spirit World Manifestations*, Joseph Lyon and Assoc. (Salt Lake City: DBA Magazine Printing and Publishing, 1978), 84.
9. Ibid., 86.
10. M. R. Sorenson and D. R. Willmore, *The Journey Beyond Life*, Vol. 1 (Midvale, Utah: Sounds of Zion, Inc., 1988), 65.
11. Ibid., 44.
12. Oprah Winfrey Show produced by Harpo Productions, Inc., Chicago, October 8, 1993.
13. Louis E. LaGrand, *After Death Communications: Final Farewells* (St. Paul, Minnesota: Llewellyn Publication, 1997), 185–86.

14. Leaun G. Otten and C. Max Caldwell, *Sacred Truths of the Doctrine & Covenants,* Vol. 1 (Salt Lake City: Deseret Book, 1982), 63.

15. M. Morse, *Closer to the Light* (New York: Villard Books, 1990), 159–61.

16. Smith, *Teachings of the Prophet Joseph Smith*, 296.

17. *Man's Search for Happiness*, 1964.

CHAPTER NINE

Murder, Suicide, Disaster, War, and Terrorism

THE DEATH OF A LOVED ONE USUALLY REQUIRES adjustments and grief work. When someone loses a loved one to murder, suicide, terrorism, war, or a natural disaster, the adaptation may be more complicated and the duration of adjustment lengthened.

Murder

Murder is a serious sin. It can compromise the victim's agency and shortens their life experience and probation time. Those who lose a loved one to murder not only have to deal with the loss of their loved one, but additionally the traumatic way he died and a judicial system that may seem more concerned with the perpetrator's rights than the victim's. It can impair and assault our sense of safety, justice, and trust. Combined, these factors often complicate and prolong the grieving process, making it more difficult for some to function again at home, work, church, or even in society.

A grieving mother approached us after we spoke at a bereavement conference stating: "A few years after the death of my husband, my daughter was murdered. I am the one who found her battered body in her apartment. Words cannot describe the intense trauma, pain, loss, and anger that I feel. I felt I had pretty much recovered from my husband's death when my daughter died. However, I can't seem to recover from this one. It's been five years now and I am still in therapy."[1]

145

Death caused at the hand of a murderer becomes complicated because it could have been prevented. People feel intensely violated when someone purposely takes the life of their loved one.

A mother whose daughter was raped and murdered shared the following: "It's been seven years . . . you never forget it, you just learn to live with the pain. It's something you just don't get over."[2]

For healing interventions see Part One. Professional therapy is available through LDSFS and other licensed professional counselors.

Suicide

Those who take their own lives are usually in tremendous mental, emotional, or physical pain. We must remember God is their judge. We may not understand the depth of pain and hopelessness associated with suicidal thoughts and acts. Those left behind often struggle with difficult questions, confusion, and guilt. They often ask, "Could I have done something that would have made a difference?" Their mourning process can also become complicated and prolonged.

Bruce R. McConkie taught, "Persons subject to great stresses may lose control of themselves and become mentally clouded to the point that they are no longer accountable for their acts. Such are not to be condemned for taking their own lives. It should also be remembered that judgment is the Lord's; and he in his infinite wisdom will make all things right in due course."[3]

Each year in the United States there are over thirty thousand suicides reported to the Centers for Disease Control and Prevention. Imagine the intense pain numerous family members and friends experience as they mourn those who chose to end their lives. Included amid those reported deaths were four children under nine years of age. More than five hundred thousand adolescents and the same number of adults attempt suicide annually. It is sad to think that five to six thousand teens take their own lives and five times that number of adults die annually. It is discouraging and alarming that suicide is the fifth leading cause of death among five- to fourteen-year-olds.[4]

Most teen suicides stem from drugs and alcohol. Out of every four high school students, one will use marijuana. Most adolescents get their first drug without cost. The biggest teen killer in the United States is alcohol.

One woman expressed her fear that alcohol and drugs played a role in her son's depression:

> My son stays out late. He is always missing his curfew. He is seventeen and we have tried everything to encourage him to keep his curfew without much luck. I don't sleep well worrying about him. He has also shared with us that he has been involved with smoking and had some experience with alcohol. He does not seem to have a testimony or spiritual feelings. He is not interested in church, going only because we pressure him. We have talked with him, taken away money, the use of the car, etc., without much improvement. I fear he is suicidal.

Depression can lead to suicide when depressive symptoms go unrecognized, especially in children and teens. Others won't admit they have a problem and refuse medication, often for fear of looking weak.

Dennis's mother committed suicide on her fiftieth birthday. She left a distraught husband and two young sons still at home. Her life history contributed to her depression and suicide. Her mother moved out of the home at an early age, requiring her to quit school before completing the eighth grade to help raise her younger siblings and care for their home. Her father died at a young age after an extended illness. Over time, she began to experience phobias and suffered from severe panic attacks. The combined abuse of alcohol and prescription drugs brought about other serious health problems. Her addictions, mental illness, and deteriorating health eventually intensified her feelings of frustration and hopelessness.

Dennis wrote, "After my mother committed suicide, the hardest part for me was watching the pain my father experienced, and knowing my younger brothers would be raised without a mother."

M. Russell Ballard said, "The act of taking one's life is truly a tragedy because this single act leaves so many victims: first the one who dies, then the dozens of others—family and friends—who are left behind, some to face years of deep pain and confusion."[5]

A woman whose nephew committed suicide said, "My nephew

very much wanted to serve a mission. He tried on two occasions to stay at the MTC. His depression overcame him and he returned home discouraged both times. Soon after he committed suicide. We were all devastated. His father continues to suffer with addictions and debilitating symptoms from his grief."

A mother in a bereavement group was struggling as she tried to cope with the death of both her children. Her oldest son had died of cancer. On the first anniversary of his death, her daughter, who was still grieving his death, committed suicide. Following such a devastating loss, she said, "The pain and sadness is just too much for me to handle. I really would like to join my children in the Spirit World. I think about it a lot."

Other bereaved parents of children who committed suicide have stated to us years after their losses that they were surprised to still be alive yet proud to have made it through!

Guilt is a common emotion for those siblings left behind. Notice the guilt this young adult felt after her brother committed suicide.

"My brother's last words to me were 'Help me.' Three weeks later, he committed suicide. I was left haunted. Haunted by my failure as a sister to save my only sibling's life. Haunted too by a wide range of emotions, which I chose to bury for twenty-seven years. I have been frozen in the grief process."[6]

It's important to know that once someone has made up his mind to take his life, no amount of talking, interventions, or effort on our part alone will guarantee that they will not attempt suicide. Consequently every threat and suicidal gesture must be considered valid and potentially lethal.

For healing interventions see Part One. Professional therapy is available through LDSFS and other licensed professional counselors.

Natural Disasters

When a natural disaster occurs we often hear the question, "Did God cause this?" This thought process can cause hurt, anger, and spiritual injury for those who may feel they are being punished by God.

There is some scriptural and doctrinal evidence that the Lord on occasion has controlled the weather. President Spencer W. Kimball said, "The Lord uses the weather sometimes to discipline his people for the violation of his laws."[7]

God said to the children of Israel,

> If ye walk in my statues, and keep my commandments, and do them; Then I will give you rain in due season, and the land shall yield her increase, and the trees of the field shall yield their fruit. And your threshing shall reach into the vintage, and the vintage shall reach unto the sowing time; and ye shall eat your bread to the full, and dwell in your land safely. And I will give you peace in the land, and ye shall lie down, and none shall make you afraid: . . . neither shall the sword go through your land. (Leviticus 26:3–6)

Most natural disasters are equally devastating to both the righteous and the unrighteous, the saint and the sinner. The rain truly does fall on the saint and sinner, "For he maketh his sun to rise on the evil and on the good, and sendeth rain on the just and on the unjust" (Matthew 5:45; see also 3 Nephi 12:45).

The Prophet Joseph Smith taught that "all flesh is subject to suffer and the righteous shall hardly escape; . . . it is an unhallowed principle to say that such and such have transgressed because they have been preyed upon by disease or death."[8] The Apostle Paul was aware of this reality when he spoke of the Savior. He said, "Though he were a Son, yet learned he obedience by the things which he suffered; And being made perfect, he became the author of eternal salvation unto all them that obey him" (Hebrews 5:8–9). No one would suggest that the Savior's sufferings were the result of transgression on His part.

There is also scriptural evidence that the weather on occasion can be tempered as people repent: "When heaven is shut up, and there is no rain, because they have sinned against thee; if they pray . . . and confess . . . and turn from their sin . . . then hear thou in heaven, and forgive the sin . . . and give rain" (1 Kings 8:35–36).

Losing a loved one to murder, suicide, terrorism, or a natural disaster brings unique and often complicated issues for grieving individuals to consider.

When Dennis traveled to Indonesia to train mental health workers on loss and grief, he found many there who believed that God was punishing them through the tsunami. This thinking caused significant pain and suffering to many who had lost loved ones. Some had lost everything; not only their loved ones, but homes, land, and personal possessions. Such trauma to their mind, body, and spirit would not heal easily. LDS Humanitarian Services provided millions of dollars worth of assistance that included everything from body bags, washing machines, housing, and motorcycles, to training professionals on providing loss and grief counseling. Fifteen professionals consisting of physicians, psychologists, and clergy received training from Chris Anderson and Dennis, both LDS Family Services staff sent by Church Humanitarian Services.

Once trained, these professionals would provide the loss and grief training to counselors who in turn would go out and provide therapy to grieving individuals and families. One physician receiving this mental health training asked Dennis why a small Christian church ten thousand miles away could care and provide resources to a people of another faith. He assured her that the Church members he represented worship the same God, mourned over their burdens, and desired to provide comfort in the midst of their adversity. She asked if she might visit Utah some day to learn more about LDS Humanitarian Services and meet staff from the University of Utah and Brigham Young University.

War and Terrorism

We are blessed to live in America where we enjoy freedom. It comes at a great cost. We are grateful for those who leave their loved ones and safety to protect us. Our hearts go out to those families who are grieving for a loved one lost to war or terrorism. When a death was preventable it can increase the intensity and duration of grief symptoms.

A few years ago Dean Byrd and Dennis had the opportunity to help coordinate LDS Humanitarian and Family Services relief efforts to Kosovo refugees seeking asylum in Albania. While comforting the refugees, Dennis and Dean witnessed and experienced firsthand many sad and tragic challenges. After speaking at a missionary conference where they shared ideas on helping families deal with loss and grief, two missionaries offered to introduce Dennis and Dean to a family they had recently made contact with. The family escaped across the border of Kosovo into Albania after experiencing catastrophic losses. The next afternoon Dean and Dennis met with the family and heard their horrific story. Soldiers had accosted the family as they participated in a large family gathering. All the men were taken outside of the house. Women and children were ordered to draw the blinds, remain inside, and not make any attempt to look out or leave the house. Within a few minutes, which seemed to last for hours, gunshots rang out into the dark, cold evening. The oldest member of the family, who told the story, had just lost her husband, son, and grandson. The living members of the family remained in either their house or the basement of a neighbor's house for nearly a month, leaving only briefly in the evenings to secure a scant ration of food and water.

Dean and Dennis found it difficult to listen but knew as professional therapists that the first step to recovery is allowing the process of mourning as the bereaved share their personal, unique pain. The feelings that come through expressing one's deepest hurt and loss are often healing. They were both surprised a day later when the missionaries returned to invite Dennis and Dean back to visit the family. The Kosovo family indicated that they trusted and felt safe with these humanitarian workers sent by the LDS Church. They asked if they could share additional details surrounding the death of their loved ones.

In the second meeting, the family revealed that they had smuggled a videotape out of their country that chronicled their horrific experiences. The preservation of the tape was important enough to overcome their fear of being caught with such evidence as they escaped in the dark of night across the border to freedom and friends.

The video included scenes of mothers, wives, and daughters as they kissed and patted the heads of all the deceased men and boys who had been ruthlessly taken from their family circle on that awful night. The bodies had been gathered to the home in the darkness, where they had been washed, clothed, and eventually secretly buried. It was important that their loved ones' mortal bodies not be burned or mass buried by the soldiers. A tattered yet sacred piece of hastily torn paper indicated the precise location of each loved one's makeshift grave.

Dennis and Dean found exposure to such carnage difficult, yet realized that allowing the family to share in detail their personal burdens provided a small measure of comfort and meaning to the grieving family.

Alma's preaching at the Waters of Mormon remind us of the sacred promises we make as members of Christ's Church to be willing to bear one another's burdens, provide comfort, and perhaps most important, mourn with those who are mourning (see Mosiah 18).

It is amazing how resilient the human soul is. Most can and do survive catastrophic and horrific events.

Many of the refugee shelters and tents that Dennis and Dean visited were filled with young children who had lost their parents. One hot afternoon as they were standing in a tent city of over one thousand refugees, Dennis and the other humanitarian workers witnessed an act of kindness, which helped them realize what they could do in return to help lighten the refugees' burdens.

A senior humanitarian missionary, exhausted by the heat and many hours on his feet, found relief leaning against a steel pole. An elderly Kosovo refugee sitting on a large cinder block brick noticed the missionary's exhaustion. He stood up and walking backward, dragged his makeshift chair to the humanitarian missionary. His cinder block brick represented the only seat in this community of over two hundred tents. The humanitarian workers were touched by this act of compassion and quickly identified what they could do to help, in a seemingly small way, to bear another's burdens.

A few days later the humanitarian workers returned to this tent city with a gift. They had purchased hundreds of plastic chairs. When the children saw the missionaries approaching, they surrounded them, pulling on their clothing.

The translator told them that the children were expressing thanks for the generous gift and pointing in the direction of their families' tents. Each child feared that there might not be enough of the chairs for each family in the camp. Returning weeks later, the missionaries learned that the school tents were the first to receive chairs. They were additionally impressed as they walked down the many rows of tents. Each family had received one chair and that chair was prominently placed in each clean, makeshift home. The valued gift was equally shared among all the families. No one in the camp had claimed more than one chair for his family. The teachers' and mothers' burdens were lightened a little that day as they were now able to rotate from their chairs to the ground while they taught and cared for the young children.

The humanitarian missionaries also had the opportunity to visit families from Kosovo who were housed by Albanian families. Arbin, a convert to the Church and interpreter, invited LDS Family Services staff to his home to meet a refugee family staying in his home. Several months earlier, Arbin's father had a surprise visit from a Kosovo business associate that he traded with one day every other year. His business associate stood at Arbin's door and said, "I've lost my home in Kosovo." Arbin's father responded without hesitation, "My home is your home." His associate then confessed that he had not come alone; other survivors were secluded outside the apartment. These twelve extended family members did not want to embarrass their potential host. After all, his home consisted of only three small bedrooms, a living area, and kitchen. It was barely enough room for the home's four current occupants.

When the representatives of Family Services arrived, they were invited into Arbin's former bedroom. Arbin had given his room to five of the thirteen house guests. For the past three months he had been living a week or so at a time with different members of the Tirana Branch so there would be room for these afflicted guests.

With eighteen refugees plus family members and visitors in the small bedroom, there was only room if everyone sat shoulder to shoulder against the walls. Dean Bird and Dennis contemplated what they might say to express their deep concern. They felt inspired to let the host family and refugees know how much they loved them and were deeply sadden by their suffering. Dennis also felt impressed to mention that there were thousands of members of our Church worldwide who would have gladly come in their place if they were given the opportunity. The senior member of the Kosovo family responded apologetically, "But do you know we are not members of your church?" Dennis and Dean's response, without hesitation, was, "Yes, we know. But we believe we all worship the same God." Their honest response brought peace and instant friendship.

Our charge as members of the Church to love all of God's children was reflected in the words of the Prophet Joseph Smith more than 150 years earlier: "A man filled with the love of God would not be content with blessing his family alone, but ranges through the whole World, anxious to bless the whole human race."[9]

He also said regarding the duties of members of the Church toward all their fellow men: "He is to feed the hungry, to clothe the naked, to provide for the widow, to dry up the tear of the orphan, to comfort the afflicted, whether in this church or in any other, or in no church at all, wherever he finds them."[10]

Following Dennis and Dean's expressions of love, concern, and common brotherhood, the family spontaneously and in unison expressed three times aloud their appreciation by bowing their heads and repeating, "Thank you very much, thank you very much, thank you very much." From that moment on, there were no barriers of race, color, religion, or custom that could separate those present from the love of God. Before they left that evening, Dennis and Dean, now referred to as honored guests, were invited to have refreshments from the families. They both declined initially, recognizing how very little food the two families had to eat. Ultimately they realized that the refugees' grief work included giving and sharing as well as expressing thanks for what they had not lost, including their own lives.

That evening everyone ate from one small plate, gratefully passed like a sacrament tray from person to person. The plate held one apple cut into very small slices. Next, the special guests were offered a small, carbonated orange drink. Dennis soon realized that only five individuals had a glass. He quickly finished his drink and returned the glass to the serving tray. The glass was quickly removed from the room by one of the teens, where it was washed, refilled, and shared with the next oldest member of the gathering. Dennis has expressed how the reverence and spiritual healing of that moment will never be forgotten. A few days following Dennis and Dean's visit, two of the teenagers present that night began missionary lessons with the full-time elders in that same small, humble home.

The death of a loved one usually requires adjustments and grief work. When someone loses a loved one to murder, suicide, terrorism, or a natural disaster, the adaptation may be more difficult and the duration of adjustment period lengthened. However, the Lord has assured us that he will be with us: "I will not leave you comfortless" (John 14:18); "Fear not, let your hearts be comforted . . . waiting patiently on the Lord" (Doctrine and Covenants 98:1–2). For coping and healing interventions see Part One.

NOTES

1. Ashton, *Jesus Wept*, 21–22.
2. —————— , *Loss and Grief Recovery*, 169.
3. Bruce R. McConkie, *Mormon Doctrine.* 2nd ed. (Salt Lake City: Bookcraft, 1966), 711.
4. G. Anderson, *Our Children Forever* (New York: Berkley Books, 1994), 186.
5. M. Russell Ballard, *Some Things We Know, and Some We do Not* (Salt Lake City: Deseret Book, 1993), 8–9.
6. J. Stanford, *The Forum Newsletter,* Association for Death Education and Counseling, March/April 1999, 15.
7. Kimball, In Conference Report, April 1977, 4–5; *Ensign*, May 1977, 4.
8. Smith, *Teachings of the Prophet Joseph Smith*, 162.
9. Joseph Smith, *History of The Church of Jesus Christ of Latter-day Saints*, Vol. 4, edited by B. H. Roberts (Salt Lake City: The Church of Jesus Christ of Latter-day Saints, 1976), 227.
10. *Times and Seasons*, March 15, 1942, 732.

Coping with Unexpected Loss

DEDICATED TO

Our three youngest children,

ANDREW, BRANDON, AND ASHLEY,
WHO MAKE US PROUD AS THEY ENDURE
THEIR INDIVIDUAL LIFE CHALLENGES
WITH FAITH AND HOPE.

Preface to Part Three

LIFE IS FULL OF CHALLENGES, LOSS, AND DISAPPOINTMENT. The "But if Not" series is designed as a guide to help you manage and find meaning in your personal tragedies. In Part One we explore helpful techniques and strategies to help you better cope and endure. We identify the unique grief symptoms and interventions available that will allow you to heal emotionally, spiritually, physically, socially, and intellectually. Part Two provides specific information and direction for those enduring disabilities, physical and mental illness, and coping with the death of a loved one. This section addresses other unexpected losses that can bring pain and suffering. Of course we can't address every possible challenge one might experience; however, we do discuss addictions, abuse, divorce, rebellious children, children's grief, early returning missionaries, unwed pregnancies, infertility, adoption, never being married, empty nest, aging, and same-gender attraction.

Inspiration for our grief series comes from a scripture passage found in Daniel 3:18, that includes the phrase "but if not." This scriptural sound bite gave us hope and comfort as we coped with the chronic illness of our oldest adult son, Darren, for a season. We knew God could deliver Darren, "but if not," we would choose to carry on and continue to be faithful and serve God. We wish you ultimate happiness and comfort on your life's journey. It is our hope and prayer that our stories, techniques, and spiritual insights will, in some beneficial way, ease your suffering and help you find meaning in your loss.

—Joyce and Dennis Ashton

CHAPTER TEN

Unexpected Losses

WE ARE SORRY YOUR LIFE'S CIRCUMSTANCES have brought you to a point where you are reading a book on loss. You probably didn't expect that these kinds of events would happen to you or your loved one and that your life would turn out quite this way. Your assumptive world has been assaulted.[1] You may struggle for some time to understand just what has happened and why.

Perhaps your pain and disappointment came to you early in life. Perhaps you experienced sexual or verbal abuse as a child. Perhaps you struggle with addiction or live with someone who does. Your daughter may have become pregnant out of wedlock; or your husband has left you for another woman, or even another man. Maybe you are currently experiencing emotional or spiritual abuse. Perhaps your parents still got divorced even after you prayed, went on a mission, and placed their names on the prayer roll at the temple. Perhaps after years of infertility and miscarriages, you struggled to adopt a child. It could be that your full-time church mission ended before the appointed time in spite of your sincere efforts to overcome unrelenting anxiety and chronic depression. Maybe you have stayed in a difficult marriage in spite of intense marital discord. Perhaps you are divorced or have never married, and are wondering if this is how you will live out your earthly life. What if the joy of parenting has turned into a nightmare as you deal with difficult or rebellious children that rob you of emotional and financial reserves? Or you may struggle with aging and the secondary losses that accompany those "golden years." Others struggle with "empty nest syndrome" as they watch their children grow up and move away. Any of these significant life challenges and losses can leave you with heartache, disappointment, and grief. (If your loss comes as a result of disability, physical or mental illness, or the death of a loved one, see Part Two.)

After Dennis and I were married, we were asked by several young women groups to come and talk about our courtship and how we came to choose a temple marriage. They requested that I wear my wedding dress and tell the girls how exciting and beautiful our temple marriage was. The goal of the young women leaders was to persuade the girls to live righteous lives so they could go to the temple and live "happily ever after." Some years later in California, a stake put on one such event. At the conclusion of the beautiful talks, including those given by a handsome bride and groom glowing in love, the stake president stood up. He said how wonderful the evening had been. After thanking everyone that participated, he said that he felt it was important that evening to also share some of life's potential tragic realities. He told the girls that evening that even if they kept the commandments and made few mistakes, it would not ensure that they would obtain a temple marriage. He told them some would never marry, some would marry and divorce, and some would experience devastating trials. He explained that the gospel was not an insurance policy to happiness and bliss.

Maybe you have experienced spiritual injury as a result of your loss. Maybe you have fasted and prayed for your situation to change, hoping for a miracle. Many faithful individuals do not receive the miracle they sincerely and desperately seek.

We may have been falsely taught that if we are righteous and faithful, we can avoid serious pain and loss. Some endure pain as a result of the misuse of agency or the destructive and sometimes sinful choices of others. The scriptures also give ample evidence that good people must endure hard times. (For spiritual injury and healing, see Part One.)

God may not remove our adversity, just as He didn't immediately deliver Alma and his people who were persecuted by Amulon. Instead, in Mosiah 24:14, He said, "I will ease the burdens which are put upon your shoulders, that even you cannot feel them on your backs." Alma the Younger, in Alma 31, discouraged with his preaching, prayed "that [he] may have strength, that [he] may suffer with patience these afflictions" (Alma 31:31). Even Christ felt forsaken and alone in Gethsemane. When He found His apostles asleep, He asked them, "Could ye not watch with me but one hour?" (Matthew 26:37). And later on the cross He asked His Father, "Why hast thou forsaken me?" (Matthew 27:46). We too may have feelings of being forsaken when we don't receive a miracle healing or when the Lord doesn't remove our adversity.

We have great hope and faith that He will strengthen and enable us in our adversity. After his resurrection He said, "I have drunk out of that bitter cup which the Father hath given me" (3 Nephi 11:11). We too may have to drink from a bitter cup.

Notes

1. Theresa Rando (lecture, Association for Death Education and Counseling Conference, Chicago, Mar. 1998).

CHAPTER ELEVEN

Abuse

MANY INDIVIDUALS CURRENTLY LIVING FAITHFUL LIVES suffer with the effects of abuse from their past. Sarah Miller reports that they may even assume that they deserved the abuse, or that somehow it was their fault. Others feel that their abuse is beyond the healing power of the Savior. Church activity can seem overwhelming to these individuals, as they compare themselves with other members and experience feelings of inadequacy. Some ask, "What's wrong with me?" Others wonder why they feel so unworthy if the abuse really was not their fault.[1]

Abuse has many faces and forms: emotional, verbal, physical, spiritual, sexual, and any combinations of the above. Abuse may be intense, violent, and obvious, or begin more subtly and innocently.

Each year in Utah, over 40,000 women (1 in 10) will be subject to physical abuse, and 194,000 to emotional abuse—74.5 percent do not report their abuse.[2]

Emotional and Verbal Abuse

We experience emotional and verbal abuse when someone attempts to control where we go, what we think, who we talk to, or what we say. It is abuse if someone subjects us to any type of physical or social isolation. This type of abuse is often due to extreme jealousy and possessiveness. Perpetrators abuse others by degrading and humiliating them through name calling and put downs. Others exercise unrighteous control or influence by withholding love, communication, and intimacy. There may be false accusation, blame, lying, broken promises, and destroyed trust. We may also receive intimidating looks, gestures, or threats that cause fear, guilt, and shame.

> My parents have threatened to never talk to or support me if I don't do exactly what they want me to do. It is so hard because I love them but I need my autonomy and feel I am only following what God wants me to do.

> It seems the majority of what my spouse says to me is with sarcastic tones, I feel like I am so stupid and of no worth. It really hurts me.

> If I don't do what my wife thinks I should she won't talk to me for hours, withholding any form of love or affection.

Some are able to exercise power over people due to status or money. Men and women experience abuse when their spouses excessively control how monies are spent, restricting access to checkbooks and financial resources including very specific purchases. A woman married to a well-educated and employed college professor reported:

> I was allowed a few dollars per week for my hair to be styled by college students. I was told what food items to buy and how most monies should be spent.

Emotional abuse can evolve into other forms of abuse, including physical abuse.

Physical Abuse

With physical abuse, someone may push, slap, kick, bite, shove, punch, strike, or restrain us. Someone may restrict our sleep, food, water, or medical care. Physical abuse may begin with verbal abuse through threats, criticism, belittling, broken promises, or intimidation.

An estimated 1.9 million women are physically assaulted every year in the United States and over 800,000 men. Most physical abuse occurs at the hand of their intimate partner.[3]

Many women who could and should get out of abusive situations don't. Eleven women in Utah die each year as a result of abuse.[4]

One distraught mother told us:

> I had begged my daughter to get out of her physically abusive relationship. It ultimately cost her life. I am the one who found her a couple of days later in her apartment. I am in total agony recovering from the death of my beautiful young daughter.[5]

"I will not suffer . . . that the cries of the fair daughter . . . shall come up . . . because of the wickedness and abominations of their husbands . . . I will visit them with a sore curse . . . ye have broken the hearts of your tender wives, and lost the confidence of your children" (Jacob 2:31-35).

Child Abuse

Children are often at risk when a spouse is being abused. Of the 4,676 domestic violence cases treated in Utah, over 44 percent were witnessed by children. In some instances, their exposure to violent acts warranted reports to Child Protective Services.[6]

In Utah, 1 in 5 children see or hear verbal abuse, and 1 in 14 will see or hear physical abuse.[7] Utah also reports that 1 in 3 girls and 1 in 5 boys are sexually assaulted before the age of 18.[8]

It is important to inform and educate individuals concerning child abuse. Then it is our duty to protect the child by reporting to Child Protective Services and our bishop when abuse is alleged or suspected. Bishops are counseled to contact the Leaders Abuse Hot Line whenever they suspect that abuse has or may occur to minor children. Reporting abuse is often the only way to hold perpetrators accountable and protect future victims.

"Many men and women have gone out of this life . . . without their vile crimes detected. They may have served in church callings; had wonderful reputations, wealth, good health, and glowing funeral services. . . . the demands of justice reach beyond the veil."[9]

Sexual Abuse

Sexual abuse is a serious concern in and out of the church. One in five women is sexually abused and usually knows their abuser. Most women never come forward. In Salt Lake City, there are over

15,000 reported sexual assaults a year. Nationally, over 17.7 million women and 2.8 million men were forced to have sex. Utah's rape rate is approximately 39.1 per 100,000 per year.[10]

Sexual abuse may include forcing sexual acts or behaviors, or hurting a partner during sex. It is also sexual abuse to force a partner to watch sexual acts or to call one's partner by sexually degrading names.[11]

> I grew up with a verbally abusive father. I especially disliked hearing him yell at my mother. I often heard him harshly demanding sex. He was very active in the church and would often apologize in a general way for his bad behavior. After my father's death, my mother would express guilt for some of the relief she felt having him gone. She said she liked living alone and had no desire to remarry. She seemed happier after his death than she was when he was living.

Unfortunately, sexual abuse occurs too frequently with children. Perpetrators are often someone in a position of power, trust, or control.

The following quote is from a young girl who was sexual abused numerous times in her life:

> Do you think differently of me now? Please don't. I already feel different. Like when my ward went to do baptisms, I did dress out and everything, but when they called me to the font I didn't feel like my body was pure enough to do the baptisms for these people. I felt really bad inside and it hurt to think that my body wasn't clean enough to do it. I stopped saying my prayers for a long time, but just a few days ago I started saying them again and boy did I feel good. I hope I have enough faith in myself that I can do these baptisms.

Then she wrote the following poem:

I said a prayer for you today
And I know God must have heard
I felt the answer in my heart
Although he spoke no word
I asked that He'd be near to you
At the start of each new day
To grant you health and blessings
And a friend to share your way.

I asked for happiness for you
In all things great and small
BUT IT WAS FOR HIS LOVING CARE
I PRAYED FOR MOST OF ALL.[12]

Most young children trust and love their parents unconditionally. They will often deny their own abuse in an attempt to protect and defend their parents or other significant adults. This is one reason why children have a difficult time getting out of abusive situations. Another obvious reason is they are only children with minimal control over their circumstances.

A lamented young man writes:

> My father died before I was old enough to confront him with the sexual abuse he had inflicted upon me.[13]

An abused woman said:

> It has taken years for me to understand how he could have abused me when I was such a small child. I've finally come to feel sorry for him, let go of the hate, and started to forgive.

A forty-year-old woman revealed that she had experienced sexual abuse as a young girl by her father. He died before she became an adult. In an attempt to help her let go and forgive her father, counseling utilizing visualization and guided imagery was used:

> In a safe relaxed state she visualized herself with a large group of people who loved her. The Savior was also present and expressed his love and acceptance of her. When she was ready, she chose to open a door and allow her father into the room. When she first saw her father, she screamed, and verbally confronted him. Through her tears and conversation she realized that he too had been abused and in this safe environment began to feel compassion toward him. She was ultimately able to offer him forgiveness and later claimed her depression had completely lifted.

In contrast to this healing experience, there are situations where abuse victims feel pressured to forgive before they are able. This premature pressure to forgive can produce added guilt. Victims who are already taking too much responsibility for the abuse they suffered now feel additional culpability for not being able to forgive their abuser.[14]

In the April 2008 conference, Elder Scott taught, "When you can forgive the offense, you will be relieved of the pain and heartache that Satan wants in your life . . . if the thought of forgiveness causes you yet more pain, set that step aside until you have more experience with the Savior's healing power in your own life."[15]

A man sexually abused as a child stated:

> I sensed as a young child it was wrong. However, I loved the attention, friendship, and relationship time my abuser offered me. When I became a teenager the sexual gratification became part of it. I knew it was wrong then, it was just hard to break away.[16]

> The sexual abuse of my husband as a young child contributed to his homosexuality, which ultimately led to our divorce.

Good people everywhere struggle with the suffering of innocent children. It is difficult to understand why adults would hurt children physically, emotionally, or sexually. God must surely cry with them. The best help for children is often a stable, loving, and supportive parent.

When such a parent is not available or sufficient, professional counseling should be considered.

Spiritual Abuse

Sadly, sexual abuse often leads to spiritual injury. How many prayers will an abused child offer, exercising faith, as he pleads with God to stop the abuse? When the abuse continues, in spite of their faith and prayers, many children experience confusion and begin to question their own personal worth. "Doesn't God love and care about me?" "Isn't this bad enough to warrant God's protection?" "Am I not worthy of an answer to my prayers?" This challenge is further complicated for some when they finally seek help from family or church leaders, only to have their claims denied by the perpetrator and not believed by those whose help and support they desperately need and seek.

> My mother got angry with me when I told her about my sexual abuse. She said, "Your brother would never do that!" Consequently, I couldn't really get the help I needed until I was an adult.

Spiritual abuse may occur when clergy or others in positions of power manipulate or exercise unrighteous dominion over the victim.

> We have learned by sad experience that it is the nature and disposition of almost all men, as soon as they get a little authority, as they suppose, they will immediately begin to exercise "unrighteous dominion" (D&C 121:39).

This form of abuse can cause spiritual injury, confusion concerning deity, and decreased self-worth.

> My church leader told me he was helping me by volunteering to take my sons on outings since I was a single mother. Sadly it turned out he was sexually abusing them.

Some Catholic priests perpetrated spiritual and sexual abuse on their victims. The cost to the Roman Catholic Church has climbed past $1 billion. Over $378 million was incurred in the past several years alone.[17]

The LDS Church and Boy Scouts of America have strict guidelines to avoid such problems. Church guidelines instruct leaders not to sleep in the same quarters with male or female youth on overnight activities. Spiritual abuse can lead to sexual and emotional abuse.

Getting Help

There is help for the abused and their families. An important principle to remember is that keeping the abuse a secret usually allows the abuse to continue.

> My father sexually abused me as a child. I never sought help because I had heard he went to his Bishop. I assumed he had changed. Many years later he sexually abused my own child. It wasn't until he was finally prosecuted that I found the burden lifted from my shoulders.

"Much abuse involves the denial of feelings and truth, so people who have been abused need to be heard and have their feelings validated . . . Bishops and other supportive members can facilitate healing by empathetically allowing the hurt to find its expression and then offering Christlike love."[18]

Holding perpetrators accountable is important. Pedophiles rarely stop offending unless the abuse is reported and prosecuted. There are therapies and support groups available to help perpetrators change their behavior from the inside out through self-control. Sadly, this change seldom occurs until they have been forced to control their behavior, from the outside in, through close monitoring or incarceration.

Victims of abuse will usually benefit from professional counseling that is consistent with the teachings of the Savior. You may contact your bishop or LDS Family Services for a referral to a professional counselor in your area. A combination of individual therapy and group therapy is often necessary to ensure successful recovery.

Adults Molested as Children (AMAC) is a valuable resource. AMAC groups offer lessons, discussions, and homework assignments as well as professional guidance and support. Most communities have shelters to temporarily protect women and children who have been or may be subject to abuse, if needed.

There are also sexual addiction support and therapy groups available in the community and through some LDS Family Services offices for sexual perpetrators.

There are often secondary losses and behaviors associated with abuse. The loss of self-esteem, poor body image, eating disorders, sexual problems, nightmares, troubled relationships, excessive need to be in control, addictions, and physical and emotional illness, are all common.

Tools that may be helpful include:

1. Writing a letter to the offender

2. Keeping a journal of feelings and memories

3. Visualizing and confronting the offender (in an empty chair therapy session or through guided imagery)

4. Individual therapy

5. Prayer, blessings, and impressions

Visions, like impressions, have been a source of knowledge and comfort for many. A stake Relief Society president came to LDS Family Services because she was feeling serious conflict in her life. Initially it seemed that she was simply over-involved in too many worthwhile projects in addition to her own busy calling and family. She gained insight as she identified self-defeating behaviors in her life and was soon able to say "no" without fear of rejection, set some priorities, and cut back.

However, throughout the therapy she didn't feel she was receiving the peace she had desired. One day as she was praying she had a vision. She saw herself as a little girl sitting on a stool in the kitchen with her feet dangling in the air. Her mother was accusing her of not telling the truth. She had just told her mother that her older brother had been sexually abusing her. Her mother told her that her brother would never do that. Her vision of this past painful experience opened up new opportunities to help her. Her recollection was followed by understanding and healing as she was finally able to deal with the true source of her pain and insecurities. Following her insight, she was able to acknowledge the pain, work through the issues, and ultimately let it go and find the peace she was seeking.

We often accept Christ's Atonement for the healing of our sins. Unfortunately, we may not realize His Atonement is infinite and equally able to offer us comfort and healing from our emotional and spiritual wounds. Remember the woman that touched the Savior's garment, hoping for healing from her twelve-year issue of blood. Dr. Terrence C. Smith reminds us that in Jewish law she would have been isolated and cast out, suffering a form of social and emotional abuse for twelve years. Through her faith in God's power she found physical, emotional, and spiritual healing.[19]

The following quote by Elder Vaughn J. Featherstone has provided comfort for the guilt-ridden consciences of many who have suffered as a result of abuse.

> When the future conduct of a violated one is warped and veers away from normal Christian conduct due to early abuse, the Lord will be extremely merciful to those thus forced and violated. It is my belief that the Lord will judge them for what they would have been had the abuse never occurred.[20]

Notes

1. Sarah E. Miller, "Hope and Healing in Recovering from Abuse," *Ensign*, Sept. 2008, 36–37.
2. http:/health.utah.gov/vipp/domesticViolence/overview.html
3. Ibid.
4. Ibid.
5. Joyce and Dennis Ashton, *Jesus Wept* (Springville, Utah: Cedar Fort, Inc., 2001), 47.
6. Utah Division of Child and Family Services, 2004 annual report, 17.
7. Http:/health.utah.gov/vipp/domesticViolence/overview.html
8. Http:/health.utah.gov/vipp/rapesexualassult/overview.html
9. Vaughn J. Featherstone, The Incomparable Christ (Salt Lake City: Deseret Book, 1996), 13.
10. Http:/health.utah.gov/vipp/rapesexualassult/overview.html
11. Http:/health.utah.gov/vipp/domesticViolence/overview.html
12. Ashton, *Jesus Wept*, 49
13. Ibid., p. 50
14. *Ensign*, Sept. 2008, 39.
15. Richard G. Scott, "To Heal the Shattering Consequences of Abuse," *Ensign,* May 2008.
16. Ashton, *Jesus Wept*, 50
17. Ogden Standard-Examiner, 11 Jun. 2005, p. 84.
18. *Ensign,* Sept. 2008, 36–39.
19. Terrence C. Smith, "An Anatomy of Troubles" (lecture, Association of Mormon Counselors and Psychotherapists Conference, Salt Lake City, Utah, Oct. 3, 2008).
20. Featherstone, *The Incomparable Christ*, 12.

CHAPTER TWELVE

Addictions

EVERY YEAR, ADDICTIONS THREATEN TO DESTROY the lives of over 28 million individuals and their families.[1] Addictions affect our physical bodies, our minds, and spirits. Not only are our jails and prisons overflowing with the devastating consequences of addictive behaviors, but many addicts are Latter-day Saints who are struggling against this powerful serpent. Addicted clientele are the single largest population seeking help from LDS Family Services in the United States.

An addiction is the compulsive use of a substance or activity. The most common addictions are alcohol, drugs, sex, pornography, food, and gambling. Although addictions come in many types and forms, it is not generally helpful to make comparisons promoting one addiction as more damaging than another. The compulsive over-eaters claim that alcoholics don't have to drink, but that they have to eat. In reality we all have to eat and drink. Alcoholics must choose to drink other beverages, just as the overeater must abstain from ingesting their trigger foods and bingeing. Some alcoholics rationalize that because alcohol consumption is legal it represents a greater temptation than illicit drugs. However, illicit drugs are small, and easily and quickly ingested, with no noticeable odor like alcohol. Compulsive overeaters may rationalize that food isn't specifically prohibited in the "Word of Wisdom" (D&C 89) like the other addictions, so their addiction is more difficult to overcome.

The sexually addicted have rationalizations and accompanying temptations as well. As computers have contributed the most to pornography addictions, addicts may not even have to leave their home computer in order to view and engage in their addictive behaviors. All rationalizations provide a way of disowning responsibility for one's self-defeating behaviors. The truth is that any addiction can ultimately destroy individuals and family relationships. Even over-doing and abusing good activities including working, exercising, shopping, and church work could cause similar problems. In excess, even "good" activities and behaviors can interfere with personal relationships, spirituality, and family life.

"Satan has a powerful tool to use [even] against good people. It is distraction. He would have good people fill life with 'good things' so there is no room for the essentials ones."[2]

Serious addictions compromise otherwise capable individuals in their most important roles: 1) home, 2) church, 3) school, and 4) work.

1. At home, a marriage suffers because trust is violated as the person dealing with an addiction has to hide, deny, and use deceit to preserve his addiction. He is consumed with his own needs (to get a fix) so he is often unable to offer time, interest, intimacy, affection, commitment, and so forth in his responsibilities and relationships. Often his children's everyday needs and demands fall to their non-addicted spouse who becomes over-taxed in her coping abilities. The one suffering from addiction fails to perform and appear at important events, causing feelings of abandonment and resentment from all involved. The associated features are fear, hurt, anger, and loss of communication and security.

2. At church, the guilt and spiritual injury induced by addictions often cause the one with the addiction to criticize and turn away from his belief system in order to cope and justify his feelings of worthlessness.

3. At school, addictions not only take time and concentration away from class and studies, but they can cause the brain to become damaged and malfunction. Sleep schedules are altered and attendance and grades soon drop.

4. At work, people dealing with addictions lose their ability to interact well with others. They are unable to be dependable or function as productively as in the past.

Over time, addictions may destroy one's physical, emotional, and mental health, as well as spiritual peace.

Alcohol is one of the top health problems in the United States. Latter-day prophets have addressed the problem through the Word of Wisdom (D&C 89), which prohibits the use of alcoholic beverages and other addictive stimulants. Other organizations, including the Catholic Church, have, in their clergy training, focused much attention to the acceptable consumption of alcohol. Learned and sincere men and women have debated for centuries as they have attempted to define what constitutes acceptable "limits" of social drinking, from a spiritual and legal perspective. The following scripture describes well their sincere, yet foolish attempts. "The wisdom of their wise and learned shall perish, and the understanding of their prudent men shall be hid" (2 Nephi 27:26; see also Isaiah 29:14). In contrast, on any given Sunday across the world, Latter-day Saint youth are called upon to share their thoughts and testimonies concerning the Word of Wisdom. They boldly testify in Sunday School, Primary, and in sacrament meetings, that the Lord has asked us not to consume even one alcoholic beverage. Unfortunately, in spite of well-intentioned anti-drug campaigns, religious commitment, and mounting medical evidence, 1 out of 12 Americans becomes an alcoholic.[3]

How Addictions Begin

Addiction often begins when the user experiments with the substance and receives a high or exuberant feeling. Following the first several events, there may be no side effects. The addict thinks it is safe or okay to seek the pleasurable feeling again and again. With time, the user finds he may need more substance to achieve the "high." It may now cost the user more time, energy, and money. Dr. Dean Belnap, MD, often explains that the more the basil ganglion of the brain is stimulated, the more it shuts off the logical decision-making executive center, and spiritual moral conscience of the brain (which is the frontal cortex). Continued misuse of addictive substances can induce similar symptoms and damage as those found in Parkinson's disease.

Due to the stress of addictive habits, the user's family may start to suspect their loved one is using. As time goes on, the user finds that he cannot feel good without the substance. However, his attempts to stop or slow down the addiction repeatedly fail even when he is aware of the consequences. He is robbed of much of his time, which is now spent finding and serving his addictions.

"Thus the devil cheateth their souls, and leadeth them away carefully . . . until he grasps them with his awful chains" (2 Nephi 28:21–22).

The following are segments from the lives of individuals struggling with addictions:

> My son has been addicted to drugs and alcohol since he was about 15. It started with alcohol, combined with his low self-esteem and depression. We have tried to get him help many times without much success. He has tried counseling and medication. He struggled to graduate from high school, and has lost many jobs. He has not attended church, nor been morally clean. I worry so much about him. I don't know how to help him. I've cried, prayed, fasted, and put his name on the temple prayer roll. My heart hurts so much as I watch him fail time and time again.

> It started at a party. A simple harmless sip. At first I didn't care for the taste, but loved the high that followed. I was freed of my shyness. Everyone laughed at my jokes. My sadness and depression lifted and life looked good. Little did I know that one sip would result in 30 years of alcoholism? It ruined my marriage and I eventually lost my family.

> My parents divorced when I was 10. I felt embarrassed around my friends. I found friends that accepted me; however, it meant trying their smokes and drugs. I have been in and out of rehab centers, searching for a way to get out of this trap. I've lost two marriages and countless jobs.

> When I discovered that porn was at my fingertips in the privacy of my own home I became addicted. One thing led to another and I lost my church membership and temple marriage.

> It started when I got stressed in the mission field. I found that masturbating relaxed me. This eventually led to a pornography internet addiction that almost destroyed my marriage.

> We had plenty of money so I felt I could shop whenever and

wherever I wished. Soon that was all I was doing. I would leave my children for hours and bring home things we couldn't afford and didn't even need.

I'm not sure what happens to me physically or emotionally. I just start putting food into my mouth and I can't stop. Even when I feel absolutely stuffed I just keep shoving in more food. Sometimes I get so physically sick, I start to throw up. Other times I make myself throw up so I don't get too fat.

After major surgery I was on pain medication for a long time. When I tried to go off of the medication, I got chills, sweats, nausea, insomnia, and an achy feeling all over. When my doctor told me these were withdrawal symptoms from the narcotic, I was shocked. [See the DSM IV p. 141 for more symptoms.] I am still struggling with trying to get off of them. It is frightening to me because my great-aunt had a similar problem which eventually took her life.

There is help and treatment for the addict. Because of the nature of addictions, help ranges from support groups to intensive inpatient recovery programs. There are many addiction recovery programs available in most areas. In 1995, LDS Family Services (LDSFS) began sponsoring support groups under its (ARP) Addiction Recovery Program.

Addiction Recovery Program

LDS Family Services sponsors group recovery meetings to assist individuals and families who desire to overcome addictive behavior. Through the principles taught in the 12-step program, participants learn that the infinite Atonement of Jesus Christ enables them to overcome addictive behavior.

Recovery meetings are ongoing, confidential, and free. Referrals are not necessary to attend. Experienced group facilitators create a safe environment where participants can share hope, encourage one another, and implement gospel principles in their efforts to recover and heal. A complete list of Addiction Recovery Program meetings is now available on the Church web site.[4]

Because many individuals struggling with addictions to drugs, alcohol, and pornography are unaware of the LDS Family Services addiction recovery program, an effort has been made to inform leaders, members, and others of this valuable resource. The following statement may be printed in weekly sacrament meeting programs:

> Know someone needing help overcoming an addiction?
> Visit http://lds.org. Click on Provident Living, Social Emotional Strength, Addiction Recovery Support Groups, Frequently Asked Questions

If there is not an LDSFS agency in your area, your bishop or branch president may be able to refer you to other community resources. You may also find resources in your area by calling your local hospital or county health department.

The Family of the Addict

Few of us realize how one family member's addictions can affect his entire family. On average, someone struggling with addiction will affect 3 out of 4 family members emotionally, spiritually, or physically. Many family members become hurt, angry, resentful, irritable, and nervous. They often try desperately to change the situation. Codependent family members and others may try to rescue the addict. They attempt to wake them in time for work or other responsibilities. They find themselves making excuses and lying about why he has missed work, stopped paying bills, or has failed to fulfil other commitments. It is not uncommon for family and friends to bail the family member out of jail, perpetuating additional self-defeating behaviors and encouraging deceptions and secrets. Family and concerned friends often pay a heavy price, including their own sanity, in frequent unsuccessful attempts to keep up appearances. It is also not uncommon for families to spend excessive amounts of time and money defending and covering the irresponsible choices and actions of those in their midst who are dealing with addictions.

Due to the denial associated with addictions, recovery often requires confrontation from friends and family members. It takes courage and love to confront the addict with the seriousness of his or her problem. As difficult as it may seem for families and friends, they must generally allow those addicted to experience the consequences of their craving-driven choices. It's very difficult, but important for family members to find ways to show love to the person dealing with addiction, while not facilitating or covering for their addictions and poor choices.

Help for Family

There are support groups and therapies available for family members who may have, over time, become as dysfunctional as the addict. They may need help discovering and accepting that they are not responsible for their loved one's addictions or recovery. They may need help letting go of the guilt, suffering, worry, obsessions, and attempts to control someone else's behaviors. Some need help understanding that they cannot assume responsibility for reforming or changing another person's unhealthy behavior. They need help detaching emotionally and "letting go and letting God." They need help realizing that relapses are part of recovery. They need help understanding they are responsible for their own peace, happiness, and recovery. They need help realizing that they are not helping by doing something for others that they can do for themselves. They may need help realizing that they are not helping by covering up. Those who have addictions need help with their distorted thoughts, selfish attitudes, and emotion-driven decision-making.

Al-Anon and other support groups help family members learn about the disease and let them know that they didn't cause the addictions and cannot control the addict or cure their addiction. Anger, rejection, and silent treatments only add to the guilt and shame that fuels the addiction, especially with those that are active in the LDS church.

Individuals with mental illnesses are more susceptible to addictive behaviors. (See Part Two.)

Tools that help those with addictions accept responsibility:

- Don't attempt to blame, bribe, punish, threaten, or preach.
- Don't play the "poor me" martyr.
- Don't cover for, take over, or hide consequences.
- Don't argue with, destroy substances, or drink with them.
- Do let them know you are studying and learning about their problem.
- Do let them know you are attending support groups for yourself.
- Do accept setbacks and be patient.

- Do spend leisure time together and find new interests.
- Do discuss your situation with someone you trust.
- Do let go of anger, look to your own self-improvement.

Counseling and support groups are available in most areas for family members of those struggling with addictions. Contact your local Bishop or LDSFS. Al-Anon and Alateen are world-wide organizations helping families live with the alcoholic. They discuss the three C's: We did not *cause* our loved ones addictions. We cannot *control* or *cure* those struggling with addictions, only love and support them as they help themselves.

Most addiction recovery support groups follow the Alcoholic Anonymous 12-step support model first introduced in 1935 by Bill Wilson, cofounder of AA and author of the AA Big Book. Recovered addicts believe and profess the following statement:

> I don't think anyone can recover from addictions without sacrifice and complete surrendering by using the principles of the twelve steps.

We will briefly list a modified version of the 12 Steps (the word alcohol has been changed to addiction), with some supporting scriptures.

1. Admit that you, of yourself, are powerless to overcome your addictions and that your life has become unmanageable.[5]

> I was in denial thinking I would never do it again . . . over and over . . . until I finally admitted that I couldn't stop the addiction without getting help. The following scriptures confirmed this to me:

> I of myself am not more than a mortal man. (Mosiah 2:10)

> Oh how great is the nothingness of the children of men. (Helaman 12:7)

> The greatness of God, and my own nothingness. (Mosiah 4:2)

> Put on the whole armor of God that ye may be able to stand against the wiles of the devil. For we wrestle not against flesh and blood, but against . . . the rulers of the darkness of this world. . . . Wherefore take unto you the whole armor of God, that ye may be able to withstand in the evil day. (Ephesians 6:11–13)

2. Come to believe that the power of God can restore you to complete spiritual health.[6]

Individual willpower, personal determination, motivation, effective planning, and goal setting are necessary but ultimately insufficient to triumphantly complete this mortal journey. Truly we must come to rely upon "the merits, and mercy, and grace of the Holy Messiah (2 Nephi 2:8). . . . Thus the enabling power of the atonement strengthens us to do . . . beyond our . . . natural capacity.[7]

Once I fully realized I could not do it alone I knew I must turn to someone with more power than I possessed.

And my soul hungered; and I kneeled down before my Maker, and I cried unto him in mighty prayer and supplication for mine own soul (Enos 1:4).

Nevertheless they did fast and pray oft, and did wax stronger and stronger in their humility, and firmer and firmer in the faith of Christ . . . even to the purifying and the sanctification of their hearts . . . because of their yielding their hearts to God (Helaman 3:35).

And were it not for the interposition of their all-wise creator . . . they must unavoidably remain in bondage . . . (Mosiah 29:19).

To bind up the brokenhearted, to proclaim liberty to the captives, and the opening of the prison to them that are bound (Isaiah 61:1).

3. Decide to turn your will and your life over to the care of God the Eternal Father and His Son, Jesus Christ.[8]

When we put God first, all other things fall into their proper place or drop out of our lives.[9]

The great task of life is to learn the will of the Lord and then do it.[10]

Counsel with the Lord in all thy doings (Alma 37:37).

But if you will turn to the Lord with full purpose of heart, and put your trust in him . . . He will deliver you out of bondage (Mosiah 7:3).

Even Christ suffered the will of the Father in all things from the beginning (3 Nephi 11:11).

Saul (before becoming Paul) when confronted by the Lord for

his sins humbled himself and asked: "What wilt thou have me do?" (Acts 9:6)

4. Make a searching, fearless, written moral inventory of yourself.[11]

I realized the addiction was only a symptom of my many problems.

And finally, I cannot tell you all the things whereby ye may commit sin; for there are diver's ways and means, even so many that I cannot number them (Mosiah 4:29).

It may help us to realize that often the root of sin is pride and we may not admit the seriousness of our sins and problems. Alma tells us, "after much tribulation the Lord did hear my cries . . . and has made me an instrument . . . in this I do not glory, for I am unworthy to glory of myself" (Mosiah 23: 10–11).

I, the Lord have suffered the affliction to come upon them, wherewith they have been afflicted, in consequence of their transgressions (D&C 101:2).

And except they repent and turn to the Lord their God, behold, I will deliver them into the hands of their enemies; [addictions] yea, and they shall be brought unto bondage; and they shall be afflicted by the hand of their enemies [addictions] (Mosiah 11:21).

5. Admit to yourself, to your Heavenly Father in the name of Jesus Christ, to proper priesthood authority, and to another person the exact nature of your wrongs.[12]

After I accepted my sin I prayed regularly to God for forgiveness. The hardest part was telling my family and seeing their disappointment and sadness.

And never until I did cry out unto the Lord Jesus Christ for mercy, did I receive remission from my sins....and did I find peace unto my soul (Alma 38:8).

6. Become entirely ready to have God remove all your character weaknesses.[13]

I wanted to change, I was ready to do it, and I just had to believe that God would help me.

My soul hath been redeemed from the gall of bitterness and the bonds of iniquity. I was in the darkest abyss; but now I behold the marvelous light of God. My soul was racked with eternal torment; but I am snatched, and my soul is pained no more (Mosiah 27:29).

Sanctification cometh because of their yielding their hearts unto God (Helaman 3:35).

Behold, he changed their hearts; yea, he awakened them out of a deep sleep, and they awoke unto God...they were in the midst of darkness; nevertheless, their souls were illuminated by the light (Alma 5:7).

7. Humbly ask Heavenly Father to remove your shortcomings.[14]

I wish I could have the experience of Enos. I am trying to humble myself, "I cried unto him in mighty prayer and supplication for mine own soul . . . and there came a voice unto me, saying: Enos, thy sins are forgiven thee, and thou shalt be blessed" (Enos 1:4–5).

Awake and arouse your faculties even to an experiment on my words. Let this desire work in you (Alma 32:27).

And if men come unto me I will show unto them their weakness . . . for if they humble themselves before me, then will I make weak things become strong unto them (Ether 12:27).

And we talk of Christ; we rejoice in Christ, we preach of Christ . . . that our children might know to what source they may look for a remission of their sins (2 Nephi 25:26).

I was discouraged one night, wondering when I would master this problem; would it ever really be possible? I came upon this scripture following my heartfelt plea to the Lord: "How is it that you have forgotten that the Lord is able to do all things according to his will . . . if they exercise faith in him" (1 Nephi 7:12).

And it shall come to pass in that day that the Lord shall give thee rest, from thy sorrow, and from thy fear, and from the hard bondage wherein thou wast made to serve (2 Nephi 24:3).

8. Make a written list of all persons you have harmed and become willing to make restitution to them.[15]

I have the most wonderful children, I feel so horrible that I have disappointed them and not been there for them. They have all reacted differently to my addiction. Some were shocked, sad, and hurt. Others were furious with me, angry that I have allowed this to be a part of our family.

But if the children shall repent . . . and restore four fold . . . thine indignation shall be turned away (D&C 98:47).

9. Wherever possible, make direct restitution to all persons you have harmed.[16]

I'm not sure how to make it up to my parents; they have been so hurt and disappointed over and over. They have invested time, money and tears.

Ye can do good and be restored unto that which is good (Helaman 14:31).

10. Continue to take personal inventory, and when you are wrong, promptly admit it.[17]

How oft will I gather you as a hen gathereth her chickens under her wings, if ye will repent and return unto me with full purpose of heart. But if not . . . your dwellings shall become desolate (3 Nephi 10: 6–7).

I learned that I may have to deal with cross addictions. Once I abstain from my addiction then other choices sometimes become an issue and I will need to be careful.

And being somewhat of a sober mind, therefore I was visited of the Lord, and tasted and knew of the goodness of Jesus (Mormon 1:15).

11. Seek through prayer and meditation to know the Lord's will and to have the power to carry it out.[18]

It was so disappointing when I would be abstinent for months and then have a slip. The longer my success the deeper the fall and failure seemed. I have, however, learned to get up faster with each fall and turn again to the Lord.

I have had sure answers to my prayers and small miracles in my recovery. The spirit has comforted me.

For I know that the Lord giveth no commandments unto the children of men, save he prepare a way for them that they may accomplish the thing which he commanded them (1 Nephi 3:7).

I try not to forget how great it feels when I pray and feel the Spirit.

Thus we see that the Lord is merciful unto all who call upon his holy name (Helaman 3:27).

The Brother of Jared was chastened for three hours because he remembered not to call upon the Lord (Ether 2:14).

Nothing can make a greater difference in our lives as we come to know and understand our divine relationship with God and His Beloved Son, our Master.[19]

What we really have is a daily reprieve contingent on the maintenance of our spiritual condition.[20]

12. Having had a spiritual awakening as a result of the Atonement of Jesus Christ, share this message with others and practice these principles in all you do.[21]

The healing power of service and lifting others had a profound effect on me.

All these things shall give thee experience (D&C 122:7).

I had learned so much, I wanted to share my hope with others. There are some simple steps that can make a difference.

And the labor which they had to look; and because of the simpleness of the way, or the easiness of it, there were many who perished (1 Nephi 17:51).

God grant me the grace to except with serenity the things that cannot be changed, the courage to change the things which should be changed, and the wisdom to distinguish the one from the other.[22]

May we have the strength, courage, and faith to master our addictions and help others in their recovery.

Thou shalt not be forgotten of me. . . . I have blotted out, as a thick cloud, thy transgressions, and, as a cloud, thy sins: return unto me; for I have redeemed thee (Isaiah 44:21–22).

For more material on addictions see the *Addiction Recovery Program: A Guide to Addiction Recovery and Healing* and the new *Family Support Manual: Support for Family and Friends of Those Who Struggle with Addictions.*

We also offer a few more self-help tools and interventions for those struggling with addictions and their family in Part One.

Notes

1. Mentalhealthlibrary.info/addhelpfamilies
2. Richard G. Scott, "First Things First," *Ensign*, May 2001, 7.
3. http://www.niaaa.nih.gov/FAQs
4. http://lds.org, Provident Living, Social Emotional Strength, Addiction Recovery Groups.
5. *Addiction Recovery Program: A Guide to Addiction Recovery and Healing*, prepared by LDS Family Services, 2005, step 1.
6. Ibid, step 2
7. BYU address, David A. Bednar, "In the strength of the Lord we can do and endure and overcome all things," Oct. 23, 2001.
8. *Addiction Recovery Program*, 2005, step 3.
9. Ezra Taft Benson, "Addiction Recovery Program," *Ensign*, May 1988, 4.
10. Ibid.
11. *Addiction Recovery Program*, 2005, step 4.
12. Ibid., step 5
13. Ibid., step 6
14. Ibid., step 7
15. Ibid., step 8
16. Ibid., step 9
17. Ibid., step 10
18. Ibid., step 11
19. James E. Faust, "That We Might Know Thee," *Ensign*, Jan. 1999, 2.
20. *Big Book of Alcoholics Anonymous,* fourth edition, 2001, 85.
21. *Addiction Recovery Program*, 2005, step 12.
22. Reinhold Niebuhr (http://www.brainyquote.com/quotes/authors/r/reinhold_niebuhr.html).

CHAPTER THIRTEEN

When a Missionary Is Unable to Serve

MANY YOUNG MEN AND WOMEN, AS WELL AS THEIR PARENTS, have looked forward to the time when they would become eligible to serve a full-time mission. Most families and church leaders know the benefits of missionary work; not only for the individual lives that are changed as they hear the Gospel, but also for the missionary's growth. We are edified as missionaries return home and share their increased testimonies, recounting wonderful faith-promoting experiences. However, many families are not aware of how difficult or painful the adjustment to the mission field can be. Most young men and women will adjust to their new circumstances and accomplish their goal and dream of bringing many souls into the fold. Unfortunately for others, the dream is shattered as they realize that for a variety of reasons, not every worthy young man or woman will be able to serve a full-time mission.

It is important that individuals, family, and ward members be understanding when a missionary's physical or mental health precludes mission service. When an individuals' desire to serve exceeds their physical and emotional capacity to serve, they need and deserve our compassion and support when they must return home early.

President Hinckley said, "Missionary service is extremely demanding and is not suitable for persons whose physical limitations or mental or emotional disability prevent them from serving effectively. . . .Those individuals are honorably excused."[1]

A new elder writes:

Reality has hit! Not a familiar face in sight. I've had long nights, trying to collect my thoughts and fall asleep on uncomfortable beds with elders snoring. I'm way out of my comfort zone. I feel like I'm losing my personality. I don't feel like the same person at all, like I never existed before the mission.

Love,
Elder I don't know any more

This loss of self-identity is a common characteristic in adjustment disorders.

Another elder in the field said:

My uncomfortable moments still seem to outlast the good ones. I get troubled and hate feeling this way. I'm not sure what it is that's bothering me [confused by his grief]. I try not to think too much because then I get even more stressed out. [In a noble attempt to focus on missionary work, he denies his grief.] I've developed a lot of ways to deal with things [coping mechanisms]. It's overwhelming.

Recently, a 40-year-old woman told us of her shock when at 21 she arrived in a foreign country to serve her mission. She woke up with flea bites, bleeding through her clothing. She wondered how she could last. She said no one had prepared her for how hard it was going to be. Fortunately she made the transition and loved her mission.

Here are some general qualifications for missionary service that may help us understand why some otherwise worthy members are unable to serve.

1. **Physical**

Missionaries must be able to work long hours, up to 16 hours a day. They need to be able to walk up to 6 miles a day and ride twice as far on a bike. This routine is physically taxing. A missionary must have healthy eating and sleeping patterns.

2. **Emotional and Intellectual**

Missionaries should be able to read, learn, and memorize.
A recently called elder with Attention Deficit Disorder writes:

While reading aloud to my companion through all the rules and things I had to learn in my binder, I stopped as I felt overwhelmed and tears started hitting the pages. It reminded me of preschool when I couldn't cut on the lines and tears fell on my work. However, mom came and rescued me then! Mom, where are you now?

Can he or she drive a car and obtain a license? Can she control her emotions? Does he have a temper? Can she interact socially with others? Does he know how to set and accomplish goals? Does he respect authority and follow rules? Can she speak in public settings?

3. Mental

Just as the physical body is subject to illness and malfunction, so is the brain. Serious malfunction of the brain can cause mental illness. (See Part Two.) Mental illness can cause distortions in thoughts, feelings, and behaviors. Serious mental illness cannot simply be willed away with a positive attitude.

One missionary shares:

> Our family has a history of depression going back several generations. I was confused and frustrated when after several attempts to serve a mission I too, was diagnosed and sent home. It's hard to feel like a failure.

President Hinckley reminds us: "Whatever ailment . . . a missionary has when he comes into the field only becomes aggravated under the stress of the work . . . we need missionaries, but they must be capable of doing the work."[2]

Unfortunately, serious struggles and challenges have led, on rare occasions, to a few missionaries tragically ending their own lives.

> My nephew tried to go on a mission two separate times. His depression was so severe he came home from the MTC both times. After he returned for the second time, his family found him dead from a self-inflicted wound.

Individuals with serious mental illness may require professional treatment just as the cancer patient does. Significant mental illness not only affects the missionary, but may also adversely affect his companions and leaders. Missionaries with the following conditions are often not recommended for missionary service: Asperger's disorder, autistic disorder, bipolar disorder (with a history of moderate to severe symptoms), dissociative disorders, eating disorders (moderate to severe symptoms within the past 18 months), mental retardation or borderline IQ (85 or lower), pedophilia (sexual attraction to children), schizophrenia, and other psychotic disorders. Also, extensive use of drugs or alcohol, or individuals with a past history of suicidal ideation or risk may not be recommended to serve. Additionally those needing certain medications such as anti-psychotics may not be recommended to service full time. (For more information see Part Two.)

"Candidates . . . who have had significant emotional [mental] challenges or who are dependent on medication are to have been stabilized [6 months] and found to be fully functional before being recommended."[3]

4. Spiritual

Spiritual preparation is very important for missionary work.

President Hinckley said, "It demands faith, desire, and consecration. It demands clean hands and a pure heart."[4]

Moral worthiness requires that:

> Prospective missionaries who have been guilty of fornication, heavy petting, other sexual perversions, drug abuse, serious violation of civil law and other transgressions are to repent and be free of such for sufficient time (generally not less than one year from the most recent offense). Individuals who have been promiscuous with several partners or who have been with one partner over an extended period of time in either a heterosexual or a homosexual relationship will not be considered for full time missionary service.[5]

Pre-Mission Evaluations

There is a pre-mission evaluation process through LDS Family Services available for missionaries whose psychological health may compromise their ability to serve or whose applications are questionable. LDS Family Services Missionary Clinics provide, at no cost, pre-mission assessments for prospective missionaries. These services (where available) include psychiatric evaluations, medication management, as well as individual and group counseling. Prospective missionaries may be self- or family-referred. They may also be referred by their church leaders or the missionary department. Pre-mission mental health assessments include professional recommendations regarding the likelihood of the candidate's success as a full-time missionary. Written recommendations are provided to the candidate's stake president and bishop. Decisions concerning a call to serve a full-time mission are prayerfully made by priesthood leaders, after considering the pre-mission assessment recommendations.

Doctors and other professionals in the missionary department also review missionary applications from a medical and mental health perspective. If there is a significant history of mental health issues, the candidate may be referred to an LDS Family Services office or a physician for additional mental and physical health pre-mission assessment.

Early Returning Missionaries

LDS Family Services provides gospel-based counseling, psychiatric evaluations, and educational services for both prospective missionaries and early-released missionaries and their families.

There are also limited counseling services provided by LDS Family Services at the Missionary Training Center (MTC) to help struggling missionaries. Priesthood leaders (following counseling at the MTC or agency pre-mission assessments) will recommend a continuation of missionary service or determine that the missionary should be honorably excused from additional full-time missionary service.

Anxiety is the most common troubling mental health condition seen by LDS Family Services MTC staff. It is commonly manifested as an adjustment disorder, obsessive-compulsive disorder (OCD), or separation anxiety. Other commonly diagnosed conditions include depression, attention deficit hyperactive disorder (ADHD), and learning disabilities.

If a missionary returns home early with serious emotional struggles, LDSFS missionary clinics in Provo, Salt Lake, and Layton provide psychiatrists, professional counselors, and support groups to assist the missionary and his family. Missionary clinics ensure that counseling, medical, and psychiatric services are offered immediately upon the missionary's return home. Separate support groups are offered for parents and the missionary to assist everyone affected by the missionary's unanticipated early return home from the field.

Services are provided or referrals given until stabilization is achieved. If a missionary decides to return to the mission field, he generally must demonstrate stability for six months and have received a favorable recommendation provided by a professional counselor to his stake president and bishop. LDS Family Services and other approved professionals can provide these evaluations. Regardless of the counselor's recommendations, final decisions concerning future service are always made by appropriate church leaders after prayerful inspiration.

A follow-up study on missionaries served by the LDS Family Services missionary clinics revealed that 97 percent of the early returned missionaries seen identified themselves as being 100 percent active in the Church two years following treatment.

Preparing Future Missionaries

Brent Scharman lists some basic tools that parents can implement with their children to help them adapt to missionary life.

1.   Teach our children to set and accomplish realistic goals and standards.

2.   Teach them how to evaluate and solve problems.

3.   Teach them to work and manage their time effectively, including getting regular exercise and sleep.

4.   Help them to understand the difference between discouragement, everyday ups and downs, and more serious depressions. Excessive worry, guilt, or perfectionism makes it difficult to serve.

5.   Teach them basic nutrition facts and not to deal with their emotions through over or under eating or using other substances. Obesity and other eating disorders are very difficult to manage in the field.

6.   Teach them about social cues, domestic skills, and money management.

7.   Missionaries often struggle with severe homesickness; prepare children to spend time outside their home by encouraging them to attend Church and scout camps, or go away to school.

8. Teach them the Gospel, to love the Lord, to serve, feel the Spirit, and to gain a testimony.[6]

After all our love, hard work, faith, and teaching, we then must learn how to accept our own or our children's limitations.

For more coping interventions see Part One.

Notes

1. Statement on missionary work from the first presidency and the quorum of the twelve apostles, Dec. 11, 2002.
2. Gordon B. Hinckley, "Missionary Service," first worldwide leadership training meeting, Jan. 11 2003, 17–18.
3. Ibid.
4. Ibid.
5. Ibid.
6. S. Brent Scharman, "Preparing your Future Missionary," *Ensign,* Oct. 2004, 17. (Or Dr. Donald Doty, "Missionary Health Preparation," *Ensign,* Mar. 2007, 63.)

CHAPTER FOURTEEN

Coping with and Helping Our Children

RAISING CHILDREN IN TODAY'S WORLD CAN BE CHALLENGING. Parenting is one of the toughest stewardships we may ever face. Most of us have little preparation, and soon learn child-rearing can be difficult even under the most ideal situations. In this chapter we will discuss raising children who are experiencing adversity or dealing with loss and those being raised in blended families after the loss of a parent due to divorce or death.

Rebellious Children

Often, in spite of our efforts to provide a loving gospel-centered family, our children may choose not to follow our teachings and examples.

> Many of our children shall perish in the flesh because of unbelief, nevertheless, God will be merciful . . . and our children shall be restored, that they may come to that which will give them the true knowledge of their Redeemer (2 Nephi 10:2).

A mother writes:

> Why did I think I would escape having rebellious children? Why did I assume I was beyond enduring the heartache I had seen in other parents? Did I assume that I was a better parent? How wrong I was to assume other parents had complete control and could have taught their children better. I had taught my child everything I knew to help her make right choices. We held weekly Family Home Evening.

I sent her to good schools where I worked with her teachers. I taught her to be responsible and work hard. I taught her not to steal and return things when she borrows them, she doesn't. I taught her to pay her tithing, she won't. I taught her to live the Word of Wisdom, she doesn't. I taught her to keep a curfew; she won't. I thought I taught her to show respect and obey, but she isn't doing it.

Elder Featherstone suggests that parents who have wayward sons or daughters experience profound and lasting suffering.

He makes the point that losing someone to sin can bring about an eternal loss. In contrast, when we lose a righteous loved one to death, we take comfort in the promise of being reunited with them in the Resurrection if we live worthy:

"Parents of a wayward one have a void and heartache that will not go away until the straying one returns."[1]

The parents of wayward children are often innocent of wrongdoing; however, they suffer deeply watching their child stray.

"If Christ can carry the burden of our transgression, it would only be 'just' that the innocent [parents could] have their pain and afflictions removed."[2]

I have no greater joy than to hear that my children walk in truth (3 John: 4).

On my daughter's sixteenth birthday, she asked for leather-bound standard works for her mission preparation class and a CTR ring in gold. She was a 4.0 honor student attending seminary daily. Five months later she ran away from home with a boy in the band at her school. His family hid her for three months until the boy broke up with her. She was sent back to us a different girl. She broke our hearts. She lasted at home for a couple of months. The drugs, alcohol, sex, and party life had changed her. The anti-church environment and anti-Mormon doctrine turned her into a purple, frizzy-haired, modern hippie.[3]

We suspected our son was involved with alcohol and smoking. We discussed it with him often; however, it didn't seem to make a difference. Eventually it led to worse things. His grades dropped, he lost jobs, and pulled further away from family support. The most difficult event was when he confessed to us he had sex with a girl after drinking. He doesn't care for or even really know this girl!

Our 19-year-old son has dated the same girl steadily for two years. They are hugging and kissing every day. We have discussed this close contact with him; however, he doesn't seem to change. We tell him it could lead to an unwed pregnancy. He could lose his opportunity to accomplish his (and our) goal to serve a mission and attend BYU.

Many parents have wondered:

Do we allow her to skip homework, pierce his ear, not pay her tithing, and skip Seminary class, church, or school? Can he date this girl or "hang out" with those guys? How should we discipline curfew violations or too many school tardies? How should we respond to the teen who refuses to do chores, or those who use drugs, cigarettes, or alcohol?[4]

The scriptures provide important insight on the appropriate use of power and influence:

No power of influence can or ought to be maintained by virtue of the priesthood, only by persuasion, by longsuffering, by gentleness and meekness, and by love unfeigned; by kindness and pure knowledge (D&C 121:41–42).

Boyd K. Packer wrote, "The measure of our success as parents . . . will not rest solely on how our children turn out. That judgment would be just only if we could raise our families in a perfectly moral environment, and that now is not possible. It is common for responsible parents to lose one of their children, for a time, to influences over which they have no control."[5]

Elder Packer continued, quoting Elder Orson F. Whitney of the Quorum of Twelve Apostles, "Though some of the sheep may wander, the eye of the Shepherd is upon them, and sooner or later they will feel the tentacles of divine providence reaching out after them and drawing them back to the fold. . . . Hope on, trust on, till you see the salvation of God."[6]

For I pray continually for them by day, and my eyes water my pillow by night, because of them; and I cry unto my God in faith, and I know that he will hear my cry (2 Nephi 33:3).

Brother Robert L. Millet teaches, "If our children are sealed to us, we have claim upon the sealing covenant and promise that they will return to us, if not on this earth then in the next. Remember, they were His 'sheep' before they were our children."[7]

Where is My Wandering Boy Tonight?

Where is my wandering boy tonight?
The boy of my tenderest care;
The boy that was once my joy and light,
The child of my love and prayer.
Once, he was pure as the morning dew,
As he knelt at his mother's knee;
No face was so bright, no heart more true,
And none was as sweet as he.
O, could I see him now my boy,
As fair as in olden time,
When cradle and smile made home a joy,
And life was a merry chime.
Go for my wand'ring boy tonight,
Go search for him where you will;
But bring him to me with all his blight,
And tell him I love him still.
Where is my boy tonight?
Where is my boy tonight?
My heart o'erflows, for I love him, he knows,
O, where is my boy tonight?
(Unknown author)

The following scripture reference found in Jacob 5 may apply to the challenge of raising rebellious children; the Servant and Master work long and hard in the vineyard with the tame and wild olive trees:

> What could I have done more . . . should I give up and burn the vineyard? But behold . . . the servant said unto the lord of the vineyard, spare it a little longer (verse 50).

Many members of the Church have had their hearts broken and mourn the loss of their children who choose not to live the commandments. According to scriptural accounts, God lost a third of his children following the war in heaven. We can also read of Enoch's grief and disappointment as he was shown the wickedness of God's children prior to the flood (Moses 7:28, 29, & 37). He cried as he was shown the rebellious children that were drown in the depths of the sea and could not board Noah's Ark (Moses 7:44). However, we can find comfort knowing, "all they that mourn may be sanctified and have eternal life" (Moses 7:45).

It is tragic to see how one child can break the tender hearts of their parents and wreck the spiritual climate in a home. The shattered expectations we have for our children may develop into a significant loss and require grief processing.

We may also be dealing with family traditions and struggles passed on from former generations. Some of the mistakes we make will also be carried into the next generation. An abused child may manifest distrust that contributes to failure in his or her marriage. Children of divorce may be more willing to consider divorce in their own marriages. Generation after generation is perpetuated without a stable, loving, committed, and healthy family. However, it takes just one individual to stop the cycle.

Special Needs Children (See Part Two)

> I have an adopted daughter with ADHD [Attention-deficit Hyperactivity Disorder]. No one seems to understand how difficult it is to cope. I feel judged by her behavior; wondering if others think that I'm not a good parent. It is so draining. When my husband comes home at night he says I look so exhausted. I feel others think I am a bad mother because of her behavior. No one seems to understand that we are trying our best to help her. Many members give me advice about how to discipline her, and so forth. Teachers call, frustrated with her in classes at school and church. I didn't know having or adopting children could be so difficult and disappointing. I just don't know if I can cope. I don't see her ever being on her own.

Healthy Families

It is helpful to have a basic idea of what a healthy family is. According to The Family: A Proclamation To The World, families thrive most when parents and children communicate, listen, support, accept, laugh, respect, trust, compliment, play, work, serve, problem solve, pray, and worship together. We are blessed with and accountable to the inspired counsel found in the family proclamation.

It has been said that one of the greatest gifts we can share with our children is a loving marriage relationship. If we are consistent, committed parents, we will have the greatest impact on our children. As soon as our children see we will say "no" ten times, followed by a "yes," they learn to keep asking and we have reinforced their asking up to eleven or twelve times the next time we say "no." We must also agree on discipline and direction (joint front). When one parent gives direction or discipline, the other backs and supports them with consistency and predictability. The exception to this rule would be the responsibility all parents have to interview and protect their children from the abusive behavior of any caregiver including their spouse.

Sometimes it is helpful to ask our children what they need from us during stressful times. A mom and researcher interviewed more than 500 children to learn the kinds of things children consider *least* helpful. Here is what they said:

1.   Indiscriminate praise: Everything I do they tell me is good! Good trying, good finding, good breathing!

2.   Babying: Whenever I go anywhere, they tell me "be careful."

3.   Not listening: My dad doesn't seem to hear what I say.

4.   Not explaining: They say there are going to be consequences but I have no idea what consequences are.

5.   Not showing you care: Telling me all the things I need to do when I get home, instead of asking 'did you have a good day?'

6.   Making idle threats

7.   Public reprimands

8.   Nagging

9.   Blaming

10. Controlling and ordering, (Afraid I'll mess up).

11. Bribing. If you want this, you must do that.

12. Over-scheduling. I can never just hang out.

13. Misplacement. Ask them to do something and they will say, not now, we are busy.

14. Negativity (too much criticism).

15. If I ask why, my mom will say, "Because I said so!"[8]

The following comments are generally road blocks to communication and relationship deflators.

1. Not now!
2. You never . . .
3. You always . . .
4. Why can't you be more like . . . ?
5. Here, let me do that.
6. These are the best years of your life.
7. Stop crying. (It can't be that bad.)
8. Stop being so . . .
9. Act your age.
10. You were always such a good boy/girl.

Research indicates that children are most responsive when parents make more deposits of honest praise into their child's emotional bank account and less withdrawals that result from excessive criticism.[9]

It is helpful to understand that each child is born into this world with a different temperament.[10]

We find these temperament differences in a number of areas including:

1. Activity level
2. Emotionality
3. Sociability
4. Self-regulation[11]

"Bring up your children in the love and fear [reverence] of the Lord; study their dispositions and their temperaments, and deal with them accordingly."[12]

Self-Esteem

"It's safe to say that the self image is the core personality ingredient which directs every aspect of our being. The way we communicate, the way we handle our emotions. The way we behave publicly as well as privately is all a commentary on our image of ourselves"[13]

A child's self-esteem and self-worth affects his thoughts and behaviors. Studies have shown that the relationship we have with our children directly affects their self-esteem and confidence. It is important to have a strong spiritual climate and offer a consistent outpouring of daily love shown by physical and verbal affection.[14]

"Those with low self-esteem often perceive a discrepancy between whom they are and who they would like to be."[15]

"Unrealistic expectations can also harm self-esteem."[16]

Everyone desires to be loved and adored. All of us want to hear how wonderful we are and how much we are valued. We can offer this love and acceptance to our families, friends, neighbors, and fellow ward members. We can help others, especially children, focus on the things that they can do rather than the things they can't. This will lift their self-esteem as well as their self-worth. Often we may need to learn to accept, not expect. This does not mean that we don't have rules or discipline for our children. Children with low self-esteem often come from families where there are harsh or over-permissive forms of discipline. Most children respond best to clear, firm, consistent, and loving discipline. Accepting ourselves, our spouse, or our children unconditionally is not always easy. It may mean "letting go" of control. Interdependence is a foundation of self-esteem and may be damaged by attempts to over control individuals. Overly dependent or independent relationship styles are seldom successful in marriage or parenting.

Many children carry negative labels about themselves. They will say things such as "I am ugly," "I am lazy," "I am dumb," "I can't learn," or "No one likes me." These self-defeating statements limit our children's abilities to cope and can damage their self-image. We can help displace these thoughts with new positive labels. Of course parents cannot shield a child from all negative situations. Peers, teachers, and siblings also influence the development of these negative labels. However, "Honest and open communication is the key to preventing self-defeating behaviors from developing and being maintained in our lives."[17]

"Self-defeating behaviors based on faulty perceptions are kept alive and hidden within the individual when either good communication or sufficient love is missing. . . . In those stressful moments, people tend to say or do damaging things to children and let the damaging impressions stand unchallenged and unchanged in the child's mind."[18]

Honest and effective communication is difficult to implement if we are too busy or angry or are grieving. It's during these vulnerable moments that thoughtless or damaging words are often spoken.

"These negative concepts need to be talked out so that the child does not hold them as negative possessions that hinder individuality and limit or cripple potential."[19]

Our son Cameron had cerebral palsy and consequently did not have many of the talents and abilities most children have. We tried to help him feel he was a special child just the way he was. I remember when a little boy asked if he could play with his new Christmas truck and horse. Cameron said, "Yes!" hoping the boy would play with him as well. The young boy picked up the new toy and walked away saying, "No, I don't want to play with you because you're ugly!" Cam responded, "I am not ugly!" (He really was a cute boy, despite his disability.) He handled the situation very well; it was mom who left the room crying! I didn't want Cameron and the others to see my tears and know that my self-esteem wasn't as strong as his! He helped teach our family the true meaning of self-worth and the unique value of each human being.

Dennis would go once a week to Cameron's school and work with Cam and his physical therapist. After several visits he wrote:

> I appreciated the beautiful grin that was always present on Cameron's face when I would walk into his classroom. One week's visit had special significance. Today he was sitting on a small tricycle with his feet strapped to the pedals. He was positioned in the middle of the school hallway. Slowly and with great effort, he started to move his tricycle toward me! The pleasure, excitement, and pride I felt are hard to describe. Though he had moved only a few inches in my direction, it was the first time in his short life that he had demonstrated his ability to be independently upright and mobile. I realized at that moment that my pride in my son was no less than that of other fathers who had watched their children overcome great challenges and succeed. I knew he would never be the star quarterback for a high school football team, or even compete with his peers in most areas, yet at this moment, I felt joy and pride for a child who was doing his very best with the abilities and talents he possessed.

The things we do, our physical attributes, and the way we dress all have an impact on how we see ourselves on a daily basis and affect our fragile self-esteem. In contrast, self-worth which comes from the inside out, and is based on whom we are, can be permanent. Self-worth is personally controlled internally by those who possess it. Individuals possessing true self-worth are still affected by the loss of friends, possessions, physical health, appearances, [and so forth]. Nonetheless they seem able to find deep within themselves a worth and a value that carries them through difficult times. Unfortunately much of today's values are built upon a self-esteem model that focuses on looks, performance, and obtaining possessions. Our attempt to dress and act in prescribed ways is all designed to increase our esteem and value in society's eyes. Sadly, since the ultimate appraisal of how we are doing comes from others, outside, rather than within, it can be very fleeting. Ultimately our physical talents and possessions will be left behind, and if we do not have internal insight and love of self and others we too may find ourselves lacking the strength to go on in the face of adversity.[20]

Cameron seems to have developed a strong inner strength or self-worth. When asked, "What would you never change about yourself?" He said, "My name." "What is the most important thing you own?" "My wheelchair." "What is your most important achievement?" "To learn to read." "What are you like on the inside?" "Happy." "If your life ended today what would you like people to say about you?" "Hey, that was a neat kid! He also had a cool wheelchair." "Who do you love and admire most?" "God and my mom and dad."

We can hurt a child's self esteem by:

1. Putting them down.
2. Breaking promises.
3. Not allowing them choices and independence.
4. Not giving them respect and privacy.
5. Denying their feelings and personal identity.
6. Not being consistent.

After telling us to love our children, Joseph Fielding Smith counseled: "However wayward they might be . . . when you speak or talk to them, do not do it in anger, do it not harshly . . . speak to them kindly . . . you can't drive them; they won't be driven."[21]

The gift of moral agency applies in our parenting and child

rearing. Unfortunately, some parents seem to understand the principle of free agency and how to enforce it!

The Lord has asked us to "teach them to understand the doctrine of repentance, faith in Christ the son of the living God, and of baptism and the gift of the Holy Ghost by the laying on of the hands, when eight years old." One of the consequences of not teaching our children is outlined in the Doctrine and Covenants: "the sin be upon the heads of the parents" (D&C 68:25).

How Children Cope with Loss

A child's rebelliousness may be a way of acting out his or her pain and grief. Some may become angry at God or the church because they feel God should have prevented their tragedy or protected them. Spiritual injury may result when a child's prayer isn't answered how they hoped it would be. (See Part One on "spiritual injury and healing.")

Children can usually sense increased stress and anxiety in their home when parents or siblings are struggling with serious issues. Children should be involved in the open acknowledgement of family issues that directly affect them. Children may experience a loss of trust toward their parents if important issues affecting the family are kept from them. Including children in challenges doesn't mean parents should overwhelm them with their own grief, guilt, sin, and unrealistic expectations. Parents should never involve children in parental conflict that causes them to take sides against any another family member. Parents should never withdraw love and affection as a punishment to one another or their children. Young children cannot fully comprehend a parent's pain. They have developmental limitations for understanding grief, based on their age and limited life experience. Children look to adults, especially their parents, as examples of how to respond to life events. Seeing and sharing our own sadness and disappointments in healthy ways often validates a child's own sadness, confusion, or other emotions. It's a challenging and sobering responsibility to acknowledge that, "parents can complicate or facilitate the grief process for children."[22]

"Children can't tolerate intense emotions for very long. Children generally have a short feeling phase."[23]

Because children may not be developmentally ready to process some aspects of the traumatic event, they often remember and re-grieve certain aspects of their loss as they grow and mature. They may need to relive the experience or grieve at a later time as they mature and grow older. Our 12-year-old son (at the time of Cameron's death) did more of his grief work years later in the mission field when he had the opportunity to work with a young girl dying from a brain tumor.

"Children's emotional symptoms may be slower in surfacing than adults, or even recur later when they reach young adulthood."[24]

We cannot force a child to grieve or react how we would like. We can be available to accept and guide them through whatever phase they are currently in, assisting them when and how they may need us.

"Available evidence suggests that not to assist the bereaved child in actively dealing with the death is to predispose him to significant pathology and lifelong problems."[25]

Children often feel comfort and are reassured when parents make themselves available, share personal testimony, read scriptures, and pray together. Family home evenings can be a forum for family sharing and listening.

Children are often robbed of consistency during tragedies. We shouldn't over-indulge them; however, we should give them our time and love. If left on their own, without support and insight, they may blame themselves or feel responsible for the crisis. In very young children, we may see bed wetting, returning to the bottle, clinging, and phobias.

Encouraging open communication may aid in the healing process. Remember that young children communicate in many ways. Some may communicate subtly and more naturally through their behaviors and play. Others may communicate through art and music. Young boys often grieve through aggressive behavior while many girls become caregivers. Teens may or may not be openly communicative.

A teenage boy wrote after the death of his brother:

> I just wanted to speed my life up about two years and forget what was happening.

We can help children become healthy survivors rather than victims by offering support. We can guide children toward letting go of unrealistic blame and re-channeling their energies into meaningful and productive tasks.

Teens, Trials, and Punishment

Years ago, our 18-year-old son lived away from home for a brief time. One day he called to discuss his new adversities. I realized through this experience how careful we need to be in responding to the misfortunes of children as well as adults. He told me that he had lost his girlfriend and his job all in the same week. As we discussed his sadness, I started asking him if he was paying his tithing, attending church, and reading his scriptures. He said, "Mom, I am not being punished." I thought about his statement off and on over the next several days. I wished I hadn't tried to shame or blame him for his adversity. Then one morning it hit me. My reply to him should have been, "No, you are not being punished; however, if you are keeping the commandments, you are entitled to additional comfort and promptings from the Holy Ghost." God usually will not remove our trials; however, he can comfort us and oftentimes carries us through our most trying circumstances and challenges. His hands, though ever present to sustain and guide us, generally do not take away our trials.

Some children, especially teens, may not want to be involved with the crisis. However, they should still be given the choice.

Children, like adults, fear more bad things may happen. These fears can make them feel vulnerable, fearful, and anxious. Seeing an ill sibling, friend, or relative suffer or receive medical treatments may arouse fears that they might catch the illness or need similar treatments.[26] Children may ask or more likely silently wonder, "What will my future be like?" "Who else will divorce, leave, abuse me, get sick, or die?"

With time, reassurance, and love, a child's security can return. Encourage children to talk and share only if and when they are ready. We shouldn't push or impose feelings or grief upon them that they are not experiencing. We can help them memorialize the ill or dying by allowing and encouraging them to keep something special that reminds them of their loved one. They might benefit from performing a personally meaningful task or ritual. They could play a special game or listen to a favorite song. Some children will enjoy rubbing lotion or oil on their ill loved one's feet or back. Participating in the event is a way of expressing love and concern. Others could help plant a tree or buy a symbolic gift. These activities help children form special relationships with their loved one. The memories of these events can later bring comfort, special memories, and reduced guilt. We should also be prepared for and allow siblings to be children, recognizing their need to play, laugh, and even disagree during adversity. It is not wise to say, "Put it behind you, get over it," or "Be strong, don't cry." These statements encourage children to bury their feelings and promote unhealthy isolated disenfranchised grieving. (See more in Parts One and Two of this publication.)

Children and Pets

Caring for animals can be a healing tool for children and adults facing adversity and death. A pet can offer unconditional love and acceptance, which may be a source of significant comfort.

Caring for animals also can help children learn that death is part of life. Losing a pet may be a child's first experience with loss.

After Cameron died, we decided to get a dog named Rusty. He was an important part of our family for 14 years, and we all cried and mourned when Rusty died. Adults and children alike can bond tightly with their pets. Remember the song "Mr. Boe Jangle"? Boe and his dog traveled and performed together for many years. A strong bond was formed between man and dog as they worked side by side. When his dog died, Boe was lost for a time. He had lost his best friend as well as his employment. Unfortunately his grief turned to depression. He turned to alcohol in an attempt to numb his pain and spent time in jail.

We should resist the impulse to immediately replace our child's lost pet. We should provide them with the time and opportunity to cry and mourn. We can also help them bury their pet. We can allow them to decide if and when they desire another pet. Avoid the temptation to run and buy another pet in an attempt to negate the loss and stop your child from grieving.

Children and Funerals

Children are exposed to 8,000 murders and more than 100,000 other acts of violence on TV by the time they leave elementary school.[27] They are rarely shown the aftermath of grief that inevitably follows death. Few are prepared to deal with the realities and consequences of a significant personal loss.

A funeral may help children actualize the event and their loss. Most children can and should be invited to attend a loved one's funeral. If they are old enough to love, they are generally old enough to grieve and participate. It is appropriate to ask them if they'd like to go to the funeral. Explain what will take place, and what they will see. They could also participate in the program if they so desire. For example, they could write a letter or a song to the deceased that could be shared, if appropriate. Dennis and I left our 4-year-old home during his grandfather's funeral. When he was 15 years old he told us he wished we had let him go. We took our almost 3-year-old daughter to her brother's viewing and funeral. When she saw her brother in the casket she said, "That's not Cameron." She was visibly upset and pushed to get away! We asked a friend to sit with her in the back of the chapel during the funeral, because she wouldn't sit still. Later, she didn't want to look at the pictures of her deceased brother in the coffin, the very same pictures that brought us comfort. Fortunately, years later, she remembers none of the negative events and seems focused on her pleasant memories of Cameron. She also chose later to view his pictures.

The function of funerals or other death rituals is:
1. To acknowledge death and accept our new reality.
2. To remember and recall.
3. To receive support.
4. To express love and encourage emotional release.

Teaching Children about an Afterlife

Studies show most bereaved parents believe in life after death. They hope for a reunion with their child.[28] The following analogy may help parents verbally convey their belief and hope in an afterlife to young children:

JOYCE AND DENNIS ASHTON

Have you ever seen a butterfly? Did you know it was a caterpillar first? [Explain the cocoon and its process.] Your brother's body lying so still [use the words dead, dying, die, not asleep] is the shell he left behind, like the cocoon when the butterfly leaves. His spirit or soul has gone or flown to another place, [heaven] just like the butterfly flies away.

Another visual aid helpful for young children requires your hand and a glove:

This glove represents or is like your brother's body lying here so still in the casket. [Take your hand out of the glove and lay it down.] The glove, like your bother's body is now empty. [Move your hand toward the sky.] Your brother's spirit, represented by my hand, has gone on to another place we call heaven.

Blended Families

A blended family occurs when two people, each with children of their own, decide to marry and form a new family union. This usually occurs due to death or divorce.

Blending families can be a challenge. Knowledge and understanding of the process and what to expect can help. There are also many interventions that can help make the process more successful.

It is important to realize that children may be still grieving the loss of their former parent when the new marriage takes place. There may be fantasies that mom and dad will reconcile some day. Some children fear that their parent will love the new siblings more than their own biological children. This can bring waves of hurt and anger for children.

With the death of a parent, a new marriage may bring sadness and grief, a reminder of what has been lost. All of these changes and emotions may make it difficult to blend families; however it can be successfully accomplished.

It would be helpful for parents to learn and acquire education and information about blending and step parenting. Some information that Brent and Jan Scharman share may be helpful:

1. Realize that any major change or loss in life often takes years to adjust and adapt.

2. Professionals recommend that the biological parent do the disciplining of their own children whenever possible.

3. Both parents should keep some of the old traditions while planning and experiencing new ones.

4. Exercise flexibility with your rules and try to give each child his own space and privacy.

It is possible to successfully blend families and have love and joy again in family life.[29]

NOTES

1. Vaughn J. Featherstone, *The Incomparable Christ* (Salt Lake City: Deseret Book, 1996), 9.
2. Ibid, 10.
3. Joyce and Dennis Ashton, *Jesus Wept* (Springville: Cedar Fort, Inc., 2001), 41.
4. Ibid, 220.
5. Boyd K. Packer, "Our Moral Environment," *Ensign*, May 1992, 66.
6. Ibid.
7. Robert L. Millet, *When a Child Wanders* (Salt Lake City: Deseret Book, 1996).
8. The Parent Institute, *Parents Make a Difference* [newsletter, 1993].
9. F. Covey, "Strengthening the Family" (lecture, Association of Mormon Counselors and Psychotherapists Conference, Salt Lake City, Utah, Apr. 1999).
10. M. K. Rothbart and J. E. Bates, "Temperament," in *Handbook of Child Psychology*, 5th ed. (New York: Wiley, 1998), 105–176.
11. T. D. Wachs (1999), "The what, why, and how of temperament: A piece of the Action," in *Child Psychology: A Handbook of Contemporary Issues* (Philadelphia: Psychology Press, 1999), 23–44.
12. John A. Widtsoe, comp., Discourses of Brigham Young (Salt Lake City:Deseret Book, 1978), 207.
13. Dr. Les Carter, "Self-Esteem" (radio talk show), Minirth-Meier Media Ministries, Jun. 15, 1994.
14. Brent L. Top and Bruce A. Chadwick, "Helping Children Develop Feelings of Self-Worth," *Ensign,* Feb. 2006, 33–37.
15. Dunn and Hargett Inc., *Growing Together* [Newletter, 1993], No. 2, Vol. 9-3.
16. The Parent Institute, *Parents Make a Difference* [Newsletter, 1993], No. 4, Vol. 4-4.
17. J. Chamberlain, *Eliminate Your SDB's* (Self-Defeating Behaviors), (Provo: BYU Press, 1978), 161.
18. Ibid., 162
19. Ibid., 162
20. J. Ashton & D. Ashton, *Loss and Grief Recovery* (Amityville: Baywood Publishing, 1996), 52–3.

21. Joseph F. Smith, *Gospel Doctrine*, 5th ed. (Salt Lake City: Deseret Book 1939), 316.

22. K. Doka, "Living with Grief" (lecture, Hospice Foundation of America National Teleconference, VA, Apr. 4, 1999).

23. A. Wolfelt, "Grief" (lecture, Association for Death Education and Counseling Conference, Chicago, IL, Mar. 1998).

24. Ashton, *Loss and Grief Recovery*, 118.

25. T. A, Rando, *Grief, Dying and Death* (Champaign: Research Press, 1984), 155.

26. S. M. Thibodeau, "Sibling Response to Chronic Illness: The Role of the Clinical

27. Nurse Specialist," *Issues in Comprehensive Nursing*, no. 11 (1988): 17–28.

28. Children Television and Violence, Abelard.org/tv/tv.php, 1998.

29. Knapp, R. J., *Beyond Endurance—When a Child Dies* (New York:Schocken Books, 1986), 35.; Doka, K.J. &J.D. Morgan (Eds.), *Death and Spirituality* (Amityville: Baywood Publishing, 1993), 65.

30. Janet Scharman, "Blended Families" (lecture, Families Under Fire, Provo, Utah, Oct. 3, 2005).

CHAPTER FIFTEEN

Divorce

DIVORCE IS THE LEGAL ENDING OF A MARRIAGE. No one marries and then plans for divorce. The death of a marriage is painful, lonely, and complex, and may follow many years of painful marital discord. There are no funeral services, sympathy cards, condolence calls, or flowers sent. Divorce can affect one's personality, role, and identity in dramatic and damaging ways.[1]

Divorce is especially devastating if you've grown up in the church believing that someday, if you're worthy, you can be married "forever" in a temple of God. Establishing an eternal family is the hope and dream of many wonderful LDS couples. Fortunately, we do have many wonderful marriages and families in the church where everyone works together to realize these promises. Unfortunately, there are far too many others whose dreams are shattered in spite of their wholehearted and righteous efforts.

A divorced mother said:

> All my hopes, dreams, prayers, and energy have gone into my temple marriage. I am still in shock that it is gone. How did this happen?

Why Do Couples Divorce?

A marriage and family study lists, in order, the most common reasons couples divorce:

1. Infidelity
2. No longer in love

3. Emotional problems
4. Financial problems
5. Sexual problems
6. Problems with in-laws
7. Neglect of children
8. Physical abuse
9. Alcohol
10. Job conflicts
11. Communication problems
12. Married too young[2]

When Is Divorce Justified?

Ending a marriage is usually a heart-wrenching decision. For most Latter-day Saint couples, to let go requires much prayer, fasting, and revelation. Each couple's circumstances are different and ultimately they are responsible to determine their own outcomes. However, married couples who struggle with chronic addictions, substance abuse, psychosis, extreme mental illness, and physical or mental abuse have marriages that often end in divorce.[3]

Infidelity is listed as one of the top twelve reasons couples divorce. The truth is that many marriages can survive a sexual indiscretion; this occurs when the offended partner is willing and able to work through the initially overwhelming disappointment and loss of trust. Mira Kirshenbaum, PhD discovered that couples are able to forgive the first affair when *both* are willing to try to build trust again; however, if an affair occurs a second time, the likelihood for a successful marriage is seriously compromised.[4]

President Faust said of divorce, "In my opinion, 'just cause' should be nothing less serious than a prolonged and apparently irredeemable relationship which is destructive of a person's dignity as a human being."[5]

A divorce usually brings about a division of debts, assets, and property. It may also include the payment of spouse and child support and the assigning of parental rights.

We have watched close friends and relatives, as well as clients endure divorce. Some individuals view their divorce as an *eternal loss* because of the catastrophic consequences that they feel extend beyond earth life. Friends and family often offer comfort to those who have lost a loved one to death by reassuring them that they will eventually see and hold their deceased loved one again in the eternities. It is often much more difficult to comfort men and women who have lost an eternal mate to divorce.

A recently divorced member said:

> I grew up in the church, married a returned missionary in the temple after fasting and praying to confirm my decision. My husband and I have always been worthy and active in the church. Last year my husband told me he didn't love me anymore and wanted a separation and probably a divorce. I was overcome with shock and confusion. How could this happen? I feel so helpless and hopeless. I have prayed, fasted, and attended the temple begging for God's help. I pray that my husband will return, or that I can find some permanent peace and resolution. Neither has occurred yet. I feel I am worthy and have faith for a miracle. I have done everything possible to ensure a good life and a temple marriage. I don't feel as comfortable at church. I feel everyone is looking at me, feeling sorry for me, or wondering what I did to drive my husband away. The sacrament talks and lessons in Relief Society don't offer much comfort right now. My husband has told me he cannot afford to pay for two places to live, so I must look for work. I'm not sure I am capable of so much stress right now. What will my children do? How will they cope with their father leaving, and now me going to work? What has happened to my eternal family? It's hard to want to go on when the most important thing to me is gone.

We believe God is just and will, over time, compensate for the pain parents and children experience because of divorce. Until then, how can we support those in the church who have experienced what many consider an eternal loss?

Even when couples consider divorce, it is common for one spouse to continue fighting for his or her temple marriage.

During and following a divorce it may be difficult for some grieving family members to attend church meetings. The following is a journal entry of a divorced member:

> Today it was hard to be at church. They showed part of a video called "Families are Forever." It's awful for a divorced person to realize that we no longer have a complete family. I feel it sometimes

pulls people away from the church . . . I need to remember to follow Christ and believe Christ. He has promised that if I do what is right I will have all that he has. That means a "forever family."

(Later) When I look through my journal now, it upsets me. I see how I was so consumed with justification that I couldn't enjoy life. . . . I was trying to do my best and I didn't feel it was good enough. My spouse said that one of the reasons he left was because I made him feel guilty. I told him I didn't mean to "guilt" him and that I would go to counseling and learn how to improve communication. "No," his mind was made up. This made me carry more guilt. One thing I would say to a person going through divorce, "Get rid of guilt, it doesn't do any good. Guilt gets you nowhere."[6]

Part of the guilt she was suffering from was "false guilt"—feeling guilty for events that were outside of her personal agency and control. In contrast, true guilt for willful wrong doing will lead us to repentance and personal growth as we change our own sinful behavior.

I called my sister today. She is in the depths of despair. She just finished her first week of full-time employment since her husband left about a month ago. She was physically and emotionally exhausted, and so sad. It was Easter Sunday and she had watched General Conference and tried to find comfort in the Atonement and the words spoken. She desperately wants to keep her husband, temple marriage, and children together. She asked me why Alma's father's prayer was answered by an Angel appearing and convincing his sons and Mosiah's sons to repent. Why didn't the same angel convince her husband to repent and stay with his family? She asks, "Why do some people receive a miracle, while others do not?" She is a worthy member, with faith as strong as any I've known. She was so sad and depressed. She thought of asking her kindergartner to come and kneel by her bed and pray for her as she lay sobbing. She wondered if maybe the faith of a child's prayer would relieve her agony. I thought of the Savior who felt the pain of the world's sins in Gethsemane. Please let this cup pass. She also said she was hoping for a car accident to remove this pain and the future without her eternal companion. I cried with her, realizing her pain was beyond my comprehension. Will a new mate be provided? When and how? Could she and the kids love him as much as their biological father? So much faith is required.[7]

A child writes about her plea to God:

> I remember getting down on my knees and asking my Father in Heaven to please help my parents to not get a divorce. When I received no answer, I felt all alone, like I wasn't getting any help for the pain I felt. It hurt for a very long time. I don't think I ever got over not getting my answer. [See "Spiritual Injury" in Part One.] With time I accepted that my parents were going to get a divorce.

A teen writes:

> My dad was excommunicated before my parents' divorce. It was embarrassing to have friends over, so I didn't do that much. My mom showed her anger even in front of my friends. I turned to my peers, especially boyfriends.

> I received some spiritual impressions and insight today. I was doing the laundry, of all things. I was feeling confused about life and God's intervention in it. I had just talked to several women whose husbands had left them and their families. As I listened to their pain, I wondered how God could stand to watch their suffering and not cause a great miracle and take away all of the pain. Why didn't he intervene and change their situations? The words that came to me were simple. I had heard them a hundred times before. But now the power of the spirit overwhelmed me. What I heard in my heart was this: "The Lord, God, knows the end from the beginning." (Isaiah. 46:10; 1 Nephi 9:6)

Robert L. Millet comes to a similar revelation as he shares the time he was struggling with "wandering souls" in his family. A caring colleague asked him if he thought Heavenly Father moped around the heavens over his straying children. After he said no, he concluded that the reason was God, "[knows] the end from the beginning," or His eternal perspective.

As we remain faithful and endure to the end, we too may find comfort in this same eternal perspective.

The divorce rate in the United States is about 50 percent.[8] Many divorced individuals choose to stay single while others decide to give marriage another try. (See chapter 18, page 249, "Never Married.")

Marrying Again

Many divorced individuals wonder if they could, or should, marry again. Of course this is a very individual decision with varied answers and circumstances. Children may still be grieving the loss of their former parent when the new marriage occurs. With divorce, children may fantasize that mom and dad will reconcile some day; thus, a new marriage can bring waves of hurt and anger. With death, a new marriage may be seen as a betrayal of their loved one and their memories. Blending families with all of these emotions will be difficult, but can be successfully accomplished.

Marriages often fail as a result of the stress experienced from a significant loss. The loss of a child, for instance, too often results in a secondary loss of the marriage. The accumulative grief resulting from such multiple losses can be devastating to families; however, if we allow all family members to fully mourn and deal with their grief, they can usually love and live well again.

"They shall obtain gladness and joy; sorrow and mourning shall flee away. I am he; yea, I am he that comforteth you" (2 Nephi 8:11–12).

Notes

1. Association for Death Education and Counseling, *The Forum* [Newsletter, 1998], May/Jun.
2. David H. Olsen, and John Defrain, *Marriage and the Family, Diversity and Strengths* (Mountain View: Mayfield Publishing, 1994), 522.
3. Diane Medved, *The Case Against Divorce: Discover the Lures, and the Emotional Traps of Divorce—Plus the Seven Vital Reasons to Stay Together* (New York: Donald I. Fine, Inc., 1989), 121.
4. Sara Eckel (quoting author Mira Kirshenbaum, PhD), *The Lowdown on Cheating* (AOL Women's Channel), http://relationships.blogcity.com/lowdown_on_cheating_1.htm (accessed Jun. 28, 2008).
5. James E. Faust, "Fathers, Mothers, Marriage," *Ensign,* Aug. 2004, 3.
6. Joyce and Dennis Ashton, *Jesus Wept* (Springville, Utah: Cedar Fort, Inc., 2001), 38–9.
7. Ibid., 39–40.
8. Stark (2004), 381–382; General Social Survey 1972–2002, Cumulative Datafile, 2003.

CHAPTER SIXTEEN

Help for Marriage During Unexpected Loss

GOOD MARRIAGES DON'T JUST HAPPEN. Marriage is an ever-changing and demanding venture requiring constant attention. It will require extra time, patience, and love when your marriage is experiencing an unexpected crisis. Every marriage has degrees of conflict woven around love and joy. It is when needs are not met and the conflict cannot be resolved that marital discord becomes a problem. It takes hard work, flexibility, responsiveness, sensitivity, compromise, tolerance, and forgiveness to make a marriage work under any circumstances.

Many scholars believe that 50 percent of the marriages in the United States end in divorce.[1] Divorce is less likely for those in the United States who marry in a church. In contrast, the lifetime divorce rate for temple marriages is estimated to be no greater than 20 percent.[2] Church members who marry in the temple are five times less likely to divorce than church members who have a non-temple marriage.[3]

There are gospel principles, many of which are listed in The Family Proclamation, that provide support and direction to our marriages. We will discuss specific marriage practices that can contribute to successful matrimony as couples endure loss.

Common Stressors

As stated in the previous chapter on divorce, the most common reasons couples list for giving up on their marriages are: 1) infidelity,

2) no longer in love, 3) emotional problems, 4) financial problems, 5) sexual problems, 6) problems with in-laws, 7) neglect of children, 8) physical abuse, 9) alcohol, 10) job conflicts, 11) communication problems, and 12) married too young.[4]

Another common stress among church members occurs when one spouse is not as active or committed to the gospel or their temple marriage as the other. Conflicts develop as couples attempt to adapt to each other's varied differences, including spiritual issues. Differences that seem to threaten the eternal covenants are often the most painful to accept. One may feel cheated or robbed from a more ideal partnership that was imagined, expected, or even promised during the courtship, temple sealing, or early years of marriage. These lost dreams and expectations can lead to resentment and bitterness between couples. As a result the other spouse often feels judged, unloved, or condemned as not being "perfect" or "good enough."

> I have thought of divorce off and on for years; the biggest reason is the lack of spirituality in our marriage. I finally thought our spiritual life was on its way because my husband of fifteen years decided he would give up his vices and take me and our children to the temple. I was thrilled! However, my excitement didn't last long. A few months after our sealing, we bought a computer and my husband started spending time on the Internet. He has gotten into sexual conversations and pornography. I feel afraid. He has also stopped our scripture reading together and he doesn't read alone. He doesn't have much desire to attend church or the temple. I also feel trapped because getting a divorce would be more difficult now because we have a temple marriage. Does God expect me to love and accept this man when he is not living the gospel?

Expectations of how one's spouse will abide by the laws and commandments are often formed from childhood. An active Latter-day Saint wife shared the following concerning her marriage to a non-member:

> I joined the church after I was married. My husband has allowed me to practice most of my new LDS religion for 30 years now. I cannot pay tithing on his money, just on mine. He provided for our son to serve a mission and our daughter to be married in the temple. He doesn't want me to go to the temple because he doesn't want me

to wear garments. He drinks; however, he doesn't pressure me to. He allows us to attend church on Sunday; however, afterwards he expects us to do what he wants to do or go where he wants to go. It is very hard. I have thought of divorce off and on over the years, but have chosen to stay, hoping someday he'll convert.

Marital discord may also be a result of a couple enduring difficult life challenges and loss. They may experience grief and pain as they struggle to keep their marriage intact.

A grief-stricken father stated after losing a child:

My wife is not the same person that I married and neither am I. We are suffering so many losses.

At times bereaved parents experience grief that is so intense that their "physical or emotional symptoms and defenses block the growth in the relationship."[5]

Basic Human Needs

Humans need water, food, shelter, and love to survive. It is helpful to understand some of the basic needs of individuals in a marriage relationship as well:

1. Affection and touch
2. Acceptance and belonging
3. Communication
4. Friendship, freedom, and fun together
5. Security and trust
6. Sexuality
7. Spirituality

For varied reasons, couples may not be able to provide these essential needs for each other. In fact, when men and women are asked to prioritize their needs in order of importance, we often find striking differences. A common difference is that men list the importance of sex higher than women do; while women list the importance of communication and understanding of their feelings higher than men do. It is helpful for couples to realize how contrasting their preferences can be. Some call this "learning your mate's love language." For example, I promise Dennis a long back rub (touch and affection are his love language) if he will do chores around the house for me. (My primary love language is tasks.) Dr. Willard F. Harley's research revealed that men listed the following in order of preference from their wives:

1. Sexual Fulfillment
2. Recreation Companionship
3. An Attractive Spouse
4. Domestic Support
5. Admiration

Women listed the following preferences in order from their husbands:

1. Affection
2. Conversation
3. Honesty and Openness
4. Financial Security
5. Family Commitment[6]

Difference in Men and Women

We are very aware of men's and women's biological differences. In addition, young girls are often raised with different expectations than boys are raised with. For instance, boys are generally encouraged to be strong and silent, while girls are encouraged to express their emotions. Society encourages numerous divergent roles for men and women that become blended with cultural and other stereotypes. The following four P's elaborate on some of these differences.

The Four P's

1. **PROTECTORS:** Men learn early that their primary role in society is to protect their family and property from harm. A bereaved father said: "When our daughter died, I felt as if I had failed to protect her. I think there were things I could have done to prevent what happened." Men also feel a specific responsibility as patriarchs in their homes. When challenges occur, men often feel a sense of failure. He may have prayed, fasted, and offered blessings that didn't seem to help. Watching his wife or family suffer due to a major challenge constitutes an additional secondary loss for men. If women are

single, they may assume the protector role for their children.

2. **PROVIDERS**: Most men feel more responsible for the finances than women do. It is often the man who returns immediately to work after a challenge or tragedy. The woman may spend more time at home in nurturing activities for her and her children. A man may push his worries aside by working the long hours he perceives are needed to more adequately support his family. He may also use his work to escape his painful realities. One woman's reaction to tragedy was evidenced by her response to her husband's attempt to cope with his own pain:

> I couldn't understand how he could just go right back to work after our tragedy. I would lie awake at night worrying and listening to his peaceful snore.

3. **PROGRAM CONTROLLERS**: Both men and women like control. However, men generally cannot handle feeling helpless or out of control as well as women do. Often when tragedy comes, so does the fear of losing control over their stewardship. Their assumptive world has been assaulted.[7]

One widower writes of his helplessness:

> The loss of control in my life is, at times, as overwhelming as my spouse's death.

Women frequently report feeling overwhelmed when confronted with the realization that there is not enough time to do all that they want to do and or feel is required of them.

4. **PROBLEM SOLVERS**: Men are often programmed more than women to "fix" everything. They feel responsible to find a cure or solution. When men or women learn they cannot fix or change their circumstances, they may feel a sense of failure and guilt. Men seem to struggle more than women do when they feel powerless. One man writes after the drug-induced death of his son:

> I was so mad at our son for putting us in this position. I also felt guilt at not being able to help him with his problems.

It may be helpful for couples to realize that differences between men and women are common and should be expected and accepted. It will take time, energy, tolerance, and healthy thought processes to work through each couple's unique issues.

In addition to men and women's bodies being biologically different, there also seems to be a difference in how men's and women's brains function. These functional differences can affect thoughts, moods, and behaviors. Additionally, men and women have different hormones that influence feelings and behaviors.

Men and women may evaluate their lives from different paradigms as well. Women generally see their lives as a "whole." If something goes wrong, such as a small flaw in her life, personality, or behavior, they often judge themselves (or their whole life) harshly. This is sometimes called, "all or nothing thinking." An example might be a sister teaching a Relief Society lesson. She has worked on her lesson for weeks, has beautiful visual aids, handouts, and so forth. However, when the special recorded music fails to function properly, she leaves discouraged, thinking her whole lesson was ruined. If you go down the hall the same Sunday to the high priests quorum, you might find that a quorum instructor has forgotten altogether that it was his turn to teach the lesson. He calmly asks if someone brought their manual which he quickly borrows as he and the other brethren begin to discuss the lesson. He and most of the other men go home thinking the class went well while debating and kidding about who will win the next big game!

It may also be helpful to remember that husbands and wives each have unique and changing needs relative to closeness and separateness. Problems may occur when one person's need for closeness threatens the other person's need for separateness.

Men often view, evaluate, and segregate their conflicting thoughts and behaviors individually into independent compartments within their consciousness. For example, a man can be a wonderful father and church leader and still not feel guilt from speeding on the highways, or cussing and losing his temper during a church basketball game. The predisposition of not focusing on conflicting behaviors diminishes his feelings of guilt. Men are usually able to positively view their overall life and self, even when they struggle and fall short in certain areas. On the other hand, women seem to focus more on their weaknesses and are not as likely to rationalize or ignore their faults as easily as men. When you add all these differences to other variables such as family background, coping style, personality, past modeling, beliefs, and values, you can see why a husband and wife may react differently over the same experience or difficulty. A mother raising a disabled teenager now fearing she's pregnant with a Down's syndrome baby writes to her deceased two year old daughter:

> I think I would be able to handle things a lot better if I knew this baby was okay. *Is it okay?* I keep thinking over and over of the night you died. It breaks my heart! Am I missing something, am I forgetting something, did I do something wrong to make you die, to leave us? Why did we lose you? You were the best thing to happen to our family. The other two kids have had a lot of problems lately. What is to become of us? Can we ever feel peace and joy in this life ever again? It is so hard for me to talk to people in the ward about my troubles. They don't understand. *Even daddy doesn't understand how I feel!* I love you. Mom.[8]

With time this mother was able to understand and accept that others, including her husband, grieve in different ways.

Prophets have spoken on the different roles of men and women in a harmonious marriage. For further reading on this subject, review The Family: A Proclamation To The World.

Self-Help Tools

What we like to refer to as the "Four Marital C's" can significantly influence and strengthen marriage relationships during difficult times including unexpected loss and stress:

1. Commitment
2. Communication
3. Cooperation and Tolerance
4. Conflict Resolution

1. **COMMITMENT**: Being committed to each other and to the marriage is a powerful ingredient found in marriages that endure serious life challenges. Those who do not consider divorce as an option, before they exhaust all other possibilities, are more likely to find mutually acceptable solutions that help keep their marriages intact.

2. **COMMUNICATION:** Lack of communication often contributes to a couple's decision to divorce. One partner may blame, the other then isolates or withdraws from the relationship. The absence of disclosing and responsive interactions can begin the process of relationship distress. When couples are exhausted, stressed, or mourning, it is difficult to find the time and energy vital for interaction. Remaining open and honest, and frequently discussing trials and challenges will enhance meaningful communication.

It's important for men to remember that most women process their thoughts, concerns, and decisions verbally. They think aloud and may say things they are only considering and espouse solutions when they are actually questioning. Women (especially prior to their menses) are usually more expressive with their emotions than men are. Women will do well to understand that men often process thoughts and ideas silently. It may take a man several minutes, an hour, or longer before he is able to reveal his innermost feelings in verbal answers to his wife's questions.

It is estimated that men speak about one third as many words per day as women. Men often use up their comfort level of words at work, which explains their silence at home. Mothers and homemakers who spend their days with children may have most of their words left in reserve waiting to be expressed in adult conversation with their husbands at the end of the day. Too often when her husband finally arrives home, tired from all his work and adult conversation, he is ready for peace and quiet.[9] If a husband can listen and validate his wife's feelings, and if a wife can avoid pressuring her husband to speak or answer all her questions immediately, their relationship will develop more smoothly.

Allowing for the expression of negative and ambivalent feelings can be healing. It is hard for some individuals to accept and share their feelings because they fear being judged or labeled. Acknowledging and validating feelings and opinions is more valuable than attempting to judge those feelings and opinions as being right or wrong. One's feelings are usually present for a reason. Negative feelings often go away more quickly when *accepted* and *expressed*. When repressed feelings are not expressed verbally and openly, they become expressed in other ways. Unfortunately, these repressed feelings often resurface in the form of unhealthy mental, emotional, or physical ill-nesses. We can avoid discounting each other's true feelings by avoid-ing the use of communication roadblocks such as "yes, but . . . ," "should," or "shouldn't," and so forth.

The following simple technique can enhance communication through the use of "I messages." It allows the sender and receiver to understand the true feelings that often drive our behaviors, yet remain unspoken, or lost in blaming and shaming defensive responses.

I feel _____ about _____ because _____.[10]

"I *feel* sad and lonely *about* you spending so much time at work, *because* I'm worried that you enjoy your work more than you enjoy being with me."

A healthy response could utilize reflective listening to repeat back what was said in order to clarify understanding:

"You *feel* I don't love you *because* I seem more concerned with my work than with you?"

During adversity we may find ourselves irritable and impatient. If we can focus our anger and disappointments on the challenges and issues we are facing rather than each other, we are more likely to stay connected.

3. COOPERATION AND TOLERANCE: Many professional therapists have discovered that "Tolerance Therapy" saves more marriages than other confrontational communication-based therapies. It's difficult to "accept, not expect" in a marriage; however, most marriages do better when couples tolerate each other's differences while recogniz-ing, focusing on, and encouraging their spouse's good qualities. It is difficult and often unproductive to focus our energies on chang-ing our spouses. Change and growth are more likely to be realized when we focus our efforts on accepting, "receiving" (see *Receive Ye One Another*, by Larry Lewis), our spouses while positively changing ourselves.

Tolerance, cooperation, mercy, and "giving in" can break down barriers and power struggles. Larry describes the power of "going the second mile" or working from a celestial perspective which goes beyond tolerance or "giving in." In other words, I may think it only fair that my spouse come home from work, feed the kids, and help me clean up before resting on the couch. But maybe my second mile offering would be to do the work even if I have also worked a long and hard day. This principle goes beyond fairness or justice; it focuses on mercy and celestial thinking.[11]

4. **CONFLICT RESOLUTION**: "Sometimes our inability to resolve conflict keeps love out of a marriage."[12] All marriages have conflicts, and not all issues can be solved easily. It is helpful to know and understand each other's family backgrounds, past losses, and personal struggles. We bring many personal issues to our marriage. Couples may have to *agree* to *disagree* on some issues. However, some conflicts cannot be ignored. A marriage may fail over time if addictions, abuse, abandonment, or serious mental illnesses are not being addressed appropriately.

Patience and Forgiveness

Affairs pose a significant threat to marriages and families. The act of betrayal can produce a potentially devastating crisis, resulting in grief, despair, anguish, and intense anger. Many couples successfully survive this devastating crisis by utilizing marital therapy. Success is most predictable when couples care for each other and both are equally committed to making the marriage work. Attachment and bonding are vital to a secure relationship. The task in crises is finding a realistic balance between hope and reality. Couples who educate and celebrate the unique needs and differences between men and women can greatly improve their marriages.

Couples often ask how much forgiveness is required when one partner has betrayed his or her marital covenants.

> My husband got involved with another woman. It has hurt me beyond words. We are trying to save our temple marriage. He is repenting and still attends church. However, I fear I don't trust him. I wonder who he is thinking about. Does he really love me? Will he stay? Can I forgive?

The following quote adds evidence concerning the value of patience and forgiveness:

> Because so many marital challenges involve a needed change of heart, repentance, and sometimes careful re-building of the

relationship; partners who wait patiently through the process are a great strength and blessing to their spouses.[13]

Touch and Massage Therapy

Touch can be a healing tool. Massage therapy has been a healing art for centuries. It can bring comfort to those who are emotionally or physically ill.

Touch helps couples stay connected. Touch can dissolve anger and frustration, and melt away tension. Touch or massage therapy can, but does not have to, involve sexual intimacy in marriage. One partner may find comfort in intimacy during adversity because touch, tenderness, and intimacy may serve as a reminder that not all is lost. Others, however, may not be able to participate in physical intimacy during or immediately after a crisis. They may wonder how anyone could think of being intimate during their crisis.

The following touch technique may help bring healing and bridge the gap between partners. Couples will need to plan to be alone and undisturbed for about an hour. Realize this time together may be one of the most important exercises that can be done to sustain a relationship.

Each partner takes a turn massaging the other. Start with the back and neck, and then move onto limbs, hands, and feet. Lotions or oils can be used if desired. Rub deep into grief-stricken muscles. Couples can talk about their concerns, or just take the time to totally relax in silence. After spending this time together, most individuals will function better emotionally and cognitively. Some couples will also notice that over time, their stress and anxiety decreases or softens.

It's also important for couples to get away and spend quality time alone together. A weekly date is worth the money and effort. Many years ago, our stake president counseled the members of our stake to borrow money for only two things: a home and a date. He also encouraged couples to spend a night away together when possible. His counsel has had a positive impact on our marriage. Communication and conflict resolution cannot occur if effort is not made to be alone together on a regular basis.

Couple's Therapy

Many couples have been helped with professional therapy. They may have developed negative or enabling behaviors or cycles that, with the help of counseling, can be altered. If couples are willing to do the work required to stay together, most marriages can become successful. Couples who want to stay together and rekindle the love they once had for each other can also benefit from couple's therapy or marital enhancement programs. Couple's therapy and marital enhancement programs and retreats help guide "the distressed couple from negative and rigidly structured responses toward flexibility and sensitive responsiveness . . . couples need."[14]

Research has shown that emotionally ill individuals can have successful marriages. Emotionally-focused therapy may be helpful. Therapists can help couples refrain from focusing on each other's weakness and teach them how to de-escalate negative cycles. Example: "I withdraw because you nag, and you nag because I withdraw." This kind of couple's therapy can help soften the blamer and help the withdrawn spouse to re-engage. An individual can move from defense and self protection to openness, where partners can become a source of security, protection, and comfort for each other. They may need help forgiving or trusting again or learning conflict resolution and communication skills. They might need to work on relationship issues and how to improve their friendship. Your bishop or local LDS Family Services can guide you to marriage counselors in your community.

When Should We Divorce?

As stated in the previous chapter, marriages impacted by chronic addictions, substance abuse, serious mental illness, physical or mental abuse, and infidelity are predictably more likely to end in divorce.[15]

Ending a marriage is usually a very difficult experience. There are some who will not have a choice.

God knows that many are suffering unfairly, often at the hand of others. God generally does not take away the agency of spouses or others who choose to harm us.

We are not required to stay indefinitely in harm's way. (See chapter one, "Abuse.") Each couple's circumstance is different and ultimately each party must be responsible to determine his own course and take responsibility for his choices and actions. God has not left us alone; inspired church leaders, LDS family service, and faithful Latter-day Saints in public and private practice can help us improve our marriages. Inspired church leaders can also provide support for those who must prayerfully determine if divorce is the best option. God has also through his Son provided the Holy Ghost to guide and comfort us, especially in those moments that we face the "but if not's" in our personal lives.

I will not leave you comfortless: I will come to you. (John 14:18)

Notes

1. Craig H. Hart, *Helping and Healing our Families: Principles and Practices Inspired by The Family: A Proclamation to the World* (Salt Lake City: Deseret Book, 2005), 32.
2. Ibid., 39
3. Ibid., 38
4. David H. Olson, and John Defrain, *Marriage and the Family, Diversity and Strengths* (Mountain View: Mayfield Publishing, 1994).
5. M. Gamblin "Forgiveness" (lecture, Association of Mormon Counselors and Psychotherapists Conference, Salt Lake City, UT, Oct. 1997).
6. Willard F. Harley, Jr., *His Needs Her Needs: Building An Affair-proof Marriage,* 4th printing (Grand Rapids: Baker Book House, 2000), 12–13.
7. T.A. Rando "Grief" (lecture, Association for Death Education and Counseling Conference, Chicago, IL, Mar. 1998).
8. Joyce and Dennis Ashton, *Loss and Grief Recovery* (Amityville: Baywood Publishing, 1996), 116.
9. John Gray, *Talks from John Gray, author of Men are from Mars, Women are from Venus* (New York: Harper Collins, 1992).
10. The Church of Jesus Christ of Latter-day Saints Social Services Department, *Becoming a Better Parent* (Salt Lake City, 1974), 33.
11. Larry W. Lewis, *Receive Ye One another: Taking Temple Marriage the Second Mile* (Springville: Cedar Fort Inc., 2006), 55.
12. "Mending our Marriage," *Ensign*, Oct. 1996, 51.
13. Ibid.
14. Susan M. Johnson, *The practice of Emotionally Focused Couple Therapy* (New York: Brunner-Routledge, 2004), 17.
15. Diane Medved, *The Case Against Divorce: Discover the Lures, and the Emotional Traps of Divorce—Plus the Seven Vital Reasons to Stay Together,* (New York: Donald I. Fine, Inc., 1989), 121.

CHAPTER SEVENTEEN

Unwed Pregnancies, Infertility, and Adoption

WHEN INDIVIDUALS HEAR THE WORD ADOPTION, they may only picture the joy of uniting a wonderful family with a beautiful child. Few of us realize the adjustment and grief that may be a part of this joyous experience. Although we should acknowledge the joy, it is also fitting to include the impact of loss and grief when discussing the adoption process. All parties involved in an adoption will experience some symptoms of grief.

Every year, more than one million unwed pregnancies occur in Canada and the United States. Approximately 15,000 of those pregnancies involve LDS birth mothers. This averages out to be one birth mother per ward per year.[1] Whether the birth mother decides to be a single parent and raise the child herself, marry, or place the infant for adoption, it can become a stressful cascade of losses and disappointments for everyone concerned and involved.

The bereavement process often begins long before most are even aware. When the unwed biological mother discovers she is pregnant, she experiences a flood of emotions and challenges that must be addressed. Could or should she marry? Can she keep her child? Could she stay in school and support herself? Would family and friends support her decision to give her child to strangers? How will she handle her changing body image? What other changes and loss must she adjust to?

Grief experts discourage individuals from making major decisions while experiencing acute grief. Unfortunately, birth parents and adoptive applicants have limited periods of time to make major decisions that will affect their own lives and the life of the unborn child. Many of these decisions have eternal consequences.

> What do I say? It's so overwhelming. When I placed my baby for adoption, all I could think about was how much better he would be without me for a mom. I get so depressed when I think of where all this has come to (birth mother, age 16).

Birth Mothers

Statistics show that most LDS birth mothers who keep their baby and become single parents will not marry in the temple. Those who place the child with adoptive couples are more likely to eventually marry in the temple.[2] An infant placed with an LDS couple who were sealed in the temple and hold current temple recommends will almost always be sealed in the temple to their adoptive family and inherit covenant blessings.

> I can't marry right now and as hard as it seems for me to give my baby to someone else, I want him to be sealed to parents in the temple (birth mother, age 18).

> Once I became pregnant, I knew I had to become active in the church—even if I had to go by myself. I took this responsibility very seriously. I remember sitting in meetings and feeling so alone. I felt that everyone around me had this perfect happy home, married to a priesthood holder, and sealed in the temple. I didn't have this (birth mother, age 20).

Birth Fathers

When the biological father receives the news, he wonders if he should become a father to his child. Is he ready to marry and support the birth mother and a baby? What about his education and career plans? Will his friends change? What are the changes and losses he must adapt to?

> I got drunk with a friend one night. Afterwards we went to visit some girls and one of them was very aggressive and knew what she was doing. The alcohol seemed to soften my previous resistive powers. I lost my virginity. Now she thinks she is pregnant! (young man, age 18).[3]

> How can I ever provide for this baby? (birth father, age 17).

Grandparents

When future grandparents of the baby receive the news, they begin to deal with their own grief, loss, and disappointment. Will their son or daughter drop out of school? Should they encourage the children to marry or place the child for adoption? Should they try to keep the pregnancy confidential? Is their child mature enough to become a parent and/or marry? How will they cope with losing a grandchild? Should they step in and offer to parent the child? Their grief often produces sadness, hurt, frustration, and anger.

> I can't believe my child has given up a temple marriage and a college education. My hopes for his future are shattered or at least altered. I feel hurt, angry, and afraid for him.

Adoptive couples

Adoptive couples experience loss as they confront their infertility and/or miscarriages. Often, feelings of failure, discomfort, and spiritual injury accompany them to the adoption agency.

> I worry some people have thought we were selfish because we haven't started our family. They see our new home, cars, and boat and probably wonder if that's why we have postponed having children.

> We were so thrilled to finally be pregnant! We had been in and out of fertility clinics for five years. We had finally conceived through IUI (Intro-uterine Insemination). We were 19 weeks along and went in for our usual check up. The doctor sent us for a routine ultrasound which showed that our baby had died; we couldn't believe it! The previous week the baby had a strong heartbeat! How did this happen? Everyone around us was having children. Why us? I was in shock for days! As I anticipated being induced to deliver my baby, I still wasn't sure it was all happening. Even after delivery, I thought I could still feel the baby moving. It took a long time for me to believe I had lost my baby. My grief lasted for over a year. Most people didn't seem to understand. They claimed I never knew my child who wasn't even born yet, so why was my grief so long and so hard? I really didn't feel happy again until I was pregnant and finally delivered a healthy baby. And even now I wish I had both babies![4]

> I had three ectopic pregnancies. The first one destroyed my right tube and the third one my left. The hardest part is realizing I cannot

conceive again. I always just wanted to stay home and be a mom. Now I have to replan my life. I cry a lot.[5]

Grief

Most individuals within the adoption triad can intellectually understand the challenges associated with the adoption process. However, birth parents and adoptive couples considering adoption often struggle emotionally and find it hard to deal with the ongoing impact of this event in their lives. Some birth parents ask the following: "Why me?" "I'm trying to repent, why can't I handle this?" "Why am I struggling so much?" They may think: "I hope I miscarry." "What about abortion?"

Adoptive applicants enduring miscarriage and infertility ask: "Where did I go wrong?" "I have faith; I live the Gospel. Why can't I have a child?"

Parents of birth parents often endure pain as a result of the misuse of agency and poor choices of their children:

I can't believe my son has brought all this stress into our lives.

Biological grandparents often experience fear and shame. Some of their fears include being judged negatively, especially if they feel somehow responsible for the negative choices their child has made. Their guilt can further complicate the grieving process, causing them to experience shame and a loss of control over their lives.

Why am I having these feelings? I really must be a weak or bad person.

No one seems to understand how hard it is to think of our grandbaby being given to another family.

Secondary Loss

Secondary loss is defined as those challenges that follow the primary event or primary loss. Secondary losses are unique to each individual in the adoptive process. For example, an unwed mother choosing adoption may have to sacrifice her education, body image, reputation, and immediate dreams of a temple marriage, in addition to mourning the loss of her child. All of these challenges, or accumulative losses combined, tend to complicate the grieving process and compromise her decision making:

> My dream of a temple marriage, college education, and the perfect body in my wedding dress are gone (birth mother, age 17).

No one involved in the adoptive process will ever be quite the same again. They see through new eyes and are forever changed as they begin to establish their "new normal."[6]

Disenfranchised Grief

When someone cannot grieve openly or others do not validate their loss, it is called disenfranchised grief. An example of this occurred some years ago when an unwed mother decided to move away from home in order to keep her pregnancy confidential. After placing her child, she moved back home and began dating a young man that had no knowledge of her pregnancy. One night he shared that he was adopted and couldn't understand why or how his mother could have "given him up." This young woman desperately wanted to share that she knew through experience how much his mother loved him and that she had done what she felt was best for him. She wanted to share how much she loved the child she had placed with a wonderful, worthy family, and how she was giving him spiritual opportunities and a better life. She felt "she hadn't given him up, but she had actually given him more" (LDSFS ad mantra). Unfortunately, her prior choice of confidentiality now limited her ability to help this young man. Nevertheless, her personal choice of confidentiality may have been in her best interest in the long run.

Disbelief, Denial, Shock, and Numbness

Disbelief, denial, shock, and numbness, are common emotions experienced by members of the adoption triad and their families.

> There is no way that my son is responsible for this pregnancy!

> I can't believe after 10 years of marriage and infertility that the doctors can do no more, and that God hasn't answered my pleas to get pregnant and deliver a child.

I didn't tell anyone that I was the father because I just couldn't believe it myself!

Some individuals become unable or unwilling to acknowledge their true struggles and limitations.

I kept my fears and feelings to myself. What would the ward think of me if they knew I couldn't handle this?

Some adoptive couples are unwilling or unable to acknowledge their pain and use avoidance patterns and denial to cope. They may consciously or unconsciously desire the biological mother to disappear after placement. Some fear if they maintain contact she may attempt to reclaim their child. This is a rare occurrence. The biological mother usually benefits from limited contact, negotiated with the adoptive couple, which allows her to know that her baby is well, happy, and keenly aware of her love. This knowledge, reassurance, and occasional contact provide confirmation to her that she has made the right decision. As the child moves into later childhood and early adolescence, being involved with emotionally healthy biological parents can often help the child in their emotional growth and be a positive adjunct to the adoptive parent's parenting.

Many birth fathers are consciously or subconsciously the source of additional anxiety and consternation for the birth mother. Over time, some birth mothers begin to feel it best to give their baby a home with a temple married couple. Some birth fathers agree with her plans, and unitedly they both choose adoption for their child. A smaller number of birth fathers express a sincere desire to parent the child themselves, without the birth mother's involvement. A significant number of birth fathers are unwilling to support the adoption desires of the birth mother. These same birth fathers often demonstrate little effort to assume financial responsibility and fail to actively prepare for the baby's future.

Experience has revealed that many unwed fathers who express opposition to adoption do so in attempt to maintain control or influence over the birth mother. At this stage, the potential loss of his unborn child is often a secondary loss for the birth father. The primary loss he is experiencing actually results from the ended or altered relationship between him and the birth mother, not his future relationship with the baby. His assumptive world relative to his and the birth mother's future has been assaulted or altered.

As the pregnancy progresses, the birth mother's focus changes from her and the birth father's future to her baby's future. This change in focus for many birth fathers constitutes a significant loss, resulting in increased vulnerability, anger, and attempts to control the birth mother.

Anger

Anger is a common emotion with any loss. Birth mothers often become angry with the birth father if he refuses to cooperate with her inspired and selfless plans to provide for the child through adoption. A birth mother's ability to make decisions, defuse anger, exercise control, and sacrifice for the baby's future is influenced by her own grieving processes.

Irritability is often a manifestation of anger. The mother of a pregnant young woman said:

> Since my daughter's unwed pregnancy, I don't seem to have any patience with my other children!

Anger directed towards deity or church leaders representing God is common among all religions during loss. Anger may be more intense for faithful members who believed that God should have blessed them by preventing or removing their adversity. An infertile couple lamented:

> It is hard to accept that God has allowed our infertility and multiple miscarriages. We have fasted, prayed and had special blessings. Where is our miracle? Aren't we worthy to be parents?

> I taught my child the Gospel and provided a shield for every temptation. I can't believe God allowed this and I find myself questioning if the Church is really true now that my daughter is pregnant.

Clichés

One may mean well using clichés that are intended to comfort; however, clichés can minimize a loss and suggest that someone has no legitimate need to grieve. Clichés often cause individuals to feel scruti-nized and judged. Examples of well meaning, yet hurtful clichés include:

> You are young and will have more chances to have children, or you can always adopt a child.

Many struggle spiritually when they hear the following types of clichés:

> This was God's will.

> God could have prevented this if you were worthy, fasted longer, prayed more, or had more faith.

Guilt

Guilt is an emotion that is common with any adoptive placement. The adoptive parents may wonder if they are somehow responsible for their infertility and their inability to bear children. The parents of an unwed mother may wonder if there was something wrong with their parenting skills, or the spiritual direction and example in their home. Biological parents often feel guilt concerning the commandments they haven't kept, and for the situation they have put themselves and their baby in. They struggle with guilt as they try to decide to place or keep the infant. For many, guilt is the most exhausting and difficult emo-tion to deal with. At times, the painful consequences of prior choices become confused with the painful, yet favorable, decision to place the child for adoption.

> I hurt so much when I consider placing my child for adoption.

> I did so many things wrong. If I had just done things differently this wouldn't have happened.

> My parents feel I should give my baby to them to raise. They don't seem to realize how hard it would be for me to see my child on a daily basis and not be involved (birth mom, age 20).

Some childless couples experience false guilt, feeling guilty for shortcomings and imperfections in their lives that they now attribute to their infertility.

If I had lived a better life, or exercised more faith, I wouldn't be infertile now.

Vulnerability and Loss of Control

Feeling vulnerable and out of control is a common reaction with the unwed mother placing her infant. She fears she will never know how the child is doing and if she made the right choice. She is often comforted by her decision to place if the adoptive couple can reassure her periodically that her child is doing well and will grow up knowing of her love.

The adoptive couple feels more control when they finally receive their baby; however, their vulnerability and accompanying need for control may cause them to resist the biological mother's attempts to find meaning, purpose, and peace in her adoption decision through ongoing periodic contact. Some adoptive couples reason:

> What if the biological mom wants more information so she can come looking for her child?

> We are hesitant to share the very best pictures of our adoptive son with his birth mother, because we fear seeing the pictures will make her want him back.

This is a frightening task for the adoptive couple; however, their willingness to give information and support actually calms the vulnerability, grief, and loss of control the unwed mother is feeling. The likelihood of her rescinding her decision is lessened when she is given sufficient feedback and reassurance that allows her to "feel and heal."

All of the above emotional reactions can stress the body, causing physical reactions. The physical symptoms may include breathlessness, restlessness, palpitations, headaches, fatigue, and changes in appetite, sleep, bowels, or sexual desire.

> After years of infertility and 6 months after losing our baby I started having lots of unusual physical symptoms. The doctors did some tests and concluded my physical problems were a result of all that I had been through emotionally. I had a lot of anxiety.

It may be difficult to concentrate on anything except what has happened. This preoccupation can lead to absent-mindedness, ruminations, confusion, and disorganization for an extended period of time. When trying to make some sense of what has occurred, one may repeatedly ask the same questions over and over again.

> I go over and over what happened the night I got pregnant. I think about all the decisions that led me to this point in my life.

This mental repetition (rumination) is a desperate attempt to consider other solutions that could have altered the outcome. An infertile couple questioned, "What if I had attempted to conceive earlier?" or "What if we had gone to the doctor sooner, would I have miscarried?"

The biological mother thinks, "If I hadn't dated him, I wouldn't be pregnant now."

The biological grandparents ask themselves what they could have done differently to have prevented the situation. They all may mentally search for a different and or better conclusion, diagnosis, or prognosis. They try to regain some control by re-creating or replaying aspects of their experience.

Some have feelings of being scrutinized and judged. An infertile couple said, "People have asked why we have such a big house with no children."

Others experience a loss of friends, which causes changes in roles and identity.

> My friends, work associates and everyone in the ward seems to be judging our parenting skills since our daughter became pregnant.

> I feel like I am under glass, people keep staring at me since they heard I am pregnant, looking at my stomach to see if I've gotten bigger.

It may be confusing for those who have strong faith, believe in miracles, and are striving to live the gospel, when they feel they were not protected or shielded from such a serious trial.

> I thought if I lived the commandments I would conceive and become a mother someday.

Finding Meaning

The most common question in the adoption process may be, "Why?" It may be "Why me?" "Why medically?" or "Why, God?"

An infertile couple wonders why medically they cannot conceive or why God has not blessed them with children. The grandparents of an unborn child wonder why they are in this difficult position. The "why's" are difficult to answer. Generally, individuals must find their own why's as they discover meaning in their unique situations. Some find meaning through the spiritual interventions of prayer, revelation, impressions, scripture reading, church and temple attendance, or dreams. We may take these interventions for granted as church members because they have always been available. Finding meaning for the unwed mother might be the confirmation from God that she is to keep her infant or place the child with loving, eager parents.

> I feel that placing my baby with a father and mother is the best thing for my child (25-year-old college student).

A spiritual confirmation helps her find purpose and solace. A similar confirmation for both sets of grandparents and the birth father is often beneficial. Hearing, contemplating, and praying for personal confirmation are never easy tasks. Some have found comfort in the following counsel from the First Presidency's 2002 letter to Church leaders concerning unwed parents:

> When a man and woman conceive a child out of wedlock, every effort should be made to encourage them to marry. When the probability of a successful marriage is unlikely due to age or other circumstances, unwed parents should be counseled to place the child for adoption through LDS Family Services to ensure that the baby will be sealed to temple-worthy parents. Adoption is an unselfish, loving decision that blesses both the birth parents and the child in this life and in eternity.
>
> Birth parents who do not marry should not be counseled to keep the infant as a condition of repentance or out of a sense of obligation to care for one's own. Unwed parents are not able to provide the blessings of the sealing covenant. Further, they are generally unable to provide a stable, nurturing environment which is so essential for the baby's well-being. Unmarried parents should give prayerful consideration to the best interests of the child and the blessings that can come to an infant who is sealed to a mother and father.[7]

President Spencer W. Kimball gave similar direction in 1976.

While speaking concerning abortion, he provided the first recorded counsel relative to unmarried parents:

> Often the question is asked, what should unmarried parents do then? Whenever possible, unwed parents should marry and build a home. When this is not possible, adoption through Church Social Services is preferred so that the infant can be sealed to loving eager parents in an eternal family. A baby needs a family, a father and a mother. The Lord intended for babies to have a family and for families to be eternal.[8]

Handbook 2: Administering the Church 2010 states the following:

21.4.12 Single Expectant Parents

When a man and woman conceive a child outside of marriage, every effort should be made to encourage them to marry. When the probability of a successful marriage is unlikely due to age or other circumstances, the unmarried parents should be counseled to work with LDS Family Services to place the child for adoption, providing an opportunity for the baby to be sealed to temple-worthy parents. Adoption is an unselfish, loving decision that blesses both the birth parents and the child in this life and in eternity.

If LDS Family Services is not available in the area, leaders should encourage the placement of the child for adoption with a temple-worthy couple through a local licensed agency. LDS Family Services may be of assistance in identifying reputable, licensed adoption agencies. Licensed agencies are designed to protect the interest of the child, screen adoptive couples before placement, and provide needed supervision and counseling.

Birth parents who do not marry should not be counseled to keep the infant as a condition of repentance or out of a sense of obligation to care for one's own. Additionally, grandparents and other family members should not feel obligated to facilitate parenting by unmarried parents, since the child would not generally be able to receive the blessings of the sealing covenant. Further, unmarried parents are generally unable to provide the stability and nurturing environment that a married mother and father can provide. Unmarried parents should give prayerful consideration to the best interests of the child and the blessings that can come to an infant who is sealed to a mother and father. (See First Presidency letter, June 26, 2002.) [9]

For members of the adoption triad, the inspired counsel of living prophets confirms that God can bless each life as we turn to him, even in the midst of our darkest despair.

> Both my daughter and I had a powerful spiritual confirmation that the baby she was carrying should be placed with a mother and father who could have the baby sealed to them in the temple. The peace that we both felt is what helped me let go of my grandchild and avoid additional feelings of pain and grief (maternal grandfather).

> I felt I should keep my baby and live worthy of a husband and temple marriage later (birth mother, age 18).

> At times I can't help but wonder why my birth mom placed me for adoption. Others have told me she did it out of love and I want to believe that is why she chose not to raise me.

Sharon Kaplan Roszia's statement captures the loss experienced in adoption well: "Everyone served by adoption loses something . . . before they gain anything."

Professionals suggest it may take 24 months or more to adjust to loss and major changes in our lives.[10] See Part One for additional coping and healing interventions.

Notes

1. Dennis Ashton and Dr. Cyril Figuere, LDS Family Services statistics, 1995.
2. Ibid.
3. Joyce and Dennis Ashton, *Jesus Wept* (Springville, Utah: Cedar Fort Inc., 2002), 44.
4. Ibid, 25.
5. Ibid, 26.
6. R. K. Limbo and S. R. Wheeler, *When a Baby Dies: A handbook for Healing and Helping* (La Crosse: Resolve Through Sharing, 1986), xv.
7. First Presidency (letter), June 26, 2002, Gordon B. Hinckley, Thomas S. Monson, and James E. Faust
8. Spencer W. Kimball, *A Visit from the Prophet*, WOF1420.
9. Handbook 2: Administering the Church 2010 (Salt Lake City: Church of Jesus Christ of Latter-day Saints, 2010), 196.
10. Glen W. Davidson, *Understanding Mourning* (Minneapolis: Augsburg Publishing House, 1982), figures 1–4.

CHAPTER EIGHTEEN

Same-Gender Attraction, Aging, and Empty Nest

SAME-GENDER ATTRACTION IS AN INTENSE INTEREST IN OTHERS of the same sex, usually leading to sexual desire. However, it often has less to do with sexuality, and more to do with the need for love, affection, and acceptance from the same gender. Experts are divided on cause; however most agree that both biology and environment play a role. Dr. Dean Byrd, PhD, an expert in the field, feels that biology plays a part in all behavior; however, homosexuality is more a derailing of biological priming. He feels there are multi-determined causes and many different factors for different individuals. There are childhood events and environmental factors. Note that it is common for children to have sexual exploration with little friends of the same gender. Homosexuality occurs if they don't turn when they are older and have a need for intimacy from the opposite sex. One may be predispositioned rather than predetermined. Nature and nurture play complex roles.[1] Here are a few common factors:

1. A child may have had an early introduction to sex by someone of the same sex. In fact where sexual abuse has occurred by someone of the same sex, same-gender attraction is 7 times more common.[2] (Find interventions for coping with abuse in Part One; also see 2 Nephi 2.)

2. A child may not have felt loved or supported by their same-sex parent. As they try to fill the void through supportive and loving friends of the same gender, sometimes reinforced sexual feelings may result as they address their emotional needs.

Elder Neal Maxwell teaches, "Our genes, circumstances, and environment matter very much and they shape us very much, yet there remains an inner zone. In this zone lies the essence of our individuality and our personal accounts."[3]

The 2000 census data reports that 594,391 same-sex couples reported living together in the United States. In 2005 it grew to 777,000. The 30 percent increase may be due to couples being more willing to report accurately; 53 percent were two men living together and 47 percent women. For the 2010 report, the census bureau has decided to use new methods for reporting, as some states have legalized same-sex marriage. The 2005 census figures show that Utah has 3,370 self-reporting households. It is estimated that 2 to 4 percent of the LDS population experience same-gender attraction.[4]

It is also estimated that over 2 million heterosexual marriages include a gay spouse. Some same-sex attracted individuals live alone, never marrying or practicing their homosexuality.

Some LDS same-gender attracted individuals choose to marry in the temple and live heterosexual lives, bearing and parenting children. Many have testimonies of the restored gospel and desire desperately to lose their attraction to individuals of their same gender. Others are sitting among us in sacrament meetings, holding and loving their children, yet feeling hurt and lonely because they believe few can or will ever understand their anger, grief, pain, and confusion.

President Gordon B. Hinckley offers compassion and important counsel:

> Our hearts reach out to those who refer to themselves as gays and lesbians. We love and honor them as sons and daughters of God. They are welcome in the Church. It is expected, however, that they follow the same God-given rules of sexual conduct that apply to everyone. . . . The Church's opposition to attempts to legalize same-sex marriage should never be interpreted as justification for hatred, intolerance, or abuse of those who profess homosexual tendencies.[5]

Listen to the struggle of this LDS man as he tries to make sense of his life experiences.

> I was sexually abused as a child. I remember thinking when I

was to be ordained a deacon that I could become "clean." I talked about it with my bishop, seeking a worthy feeling. I was active in the church and fulfilled my priesthood responsibilities. I served an honorable mission. Although I struggled with masturbation at times, I was determined to overcome my problem. I married a wonderful, spiritual woman in the LDS temple. We have several children. I have undergone years of therapy through LDS Family Services. I had many counseling hours with bishops and stake presidents. However, after children and many years of marriage we are divorcing because of my homosexuality. Now I wonder if I didn't pray hard enough. I wonder if I didn't study enough. I wonder if I gave up. Did I give it my all?[6]

The loss and grief issues emerging from homosexual lifestyles are significant, not only for the same-sex attracted individual, but also for extended family members and friends that are left wondering why their circumstances are not different.

A divorced member said:

I thought my husband would be able to overcome his homosexuality. He served a mission and married me in the temple. I love him and want him forever. However we have decided on divorce because he cannot function in the marriage. He is not sexually attracted to me. It is very painful to suffer such an eternal loss. I sometimes feel like a failure and don't want to give up. However, after all the prayers, blessings, fasting, and therapy, he hasn't changed. I think his natural death would be an easier solution. At least I would know I could have him in the eternities.[7]

After much fasting and prayer I felt impressed to marry a certain returned missionary. Little did I know that many years later he would leave for his homosexual lifestyle. Most of my children have suffered intensely from the divorce. Many have left the church, which breaks my heart.

Some same-gender attracted people receive healing or control over their same-sex attraction, others do not. It is a painful and disappointing challenge for them and their families.

A former missionary writes:

I feel like I have no choice but to either do it [recover from his same sex attraction] or live my life with a guilty conscience that would eventually drive me crazy. It is so painful to feel different, guilty, and desperate. The shame and unacceptance I feel at church is making me bitter. I'm not sure I can keep going there. I've fasted, prayed, done it all. Sometimes suicide seems the only way out . . . it seems a good option at times.

A man struggling with same-sex attraction writes:

I have done everything, the counseling, bishop and stake president meetings, prayer, support groups, sports, reading, and so forth. The only hope I see at this point is a miracle. As I weigh things out in my mind, it seems only logical and right that we should get divorced for my wife's sake. However, there is a great deal to fear: the effect on our children, financial devastation, and loss of self-esteem. Could I handle losing my family eternally? On the other hand, I would feel some relief, a decision would be made and I would be able to stop feeling like I have to pretend and cover up my real feelings. What do I do?[8]

Offering treatment to same-gender attracted individuals is controversial. The professional world is torn, not only on the cause, but the treatment of homosexuality. Many professionals feel that offering treatment wrongly suggests that an individual can change his or her sexual orientation. Yet many who suffer want to change the attraction. Seeking the right professional therapist then becomes critical for those who desire to change or find a way to deal with their attraction. Dr. Dean Bryd says that interpersonal processes can modify biology and that de-sexualizing the attraction can soften same-gender attraction.[9]

Ty Mansfield, author of *In Quiet Desperation: Understanding the Challenge of Same Gender Attraction*, said, "I know some individuals who feel they have overcome the attraction, have married, and it's not a problem for them anymore. . . . I know many more who have the type of life they want—married with a family. They still experience the attraction, but that's all they see it as."[10]

Evergreen International provides support and referral to professional therapists for those who desire change. Reparative therapy has helped many in their difficult struggle. The Church of Jesus Christ of Latter-day Saints' position on the eternal purposes of the family is defined clearly in *The Family: A Proclamation to the World*.

The proclamation encourages the abstaining of any sexual

involvement outside of marriage, whether in heterosexual or homosexual relationships. Those struggling with homosexuality and sexual addictions generally need to stop the behavior before they can successfully address the psychological and spiritual aspects of their challenges.

Never Married

For individuals who desire to marry and don't, it can be a terrible disappointment and loss. Some well-meaning friends remind singles that theirs is not an eternal loss, explaining that they will find a spouse in the next life. However, this counsel does not recognize or allow them to mourn and grieve for all they don't have here and now.

> I always thought I would marry someday and bear children. However, I am now nearing menopause and the hope of a family is fading. Everyone reminds me that I am promised a family someday . . . I guess in the next life, but I feel sad and gypped now.

Other Types of Losses

Another change we may underestimate is the impact of retirement and employment changes. The following is from a woman who lost a job she had enjoyed for 25 years.

> I miss the old way—I miss the old friends! I haven't written that grief letter about my feelings, but I do think and cry about it daily, and I am going to write it soon and hope it helps me feel better.

Empty Nest

It has been a few short months since we cared for our sweet mother in our home with the help of hospice and family. Three weeks after Mother died, our youngest daughter married. We miss having both of these great women in our home, and have discovered that even joyful events require adjustments. A few weeks following Ashley's marriage, our youngest son Brandon moved from our home to attend medical school in a different state. When we were raising five children, (one in a wheelchair) we were always busy and felt overwhelmed at times. Our young family (full nest) brought challenges, fun, and blessings. Now our empty nest family creates an equally challenging adjustment.

A close friend saying good-bye to her married daughter describes her empty nest well.

> "I know how hard it is to have a daughter get married—with my first it was so very painful! I still miss them and it can't really ever be the same. How can you raise her and teach and love her so much and then just give her to someone else? So not fair!"

One day after cleaning out my mother's home following her death, I had what I call a "grief attack." I sent the following email to all my friends and family. I wanted anyone and everyone to offer me their comfort and advice. It really helped to share my feelings and then receive back love and support.

> "I am still struggling with the fact that both of my parents are dead and now I am the "old grandma generation" and I am probably the next one to die . . . it's really weird . . . I look in the mirror and see an older face whose life could be almost over!! . . . And cleaning out Mom's house is sad and draining.

Now, months later, I realize after reading those feelings, how much better I am doing. It is a testament of how the human soul can adjust to the losses that come our way. We are resilient; we can find peace, hope, and happiness again, in spite of our life's challenges. Life is worth living, and though things will never be quite the same, most of us can find meaning as we discover our new normal.

Our New Loss: Aging

Life is full of change, loss, and adjustment. We have thought of including aging as a loss and something that many individuals grieve for. Now that Dennis and I are young senior citizens we are trying to find ways to adapt as our bodies decline. I also work with hospice patients who are most often 65 years and older. I listen to their struggles and losses as their bodies fail and they prepare for death. Many have suffered for years, while others have a quicker death. Patients tell me how difficult it is to first give up sports, jogging, and then even walking. For some, these loses will be followed by the loss of their driver's licenses and having to move out of the homes they love. I realize more fully that by the time we die we have to give up everything earthly.

Soon after Dennis and I experienced the death of our last parent, combined with our last child leaving home, I started experiencing some new physical struggles. I knew from past experience and research that bereaved individuals are vulnerable and often experience a decline in their physical health. Grief can affect us emotionally, spiritually, as well as physically (see *Jesus Wept*). I tried to keep my humor as I felt my body was falling apart, but I will admit it was frightening, and sad at times for me.

These events and losses brought about the reality and limits of our "new normal." We have felt the vulnerability of aging that includes joining the old generation. In the meantime, I will have to learn to focus on other interests and try to be grateful for the many things I can still do. This Pearl Buck quote about accepting her mentally disabled child has been a favorite for years:

> Only to endure is not enough. Endurance can be a harsh and bitter root in one's life, bearing poisonous and gloomy fruit, destroying other's lives. Endurance is only the beginning. There must be acceptance and the knowledge that sorrow fully accepted brings its own gifts.[11]

I know God can heal us physically, emotionally, and mentally, "but if not . . . ," we will continue to believe, have faith in God, and endure to the end.

"Grief becomes your companion and teacher as you learn to live with it."[12]

"My philosophy of life is that it's like being on a beach. You get knocked down by a wave and you can either lie there and drown, or you can get up and move. If you don't keep moving you die."[13]

For the Wounded

We are all likely to be wounded at sometime in our life. We must remember Christ's example when he appeared in the America's, He invited those present to touch the wounds in his hands and feet (not his strong, healthy biceps[14]). Those present experienced firsthand the wounds and pain the Savior suffered for them. He is connected to them and to us through his suffering. We too can connect to others through our own suffering.

We have not been left without the Savior's comfort. Those same wounds represent healing for each of us as we earnestly seek the Savior's Atonement in our lives.

Notes

1. Dr. Dean Byrd, "Providing Psychological Care to Men Who Present with Unwanted Homosexual Attraction: An Interpersonal Approach" (lecture, Association of Mormon Counselors and Psychotherapists Conference, Salt Lake City, Oct. 3, 2008).
2. Ibid.
3. Neal A. Maxwell, "According to the Desire of [Our] Hearts," *Ensign*, Nov. 1996, 21.
4. Ogden Standard-Examiner, Jun. 11, 2005, 1A.
5. Carrie A. Moore, "Alone in the fold: Many LDS gays struggle to cling to faith despite their yearnings," *Deseret Morning News*, Dec. 3, 2005.
6. Joyce and Dennis Ashton, *Jesus Wept* (Springville, Utah: Cedar Fort, Inc., 2001), 51
7. Ibid, 52.
8. Ibid., 53.
9. Dr. Dean Byrd, "Providing Psychological Care to Men Who Present with Unwanted Homosexual Attraction: An Interpersonal Approach."
10. Moore, "Alone in the fold: Many LDS gays struggle to cling to faith despite their yearnings."
11. P. S. Buck, *The Child Who Never Grew* (Bethesda: Woodbine House, 1950), 25.
12. D. Edwards, *Grieving: The Pain and the Promise* (Salt Lake City: Covenant, 1989), vii.
13. Robin Simons, *After The Tears* (Orlando: Harcourt Brace Jovanovich, 1985), 8.
14. Terrence C. Smith, "An Anatomy of Troubles" (lecture, Association of Mormon Counselors and Psychotherapists Conference, Salt Lake City, Oct. 3, 2008).

Conclusion

GRIEF IS HARD WORK. It is the work of thoughts and feelings. In the beginning phase of loss we may not have much control over our thoughts or feelings. However, as we acknowledge and actually pursue our "grief work," using the tools we discussed in Part One, we can gain increased control and peace. By doing our grief work we are choosing to become survivors rather than victims of our circumstance.

Our hope is that this publication on loss and grief can give you ideas for coping with the "but if not's" that will inevitably come your way, those times in your life when God's hands are there to sustain you rather than take away your adversities. We have determined in spite of our personal trials that "our God whom we serve is *able* to deliver us. . . . *But if not*, be it known . . . that we will not serve thy gods, nor worship the golden image" (Daniel 3:17–18; emphasis added).

Rather than becoming bitter when we face life's but if nots, we hope to become better as we endure. We are grateful for the gift of the Comforter, spiritual gifts, and tender mercies that help individuals endure extreme trauma in their lives. We have discovered that the human soul is resilient and most individuals will accommodate and adjust to loss across time. "But they that wait upon the Lord shall renew their strength; they shall mount up with wings as eagles; they shall run, and not be weary; and they shall walk, and not faint" (Isaiah 40:31).

May God bless you on your life's journey.

About the Authors

JOYCE ASHTON IS A REGISTERED NURSE and certified bereavement advisor. She is currently the Director of Spiritual Care for Rocky Mountain Hospice in eight offices and the Bereavement Coordinator for Davis/Weber Counties.

Dennis is a licensed clinical social worker, former bishop, and assistant commissioner for LDS Family Services. He is currently serving on the executive council of LDS Family services. Dennis was a guest on KRNS and KSL following the Salt Lake City Trolley Square shooting and Crandall Canyon Mine disaster. Dennis also represented LDS FS providing humanitarian support and training to refugees fleeing Kosovo, Tsunami victims in Indonesia, and street children projects in Mexico. He has also appeared on *Living Essentials*.

Joyce and Dennis teach at BYU Education Week and have been broadcast on KBYU-TV. They have also had the privilege of presenting at a couple of BYU women's conferences. They have authored five other books, including *Jesus Wept*; *Loss and Grief Recovery*; and *But if Not*, Volumes I, II, and III. They have also published online and journal articles.

Joyce and Dennis are the parents of six children, four of whom are living, and have several grandchildren.

NOTES

NOTES

NOTES

NOTES

NOTES

NOTES

NOTES